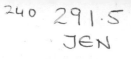

Ethics and Religion

Heinemann Educational Publishers
Halley Court, Jordan Hill, Oxford OX2 8EJ
a division of Harcourt Education Limited

Heinemann is a registered trademark of
Harcourt Education Limited

OXFORD MELBOURNE AUCKLAND
JOHANNESBURG BLANTYRE GABORONE
IBADAN PORTSMOUTH NH (USA) CHICAGO

© Joe Jenkins, 2003

First published 2003

07 06 05 04 03 02
10 9 8 7 6 5 4 3 2 1

British Library Cataloguing in Publication Data is available from
the British Library on request.

ISBN 0 435 30367 8

Edited by Eldo Barkhuisen
Designed by Artistix
Typeset by TechType, Abingdon, Oxon
Original illustrations © Harcourt Education Limited, 2003

Illustrated by TechType, Abingdon, Oxon
Printed and bound in the UK by CPI Bath Press
Cover photo: © Getty
Picture research by Jennifer Johnson

Acknowledgements
The publishers would like to thank the following for permission to
reproduce copyright material. OCR for the exam questions on pp.
29, 44, 55, 66, 86, 98, 109, 120, 135, 148, 162, 176, reproduced
with the kind permission of OCR. Edexcel for the exam questions
on pp. 21, 55, 66, 86, 135, 176. AQA for the exam questions on
pp. 29, 86, 148, 162. AQA (NEAB)/AQA examination questions
are reproduced by permission of the Assessment and Qualifications
Alliance. WJEC for the exam questions on pp. 55, 98, 109, 135.

The publishers would like to thank the following for permission to
reproduce photographs: pp. 5, 40, 57, 91 Popperfoto; p. 11 Larry
Towell/Magnum; p. 12 Neil Cooper © PANOS; pp. 14, 67 Andrew
Testa © PANOS; pp. 16, 156 Peter Marlow/Magnum; pp. 18, 54
Abbas/Magnum; pp. 24, 142 (bottom) Jayne Lennard; p. 26 Peter
Parker © PANOS; p. 28 Chien-chi Chang/Magnum; p. 31 Bruno
Barbey/Magnum; p. 34 Carl De Keyzer/Magnum; pp. 35, 102 Kent
Klich/Magnum; pp. 43, 50 Camera Press; pp. 45, 70, 84 (middle)
Fernando Moleres © PANOS; p. 47 Bruce Gilden/Magnum;
p. 58 Hulton; p. 63 Charles Moore/Black Star/Katz; pp. 64, 159
Stuart Franklin/Magnum; p. 72 Raghu Rai/Magnum; p. 75 Bill
Stephenson © PANOS; pp. 77, 142 (top), 143 SPL; p. 81 Jan
Banning © PANOS; p. 82 (top) Nick Robinson © PANOS; p. 82
(bottom) The Red Cross; p. 84 (bottom) Alastair McNaughton ©
PANOS; p. 87 PANOS; p. 88 Alamy; p. 116 Magnum/C, Steele-
Perkins; p. 119 Heldur Netocny © PANOS; p. 124 Richard
Kalvar/Magnum; p. 125 Eli Reed/Magnum; p. 127 Shehzad
Nooraniat at PANOS; pp. 129, 154 Paul Fusco/Magnum; p. 132
Rex; pp. 136, 163 Corbis; p. 138 Roslin Institute; p. 145 Kobal;
p. 149 Peter Mitchell; p. 151 Henri Cartier Bresson/Magnum; p.
164 Nick Ut/Associated Press; p. 166 Heidi Bradner © PANOS;
p. 171 Raymond Depardon/Magnum.

Every effort has been made to contact copyright holders of
material reproduced in this book. Any omissions will be rectified in
subsequent printings if notice is given to the publishers.

The author would like to thank Sarah Flynn, Sarah Flockhart, Anne
Forbes, Nicola Haisley, Robert Fisk, David Jeffrey, John Pilger and
his wife, Jayne, for their support while this book was being written.

To Idris, who was one while I was writing this book — may he live
to see a British government, for once, engaged in ethical social,
foreign and environmental policies.

Tel: 01865 888058 www.heinemann.co.uk

Websites

There are links to relevant websites in this book.
In order to ensure that the links are up-to-date,
that the links work, and that the sites are not
inadvertently linked to sites that could be
considered offensive, we have made the links
available on the Heinemann website at
www.heinemann.co.uk/hotlinks. When you
access the Heinemann website, enter the
express code **3678P**, and this will take you to
the links you want.

Word watch

Certain words and phrases have been used throughout the margins of this book,
sometimes more than once. Some of them are to be found in the Glossary (see
pages 179–188). They are useful words and phrases to get to know. Knowing what
they mean will improve your general level of understanding and self-expression. You
may know most of them but be sure to look up the unfamiliar ones.

Contents

Ethics and Religion Exam Board Matching Chart

Exam board	Qualification	Module	Pages
Edexcel	AS	Relationship between religion and morality	45–55
		Utilitarianism	87–98
		Situation ethics	99–109
		Conscience	56–66
		Freedom	22–29
		Sexual ethics	124–135
		War and Peace	163–176
	A2	Relationship between religion and morality	45–55
		Ethical theories	76–122
		Ethical language	10–21
		"Relativism, objectivism, subjectivism, law and punishment"	30–44, 80–81
AQA	AS	Medical issues	136–148
		Environmental issues	149–162
		Religious perspective on ethics	1–176
		Utilitarianism	87–98
		Kant's ethical theory	77–86
	A2	Issues raised by science and technology	136–162
		Ethics in relation to less economically developed countries	70–71, 116–120, 175
		Religious perspective on ethics	1–176
		Virtue ethics	110–122
		Free will and determinism	22–29
OCR	AS/A2	Kant and the Categorical imperative	77–86
		Utilitarianism	87–98
		Absolute and relative morality	30–44
		Religious methods of decision–making	45–66, 99–109, 123–176
		Medical ethics	136–148
		Free will and determinism	22–29
		Meta–ethics	10–21
		Moral relativism e.g. Situation ethics	30–44, 99–109
		Natural Law	41–43, 128
		Virtue ethics	110–122
		Conscience	56–66
		Environmental ethics	149–162
		Sex and relationships	124–135
		War, peace and justice	163–176
WJEC	AS	Situation ethics	99–109
		Natural Law	41–43, 128
		Utilitarianism	87–98
		Sexual ethics	124–135
	A2	Virtue theory	110–122
		Kant's categorical imperative	77–86
		Emotivism and logical positivism	10–21
		Ethical egoism	67–75
		Applied ethics: justice and conflict	116–120, 163–176

THE WORLD OF ETHICS
1 Skills

> 'The unexamined life is not worth living.'
>
> Socrates (c. 470–399 BCE)

Objectives

In this chapter you will explore an area of philosophical discussion and inquiry known as *ethics* or *moral philosophy*. **Ethics** or moral **philosophy** refers to standards of right and wrong. These standards are founded on specific virtues and reasonable **obligations** that are supported by consistent and well-founded reasons.

A community of enquiry

The Greek philosopher Socrates asked questions to elicit beliefs and values, and then presented counter-examples, to obtain clearer understanding. Socrates claimed that the self-knowledge gained by questioning may lead to true happiness.

Ethics is a *reflective* and *critical* discipline, and in this book you will be encouraged to think for yourselves. By bringing your questions and ideas to the attention of your classmates, your classroom will become a community of enquiry.

The moral maze

'Ethics' greets us each morning in the newspaper and bids us good night on the evening news. Questions and dilemmas challenge us on a personal level all the time – in our relationships at home, at school or at a club. They also confront us about the **rights** and wrongs of a whole range of issues such as criminal justice, sexual behaviour, money, drugs, work, shopping, medical technologies, the way we treat animals, 'foreigners', friends, foes, war and peace, the environment, the homeless. Dealing with these types of issues can be an intense experience – sometimes confusing, always demanding.

Ethics or **morality** asks big questions: How should I behave? How must I live? Why are some actions right and some actions wrong – who says anyway? Is honesty really necessary? Does it matter if I can get away with treating others badly? Do we have free will? Is killing a person ever justified?

Throughout life you will be confronted by many sorts of questions about right and wrong. Deciding what your actions and choices will be and which ones will lead to a successful life for you and for those around you, requires understanding and respect for ethics. This 'moral reasoning' demands intellect, stamina and patience. For many it is a sign of maturity in a person – and a significant mark of civilization.

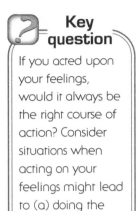

Key question

If you acted upon your feelings, would it always be the right course of action? Consider situations when acting on your feelings might lead to (a) doing the right thing, and (b) doing the wrong thing.

See Chapter 5 on religion and morality.

Key idea

Religion *can* set high ethical standards and can inspire people to self-sacrifice and heroism. But ethics *cannot* be confined to religion nor is it the same as religion.

Survey: what is ethics?

Before beginning their studies, a group of sixth formers answered the question 'What is ethics?' in the following ways.

'Ethics is about my feelings'

Sometimes people express their ethics with their feelings: 'Castrate the rapists!'; 'Hang 'em!'; 'Send 'em home!' Ethics, however, is not a matter of following your feelings.

'Ethics is about religious beliefs'

Nor should we identify ethics with religion. Although most religions aim for high ethical standards, history is littered with examples of people committing the most dreadful atrocities in the 'name of religion'. It is also littered with people committing dreadful atrocities in the name of their particular *–ism*: Nazism, fascism, Stalinism.

If ethics were confined to religion, then ethics would apply only to religious people. But 'ethics' applies to everyone – as much to the criminal as to Christ, the 'sinner' as to the 'saint', the torturer as to the tortured, the exploiter as to the exploited.

Ethics applies as much to the sinner as to the saint

'Ethics is about following the law'

Being ethical is also not the same as following the law. Would you follow 'the law' if it stated that certain groups of human beings were subhuman and should be abused, humiliated and treated as second-class citizens? Laws have existed, and still exist in the world today, that are cruel, unfair and intolerant.

First they came for the Jews
And I did not speak out —
Because I was not a Jew.
Then they came for the communists
And I did not speak out —
Because I was not a communist.
Then they came for the trade unionists
And I did not speak out
Because I was not a trade unionist.
Then they came for me —
And there was no one left
To speak out for me.

Pastor Niemoller (1892–1984)

'Ethics is about standards of behaviour society accepts'

If a society had laws that permitted husbands to beat their wives or made children work as slaves, would this society be ethical? Sometimes standards of behaviour in society can deviate from what is ethical. An entire society like Nazi Germany can become ethically corrupt. Moreover, if being ethical were simply a matter of doing whatever society accepts, then to find out what is ethical, you would have to do lots of surveys or questionnaires and then bend your beliefs to whatever society accepts as being ethical.

'Ethics is all about sex'

Some people often see ethics as simply about old-fashioned rules designed to stop people enjoying themselves, usually in relation to sex. This is a very narrow view. As we shall see in this book, ethics explores sex, among other issues, and ethics is also about the values lying behind choices, the reasons given for these choices, and the language used to describe them.

Key idea

Being ethical is *not* the same as following the law.

See Chapter 4 on relativism, Chapter 6 on conscience and Chapter 11, part 2, on contractualism.

Word watch

corrupt

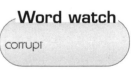

See Chapter 12 on sexual ethics.

Word watch

prescribe
rights
obligations

'Ethics is about ... help, I don't know!'

All the answers given so far in this chapter are incorrect in themselves! Here are some better answers and ideas to get you started:

- Ethics refers to accepted standards of right and wrong that prescribe what humans *ought* to do, usually in terms of rights, obligations, benefits to society, fairness or specific virtues.
- Ethics refers to those standards that offer good reasons for refraining from acts that harm others and that encourage virtues such as honesty, tolerance, compassion and loyalty.
- Ethical standards are concerned with human rights, such as the right to freedom from injury and the right to privacy. These are considered adequate standards of ethics because they are supported by consistent and well-founded reasons.
- Ethics refers to a personal study and development of one's own moral standards. Feelings, laws and social norms can deviate from what is ethical; therefore, it is necessary to examine one's standards constantly to ensure that they are reasonable and well founded.
- Ethics is the continuous effort of studying our own moral beliefs and our own moral conduct, and of striving to ensure that we, and the institutions we help to shape, live up to ethical standards that are reasonable and solidly based.

❛= Quotable quote

'At least everyone *claimeth to be an authority on "good" and "evil"'*.

Friedrich Nietzsche, *Thus Spake Zarathustra* (1891)

❞

Word watch

naturalistic fallacy

Key idea

A fallacy is an error in reasoning – a fallacious argument that seems to offer reasons for accepting a conclusion as true, but on closer examination provides no good reason for doing so.

The naturalistic fallacy

Thinking for ourselves is not easy, particularly as we are constantly being confronted and challenged in our own lives with the 'this is right, that is wrong' message from advertisers, politicians, our peers, religions, families or friends. The **naturalistic fallacy** is committed when someone offers a description of facts as the basis for accepting a moral judgement. The naturalistic fallacy is often encountered in the abortion debate. Consider these parallel arguments, one supporting anti-abortion, the other supporting pro-choice:

Statement 1: *Science has shown that at four weeks after conception the heartbeat of the embryo can be detected and therefore it is morally wrong to abort* (anti-abortion).

Statement 2: *Science has shown that before four weeks no heartbeat can be detected in the embryo and therefore it is morally acceptable to abort* (pro-choice).

Neither argument supports its conclusion. The abilities or inabilities of an embryo do not, by themselves, imply that abortion is right or wrong. What is needed is some consideration of what sorts of abilities a living thing must have to be attributed 'personhood'. Thus a further premise is required that states and defines exactly what personhood is.

Think it through

You are an international lawyer investigating the maiming of Ali Ismail Abbas a 12 year old boy in Iraq. You have to decide whether his maiming was 'justified' and make an international law for the future.

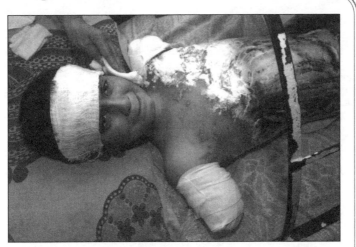

The consequences of USA and British bombing in Iraq, 2003

See pp. 171–172 for more on the just war theory.

 Hot tip

Reflect on what law will produce the most good and lead to the least harm for all involved. Respect the rights and dignity of everyone involved, ensuring that everyone is treated fairly by encouraging virtues such as compassion and tolerance.

STEP 1: What are the facts?

This first step, although obvious, is often the one most frequently forgotten.

STEP 2: What do people value?

Having the facts is not enough Facts by themselves only tell us what *is* – they do not tell us what *ought to be*. We also have to look at the way the story is presented and at other people's values – *what they believe to be good and what they believe to be bad.*

STEP 3: What international law will:

- enable the deepening of compassion and tolerance
- ensure that everyone is treated fairly
- produce the most good and lead to the least harm
- promote the common good and help everyone participate more harmoniously and happily
- respect the rights and dignity of everyone involved

STEP 4: What is the right thing to do?

After thinking, discussing and listening to the above opinions, options and questions, make your decision.

STEP 5: Reflect

How did it turn out for all concerned? If you had to do it over again, what, if anything, would you do differently?

Web quest

Find out more about the invasion of Iraq by looking at the World Messenger site and exploring the links. To do so visit www.heinemann.co.uk and click on this section.

Discussion

- Is everyone free to make moral decisions?
- If I do a 'bad' thing for a 'good' reason, does it matter?
- Is it always more important to think about the needs of others than the needs of myself?
- Should I let my heart rule my head in making moral choices and decisions?
- Is being good only about obeying certain rules?
- Is what is wrong for me always also wrong for you?

Key idea

A moral dilemma is a situation that offers two possible courses of action, each requiring a morally unacceptable action. Moral dilemmas are situations in which two or more moral obligations, duties, rights or ideals come into conflict. To begin to resolve a moral dilemma we must identify the factors involved, gather the facts of the situation, rank moral considerations, explore alternative courses of actions, and arrive at a judgement.

Moral dilemmas

A moral dilemma is a situation that offers two possible courses of action, each requiring a morally *unacceptable* action. Many moral dilemmas *are* dilemmas because of a certain kind of conflict between the rightness or wrongness of the actions and the goodness or badness of the consequences. Our duty is to do what is right, but as a practical matter, we would just as soon have things turn out as well as possible. The Greek philosopher Plato (427–347 BCE) (see pp. 38, 49, 51) presented a classic example of a moral dilemma in his teachings. A man borrows a weapon from his neighbour and gives him a promise that he will return it. The neighbour returns shortly after to claim the weapon but is in a fit of rage. He wants the weapon back so that he can kill someone. This creates a moral dilemma for the borrower. If he keeps his promise and returns the weapon, he will be an accessory to murder. If he refuses to return the weapon, he has broken his promise.

Think it through

A father's choice: You are an inmate in a concentration camp. A sadistic guard is about to hang your son who tried to escape and wants you to pull the chair from underneath him. He says that if you do not do it, he will not only kill your son but ten other innocent inmates as well. You do not have any doubt that he means what he says. What should you do?

A friend's choice: A friend confides to you that he has committed a crime and you promise never to tell anyone. Discovering that an innocent person has been accused of the crime, you plead with your friend to give himself up. He refuses and reminds you of your promise. What should you do?

Consistency

Consistency – the absence of contradictions – has sometimes been called the hallmark of ethics. Ethics is supposed to provide us with a guide for moral living, and to do so it must be rational and free from contradictions.

As a matter of fact, Joe, I never borrow from anyone, because if anyone lends me money, I always pay it back.

If a person said, 'Open the door but don't open the door,' we would be at loss as to what to do – the command is contradictory and thus irrational. There have been examples recently in the press of Roman Catholic priests who have preached **celibacy** and sexual restraint yet have been involved in child sex abuse. There are instances of politicians saying they are only concerned about peace but who then go to war. These sorts of examples point to the idea of ethical inconsistency – something we are all capable of. In its simplest form it means we say something at one point and deny it at another; like the **maxim** 'do as I say, not as I do.'

If our ethical principles lack consistency, we, as rational people, will find ourselves at a loss as to what we ought to do and divided about how we ought to live.

Word watch

consistency
contradictions

Word watch

maxim

❝ ═ Quotable quote ═══════

'If we decide that we do not have time to stop and think about right and wrong, then we do not have time to figure out right from wrong, which means that we do not have time to live according to our model of right and wrong, which means, simply put, we don't have time for lives of integrity.'

Stephen Carter, *Integrity* (1996)

❞

Word watch

equality
justify

Key idea

This is a good example of inconsistency in the application of a moral value – that of equality. The inconsistency is easily discovered if the relevant moral value (equality) is articulated in clear language and then applied to a situation.

Think it through

1 I believe that it is wrong to disobey my boss and I also believe that it is wrong to harm innocent people. Suppose one day my boss insists that I work on a project that might cause harm to innocent people. I can either obey my boss or I can avoid harming innocent people, but I cannot do both. To be consistent, I must modify one or both of these standards by examining the reasons I have for accepting them and weighing up these reasons to see which standard is more important and worth keeping.

2 To be consistent, we must apply the same moral standards to one situation that we apply to another, unless we can show that the two situations differ in relevant ways. I might believe, for example, that people should be free to live wherever they choose. Yet when a group of asylum seekers are housed next to me, I object. What is the difference between the two situations that justifies this difference in opinion?

3 We might hold consistent moral standards and apply them in consistent ways, but we may fail to be consistent in who we are as individuals. We often use the word 'integrity' to refer to people who act in ways that are consistent with their beliefs. Here, consistency means that a person's actions are in harmony with his or her inner values.

4 It is generally accepted that people should be treated equally regardless of who they are and what their background is. Slave holders in the early nineteenth century accepted this standard with respect to their own family and community, but not with respect to their slaves. There is an inconsistency here in the application of the standard of **equality** – some people are more equal than others. How did people justify this kind of inequality? There would be no inconsistency if some other relevant factor existed requiring that slaves should not be treated equally. One such factor commonly given was intelligence: a person of African descent, it was thought, was not as intelligent as someone of European descent. However, slaves were given no educational opportunities, and when they finally were it became obvious that slaves learnt just as well as their slave holders' children, demonstrating that the claim of the slave's alleged intellectual inferiority was false.

Some thinkers have argued that consistency is so important to ethics that it is the whole of ethics – if people consistently treat all human beings the same, they will *always* act ethically. Ethical behaviour, they argue, is simply a matter of being consistent by extending the same respect and consideration that we claim for ourselves to others.

But is consistency all there is to ethics? We may be perfectly consistent with respect to our moral principles and values, yet our principles may be incorrect and our values misplaced. We could say that while consistency is surely not sufficient for ethics, it is at least necessary for ethics.

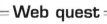

Discussion

1 'As I write, highly civilized human beings are flying overhead, trying to kill me. They do not feel any hatred towards me as an individual, nor I against them. They are "only doing their duty" as the saying goes. Most of them, I have no doubt, are kind-hearted law-abiding men who would never dream of committing murder in public life. On the other hand, if one of them succeeds in blowing me to pieces with a well-placed bomb, he will never sleep any the worse for it.'

George Orwell, *The Lion and the Unicorn* (1941)

2 'Philosophy is to be studied, not for the sake of any definite answers to its questions, since no definite answers can, as a rule, be known to be true, but rather for the sake of the questions themselves; because these questions enlarge our conception of what is possible, enrich our intellectual imagination and diminish the dogmatic assurance which closes the mind against speculation; but above all because, through the greatness of the universe which philosophy contemplates, the mind also is rendered great and becomes capable of that union with the universe which constitutes its highest good.'

Bertrand Russell, *The Problems of Philosophy* (1912)

3 Polonius, a character in Shakespeare's *Hamlet* (1601), points out the importance of integrity to the moral life when he says to his son, Laertes:

'This above all: to thine own self be true,
And it must follow, as the night the day,
Thou canst not then be false to any man.'

4 The Bible seems to imply that ethics consists of consistency:

'Do for others what you want them to do for you: this is the meaning of the Law of Moses and of the teachings of the prophets.'

(Matthew 7:12)

5 'Men are neither angels nor devils; that makes morality both necessary and possible.'

H.L. Hart, *Law, Liberty and Morality* (1963)

Web quest

For useful information see Ethics updates, BBC Ethics and Religion, Dictionary of philosophy and Episteme links by visiting www.heinemann.co.uk/hotlinks and clicking on this section.

2 Language

> 'When I use a word, it means just what I choose it to mean — neither more nor less.'
>
> Humpty Dumpty, in Lewis Carroll's
> *Alice Through the Looking Glass* (1871)

Objectives

During the first part of the twentieth century philosophers became concerned with analysing the meaning of moral terms.

In this chapter you will learn about the language of ethics with the main focuses being:

- the different ways ethical language is used – **descriptive ethics**, **prescriptive ethics** and **meta-ethics**
- to demonstrate that any complete study of ethics needs to incorporate the descriptive, the normative *and* the meta-ethical approaches
- the is/ought controversy
- the meaning of the word 'good'
- the theories of **ethical naturalism**, **logical positivism**, **emotivism** and **intuitionism** and their strengths and weaknesses.

Word watch

descriptive ethics
prescriptive ethics
meta-ethics
ethical naturalism
logical positivism
emotivism
intuitionism

Key questions

1 What is good?

2 Are ethical principles merely social inventions?

3 Do ethical principles involve more than the expression of personal emotions?

Word watch

non-moral act
non-moral judgement

Think it through

We often respond to events, situations and issues with strong moral language – words that can be used in a judgemental way:

- right – 'It is right to do what your parents tell you!'
- wrong – 'It is wrong to kill!'
- ought – 'We ought to help others!'
- should – 'We should do what the law says!'
- good – 'It is good to talk!'
- bad – 'It is bad to tell lies!'
- must – 'We must care for the homeless!'

Write down one example for each of the following:

A **moral** act – an act that is considered to be right

An **immoral** act – an act considered to be wrong

An **amoral** act – an act that shows no understanding between right and wrong

A **non-moral** act – an act not concerned with right and wrong

A non-moral judgement – a view or opinion that has nothing to do with right and wrong.

What is 'love'?

When someone says, 'I love you,' what does he or she mean? The word could convey simple lust, mindless obsession, deep affection, the desire for manipulative possession or jealous ownership, friendship, altruistic concern — the list of meanings can go on and on.

The interpretation of words by the one to whom they are addressed is conditioned by many factors: our knowledge of the speaker, the context in which the words are spoken, and, perhaps most importantly, by what in a particular set of circumstances *we want the words to mean*.

What is 'good'?

Giving up your seat on a bus to a pregnant woman is '**good**'. Pretending to be asleep so that you do not have to give up your seat is not 'good'. We seem to know what we mean when we say that something is good or that it is not good. But what do we really mean by 'good'? How does one define 'good'?

Many of you will have read the books *Harry Potter* or *Lord of the Rings* or have seen the films. They both celebrate virtues like loyalty and courage — two characteristics generally regarded as being 'good'. So are *Harry Potter* and *Lord of the Rings* 'good' books/films? Are loyalty and courage always 'good'?

Are there some circumstances when loyalty and courage are not 'good'?

The question 'what is good?' has intrigued philosophers since the time of the Greek philosopher Aristotle (384–322 BCE), and continues to do so today.

Word watch

altruistic

How do we use ethical language?

Descriptive ethics

Descriptive ethics *describe* the way we live and the moral choices we make. Descriptivists simply present facts; for example, 'Seventy-two square miles of desert appear on Earth every day.' The actual information may be correct or incorrect. It can be checked by referring to statistical information, environmental reports and satellite pictures. However, the statement does not make any moral claim about desertification, nor does it say whether it is a good or bad thing. Some philosophers, however, argue that descriptive ethics can sometimes *imply* moral judgements by the way in which information is presented. For example, does the following photograph imply a moral judgement just by the way it is presented?

Does this photograph imply a moral judgement by the way it is presented?

Problems with descriptive ethics

Sometimes facts can be mistaken for values. You need to ask yourself what is the difference between a fact and a value?

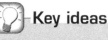

Key ideas

Descriptive ethics describe the way we live, simply presenting facts.

Prescriptive ethics prescribe what is right and how people should live.

Meta-ethics explores the meaning of ethical language.

Think it through

Does the following piece of writing contain facts or facts *and* values?

The sex tourism industry – involving men travelling to other countries to engage in sex with children – has been documented in the Philippines, Cambodia, Thailand, and in North American and Eastern Europe. Most of the children exploited in the sex trade are between the ages of thirteen and eighteen, although there is evidence of children younger than five being sexually exploited as well. Asia is the worst affected area for child prostitution, with one million children being sexually exploited. There are at least 30,000 children in India in the sex trade and countless tens of thousands of abused children in Thailand.

Prescriptive or normative ethics

Prescriptive ethics (or **normative ethics**) are concerned with rules, guidelines and norms about what is right and how people *should* live. Prescriptivists *prescribe* – tell us how we ought to behave. They might go even further and come up with definite, though not always identical, conclusions. For example, when looking at issues concerning the environment, they may come up with certain prescriptions: 'Given the evidence, a person should always join movements that work against environmental destruction,' or 'Desertification, leading as it does to famine and caused as it is by the policies of the rich world, ought to be stopped by the adoption of new policies by the rich world.'

These prescriptions *tell* people how they should behave; they do not merely *describe* how they do behave. Prescriptive ethics was considered an important part of ethics up until the 1930s when it became relatively neglected.

Word watch

normative ethics

Problems with prescriptive ethics

When arguing that things 'ought' to be a certain way it is easy to fall into the trap of preaching. This can prevent people from making consistent, objective, reasoned and informed choices for themselves (**autonomy**). In other words, it can stop people thinking for themselves and making up their own minds – pressurizing them to think in a certain way.

Word watch

autonomy

Meta-ethics or analytical ethics

From the 1930s to the 1960s, meta-ethics became a major preoccupation of many philosophers. The term 'meta' means *after* or *beyond*. Meta-ethics involves a removed or bird's eye view of ethics. Also known as **analytical ethics**, meta-ethics *analyses* ethical language and considers the *meaning* of moral judgements. Meta-ethics is concerned with meaning, not descriptions or prescriptions, and studies reasoning and language rather than content.

Word watch

analytical ethics

Problems with meta-ethics

Critics argue that the focus on minor details about language has distracted philosophers away from the bigger picture. Philosophers, critics argue, should be working out how they can help create practical frameworks for **universal** justice and peace rather than wasting time and energy arguing about definitions. They argue that **ethicists** need to engage with other disciplines and draw on the evidence provided by psychologists, professors of medicine, genetic engineers, social scientists and environmentalists. As representatives and guardians of the great traditions of philosophy, contemporary philosophers have a responsibility to help create systems of thought and action that benefit the global community.

Word watch

universal
ethicists

Write two captions, one 'descriptive' and one 'prescriptive'

The 'is/ought' gap

Consider these three statements:

- 'Sex *is* the means by which humans make babies and so people *ought* to have sex only for this purpose.'
- 'A man *is* stronger than a woman and so *ought* to use his force to get his own way.'
- 'Britain *is* a country with weapons of mass destruction so Britain *ought* to use these weapons.'

Are these statements – moving from an *is* to an *ought* – reasonable? David Hume (1711–76), in *A Treatise of Human Nature* (1740), argued that these sorts of statements are unreasonable and that prescriptive statements (*ought* ones) cannot be derived from descriptive statements (*is* ones). Hume argued that what *is* the case and what *ought to be* the case are two unrelated matters.

The bridging of this gap between *is* and *ought* has become more acceptable in modern ethical enquiry, particularly around environmental issues.

The only exercise he gets is jumping to conclusions.

Foreigners out! Bring back the birch. Single mothers are a disgrace.

Key idea

The philosopher, David Hume (1711–76) argued that there is a logical barrier to deriving claims concerning how we ought to act from descriptive claims concerning the way things are. This barrier has come to be known as the 'is/ought' gap in ethical thought.

Discussion

If *ought* is not *is*, what is?

Think it through

1 Consider the difference between the following statements:

   a 'It *is* the case that some people treat animals badly' – descriptive.

   b 'It *ought* to be that humans do not treat animals badly' – prescriptive.

   Can you see the difference? Can you think of other examples?

2 Can you think of some circumstances when supposed 'good' actions such as courage are not 'good' and might lead to 'bad' consequences?

3 Likewise, can you think of any circumstances when supposed 'bad' actions can lead to 'good' consequences?

'Good' and the naturalistic fallacy

The British philosopher G.E. Moore (1873–1958), in *Principia Ethica* (1903), argues that the notion of moral goodness cannot be defined or identified with any property. Moore argues that 'goodness' is a foundational and unanalysable property, similar to the foundational notion of 'yellowness', and is incapable of being explained in terms of anything more basic. We intuitively recognize goodness when we see it, as we similarly recognize yellowness when we see it. But the idea of 'goodness' itself cannot be defined. For Moore, philosophers who attempt to define **intrinsic goodness** commit the naturalistic fallacy – the fallacy of defining the term 'goodness' in terms of some natural property, such as pleasure.

Moore defends his argument with what has been called the *open question argument*. For any property we attempt to identify with 'goodness' we can ask, 'Is that property itself good?' For example, if I claim that pleasure is the highest intrinsic good, the question can be asked, 'But, is pleasure itself good?' The fact that this question makes sense shows that 'pleasure' and 'goodness' are not identical. Moore believes that no proposed natural property can pass the test of the open question argument. This implies that all moral theories based on anything other than immediate moral intuition fail. It is only of secondary importance whether an action produces pleasure, is in accord with the will of God, or is conducive to reason. What truly matters is whether we can simply recognize the goodness of a particular action.

Key questions

1 Can ethics be more than just value judgements?

2 Facts describe what 'is'. Values say what 'ought' to be. How can we derive a value from a fact (an 'ought' from an 'is')?

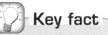

Key fact

Some modern ethicists such as Peter Singer (see p. 155) and Alasdair MacIntyre (see pp. 113–115) argue that situations exist where it is logically acceptable to move from a descriptive statement (is) to a prescriptive one (ought). For example, 'Who I am dictates what I ought to do' (for example, 'I am a doctor and therefore I ought to follow the Hippocratic Oath' or 'I am a parent and therefore I ought to behave responsibly'). These, and many other examples, they argue, are occasions when the bridging of the gap from descriptive ethics to prescriptive ethics is reasonable.

Ethical naturalism

Much of the debate about ethics in modern philosophy then, is concerned with the meaning of moral statements and the possibility of showing that they are either basically true or false. Ethical naturalism states that we can know whether something is basically good or bad or right or wrong by looking at the facts, using observation and analysis (the same tools as science).

Moral facts are not merely views or opinions but are observations based on the realities of the natural universe. For example, it can be said that homelessness is a moral blight in our affluent society – that the wrongness of homelessness is as much a fact of the universe as the fact that men sleeping rough on the streets of London have a risk of dying 40 times that of the general population (Bristol University Research, 2003).

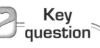

Key idea

The naturalistic fallacy: according to G.E. Moore, any argument that attempts to define 'the good' in any terms whatsoever is indefinable.

Key question

Can I conclude that something is basically right or wrong by looking at the facts?

Men sleeping rough on the streets of London have a risk of dying 40 times that of the general population

Ethical naturalists argue that moral conclusions can be deduced from non-moral premises. We can know something is wrong from observation. Consider the two statements:

'Russian troops completely destroyed Chechnya's capital Grozny in 1995.'

'Russian action was evil.'

The first statement is factual and can be proved by looking at the evidence. The second statement is a moral judgement. According to ethical naturalists, the second statement may also be proved in much the same way by looking at the evidence; for example, the legacy of Russian aggression. In this way, ethical terms can be defined and moral judgements based on the same kind of observation of the world as used in scientific observation.

Logical positivism

According to one particular view of philosophy – logical positivism (sometimes called logical empiricism) – questions about right and wrong cannot be answered by moral philosophy. If the logical positivists are right, then the study of ethics is a waste of time!

Logical positivists aimed to establish criteria so that philosophers could *talk* meaningfully. To this end they sought to establish how the truth or falsehood of certain propositions could be demonstrated. They argued that if a proposition cannot be established as true or false, then it is meaningless. After examining language, the logical positivists concluded that there are three types of statements:

- **Analytical statements** (for example, 'all bachelors are unmarried men'). Ludwig Wittgenstein (1889–1951) called these **tautological statements** in the sense that 'bachelors' is simply another way of saying 'unmarried men'. Most propositions of mathematics or logic are analytical.
- **Synthetic statements** (for example, 'Yusuf is a married man') are those that can only be verified or falsified by observation and examination.
- **Meaningless statements** (for example, 'violence is wrong'). When logical positivists call a statement meaningless, they do not mean that the statement is sheer nonsense, but rather that it *cannot be verified*. For a positivist, philosophy is essentially about theories of knowledge (**epistemology**). Ethics is not seen as proper knowledge, because ethical statements cannot be proved or disproved, unlike synthetic statements.

Criticism of logical positivism

In the real world of human experience, ethical language *does* have significant meaning. We not only *feel* that the murder of children is wrong, we also *know* that we are reasonably justified in saying it and would be prepared to support our argument. Try telling the parents of a murdered child that the statement 'murder is wrong' is meaningless!

Think it through

1 Try to think of examples of (a) an analytical statement, (b) a synthetic statement, and (c) a meaningless statement, according to logical positivists.

2 How would you argue to a logical positivist that the statement 'murder is wrong' is *not* a meaningless statement?

Key fact

Logical positivism emerged during the early part of the twentieth century. Initially known as The Vienna Circle, the movement influenced British philosophers like A.J. ('Freddie') Ayer (1910–89), Bertrand Russell (1872–1970) and Gilbert Ryle (1900–76). The Vienna Circle wanted to establish criteria so that philosophers could *talk* meaningfully.

Word watch

tautological
synthetic
epistemology

Emotivism: Boo! Hurray!

Emotivism is a theory that attempts to address the issues raised by meta-ethics. Can morality be reduced simply to how we feel about something? Emotivists say 'yes', arguing that ethical words and sentences merely express people's attitudes and feelings, which in turn generate feelings and attitudes in others. For example, a pacifist politician and a general are in debate.

The pacifist says, 'All war is murder.' The general argues, 'Sometimes the only way to overcome an evil dictator is to wage war.' The emotivist suggests that the debate may be characterized as follows:

To the emotivist, statements really express a person's *preferences* or *emotions*. To say that something is 'good' or 'right' is just another way of saying that one approves of it. The feelings of the speaker are expressed in order to influence the feelings of the hearer – any moral statements made by generals and pacifists do not state facts at all.

Can I conclude that something is morally wrong by listening to my emotions?

Criticism of emotivism

Is emotivism a moral theory at all? If all behaviour is just about how we *feel*, how can we *know* anything? Can we not prove in some rational way that telling the truth is morally preferable to lying; that caring for animals is morally more justifiable than abusing them; that being loyal to partners is more acceptable than betrayal?

The main criticism of emotivism is that it does not account for the connections between moral judgements and reasons. For an emotivist, a moral judgement is like a command – it is chiefly a verbal means of trying to *influence* other people's attitudes and behaviour. However, although our values are usually little more than the expression of our **subjective** feelings, *moral judgements can ultimately only be true if backed by reasons*. In considering questions of morality, one must ask why a moral judgement should or should not be accepted. One might have strong feelings and might choose to ignore reason, but by doing this one is opting out of moral thinking. Moral thinking is about weighing up reasons, something that emotivism as an ethical theory, which focuses on feelings, fails to acknowledge.

R.M. Hare

Richard Hare (1919–2002) was one of the principal moral philosophers of the post-war era. Hare's philosophical career started with a rejection of descriptivism – that moral judgements are no more than *descriptions* of actions and choices. However, he was also dissatisfied with the standard 'emotivist' alternatives, which allowed only an emotional element to moral judgements. Hare's work was very much influenced by the 'ordinary language' approach to philosophy; thus he took as the foundation of his theorizing the way moral terms are standardly used.

Hare argued that we are too complex to reduce all our language about good, right, bad and wrong, to emotive theories. Whereas the emotivist is concerned with the effect a moral statement aims to have, Hare, a **prescriptivist**, was *more concerned about what happens when somebody makes a moral statement*. In his book *The Language of Morals* (1952) he argued that a moral statement such as 'murder is wrong' is not simply an expression of feeling, but rather a *recommendation* or a *rule* such as 'Thou shall not kill'. For Hare, statements like these are designed to *prescribe behaviour*. They move beyond our specific or individual viewpoint and can be universalized because they are not only good for the individual but are good for everyone.

Intuitionism

Intuitionism is another theory that attempts to address the issues raised by meta-ethics. Intuitionists claim that we grasp basic moral principles by *intuition*: moral principles are capable of being true and known through a special faculty called 'moral intuition'. Two supporters of this view, W.D. Ross (1877–1971) and H.A. Pritchard (1871–1947), claimed that there *are* 'facts' about what is morally right

Key idea

Charles Stevenson, (1908–79), in *Ethics and Language* (1945), argued that disagreements about right and wrong are in fact disagreements in belief. If someone says 'abortion is wrong', all they are doing is announcing how they feel about abortion. Even if they give reasons why they believe abortion is wrong, these reasons merely appeal to others' emotions to support the original statement.

See Chapter 9 for more on Hare.

Key fact

Richard Hare served as a lieutenant in the Indian Mountain Artillery. He was captured and became a Japanese prisoner of war on the infamous Burma–Thailand railway between 1939 and 1942.

and wrong and that our understanding of these facts is sufficient enough to deserve the title 'knowledge'. We *know* that something is good by *intuition*: it is self-evident. You can define an action as being 'right' if it leads to a 'good' result.

Criticism of intuitionism

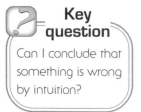

Key question

Can I conclude that something is wrong by intuition?

- The major objection to intuitionism is that if what is 'good' is self-evident, how can I still find myself full of doubts about the best way to proceed? Life is seldom straightforward and sometimes I might not know what to do. If people were always absolutely sure about what they should do, there would be no ethical debate at all. Ross – in defence of intuitionism – argued that 'shoulds' sometimes conflict with other duties and a choice has to be made. Ethical dilemmas are therefore the result of such conflicting duties.

- We do not always intuitively know the right thing to do! Think of some examples when you are torn between different choices or between 'the head and the heart'. In a pluralistic society, with different belief systems and no one single ethical tradition, people may have widely divergent views about what is ethical.

Ethical dilemmas are often controversial and open to argument and debate.

- The intuitionist's claim that 'moral facts' are known by intuition suggests that we have a faculty that reveals moral truth to us in much the same sort of way that our eyes reveal truths about our surroundings. Such a view might tempt us to accuse those who disagree with us of being 'morally blind', or to claim that their moral faculty is not in as good working order as our own. Without an account of how this faculty is supposed to work, philosophers have complained that 'moral intuition' is just the attempt to award an authority to one's own moral opinion that one is not willing to grant to others.

❛ — **Quotable quote** ━━━━━━━━━━━━━━━━━━

'Twentieth century moral philosophers have sometimes appealed to their and our intuitions, but one of the things that we ought to have learned from the history of moral philosophy is that the introduction of the word "intuition" by a moral philosopher is always a signal that something has gone badly wrong with an argument.'

Alasdair MacIntyre, *After Virtue* (1981)

❜

Web quest

For magazine articles and book excerpts that offer an alternative view look at the Third World Traveller website by visiting www.heinemann.co.uk/hotlinks and clicking on this section. Download or print any article and then study its content for (a) descriptive statements, (b) prescriptive statements, (c) meta-ethical statements, (d) emotive statements, and (e) verifiable statements.

Review

Descriptive ethics: *describes* the way we live and the moral choices we make.

Prescriptive ethics (or normative ethics): are concerned with prescriptions and norms about what is right and how people *should* live.

Meta-ethics (or analytical ethics): *analyses* ethical language by looking at the *meaning* of moral judgements.

The 'is/ought' controversy: concerns the distinction between epistemology (theory or theories of knowledge) and prescriptive ethics. Epistemology aims to describe, scientifically or logically, the way the world is constructed; prescriptive ethics aims to give an account of the way the world ought to be and the ways people ought to behave.

What is 'good'? For Aristotle, 'good' is defined as something that fulfils its own particular *function*.

Ethical naturalism: we can conclude that something is, good or bad by looking at the facts – by using the same tools as science; that is, observation and analysis.

Logical positivism: philosophy is about establishing how the truth or falsehood of certain propositions can be demonstrated. If a proposition cannot be established as true or false, then it is meaningless. So ethical statements cannot be proved or disproved and are not empirically verifiable.

Emotivism: ethical language merely expresses people's attitudes and feelings, possibly generating different feelings and attitudes in others.

Intuitionism: we can know what is right or wrong by intuition. But if what is 'good' is self-evident, why am I full of doubts about the best way to proceed?

Exam questions

1 (a) Explain and discuss why scholars claim that you cannot derive an 'ought' from an 'is' statement. (10 marks)

   (b) Examine and criticize emotivism as an ethical theory. (10 marks)
        (EDEXCEL, January 2002)

2 (a) Analyse and consider the distinctive concepts of *either* intuitionism *or* natural moral law. (12 marks)

   (b) Analyse and evaluate the application of the selected theory (intuitionism **or** natural moral law) to debates about *one* of the following:
        i   authority
        ii   justice
        iii law and punishment. (8 marks) (EDEXCEL, June 2002)

3 Freedom?

'There was once a man who said damn!
It is borne in upon me I am
An engine that moves
In predestinate grooves;
I'm not even a bus, I'm a tram.'

Limerick, author unknown

Word watch

determinism
libertarianism
free will

Objectives

In this chapter you are invited to explore the relationship between freedom and moral responsibility. The main focuses of this area of enquiry are:

* different views on freedom and **determinism**
* the concepts of autonomy, diminished **responsibility** and **predestination**
* the ethical theories of **hard determinism**, **libertarianism** and **soft determinism**, and the strengths and weaknesses of these theories
* the implications of the **free will** and determinism debate on crime and punishment.

? Key questions

1 When all the influencing and the controlling factors in my life are taken into consideration, how free am I really?

2 Do I have free will or is every action I make predetermined?

3 Can I truly choose my own actions?

4 Can I be blamed for an action that hurts someone else if I am not free?

5 Can I be praised for a 'good' action if I am not free?

❛ Quotable quote

*'Your destiny shall not be allotted to you, but you shall choose it for yourselves. Let him who draws the first lot be the first to choose a life, which shall be his irrevocably. **Virtue** owns no master; he who honours her shall have more of her, and he who slights her less.'*

Plato, *Republic* (360 BCE)

Word watch

virtue

👄 Discussion

'You will say that I feel free. This is an illusion, which may be compared to that of the fly in the fable, who, upon the pole of a heavy carriage, applauded himself for directing its course. Man, who thinks himself free, is a fly who imagines he has power to move the universe, while he is himself unknowingly carried along by it.'

Baron Paul Henri d'Holbach (1723–89), German Philosopher

'You know the alternative: either we are not free and God the all-powerful is responsible for evil. Or we are free and responsible. All the scholastic subtleties have neither added anything to nor subtracted anything from the acuteness of this paradox.'

Albert Camus (1913–60), Algerian-born writer, *The Myth of Sisyphus* (1942)

'We who lived in the concentration camps can remember the men who walked through the huts comforting others, giving away their last piece of bread. They may have been few in number but they offer sufficient proof that everything can be taken from a man but one thing: the last of the human freedoms – to choose one's attitude in any given circumstance, to choose one's own way.'

Viktor Frankl (1905–97), Holocaust survivor, *Man's Search for Meaning* (1959)

❛ Quotable quote

'Everything is determined, the beginning as well as the end, by forces over which we have no control. It is determined for the insect as well as the star. Human beings, vegetables, or cosmic dust, we all dance to a mysterious tune, intoned in the distance by an invisible piper.'

Albert Einstein (1879–1955), scientist and philosopher ❜

Free will

Imagine you were told that your supposed ability to make free choices was an illusion. Or that all human actions have a cause beyond our control. Would you still be morally responsible for your actions?

Freedom and moral responsibility are related. It is generally accepted that we should be held responsible for our actions. We must accept blame for the acts that we freely do wrong. However, if someone forces me against my will to do

Word watch

intention

something, then clearly I cannot be blamed. Likewise, if I act in ignorance, then I am not blameworthy. If I do something wrong when I am sleepwalking, I am not entirely responsible for my actions. If while sleepwalking I hit someone, I am morally blameworthy, but my crime is not as great a crime as if I had deliberately hit somebody in the cold light of day. **Intention** is important here. People who deliberately and intentionally break the law are more heavily punished than people who break the law accidentally.

❝ ═ Quotable quote ═════════════

'A man can surely do what he wills to do, but cannot determine what he wills.'

Arthur Schopenhauer (1788–1860), German philosopher ❞

'Diminished responsibility'

To have free will we must have two or more possibilities 'genuinely open' to us when we face a choice, and our choice must not be 'forced'. The concept of free will plays a central role in our thinking about the world, particularly in the way we praise and blame others, and in our finding persons *morally responsible* for things they have done. All sorts of conditions serve to diminish moral responsibility – and blameworthiness. We do not hold persons morally responsible for their actions when they are:

Word watch

diminished

- delirious and under the influence of a powerful medication producing unexpected psychological effects
- very young, since the young are unable to predict the consequences of their actions and may not have mature concepts of right and wrong
- forced (coerced); for example, by someone holding a gun to our head.

Word watch

coerced

Are there factors that might limit my ability to act freely?

The list of 'excusing conditions' has grown steadily over the years and may include:

- genetic make-up, over which one has no control
- environmental factors and upbringing
- education that, at least in one's early years, is beyond one's control.

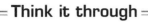

Think it through

1 Imagine you are a lawyer defending an eighteen-year-old man on a charge of grievous bodily harm. He has a history of violent behaviour and truanting. As a child he was emotionally and physically abused by a violent and drunken father. The court wants to send him to prison. Try to construct a defence for your client using one or more of the 'excusing conditions' – that is, genetic make-up, environmental factors/upbringing and education – to lessen his sentence.

2 Clarence Darrow (1857–1938) a famous American lawyer never lost a client to the death penalty in his entire career! When Darrow defended people accused of murder, he used a standard argument that his clients were not *morally responsible* for their actions:

'We know that man's every act is induced by motives that led or urged him here or there; that the sequence of cause and effect runs through the whole universe and is nowhere more compelling than with man ... The principal thing to remember is that we are all the products of heredity and environment; that we have little or no control, as individuals, over ourselves, and that criminals are like the rest of us in that regard.'

Do you agree with Darrow? Give reasons for your answer and discuss your thoughts with the rest of your class.

6 Quotable quote

'Man is condemned to be free; because once thrown into the world, he is responsible for everything he does.'

Jean-Paul Sartre (1905–80), French philosopher

Autonomy

Autonomy refers to a person's capacity to choose freely and direct his or her own life. Autonomy is restricted by factors such as the law, social tradition, responsibility to others and prevailing personal circumstances such as age, background and personality. Personal autonomy also depends upon our having a sufficient degree of knowledge or rationality to pursue our goals. This includes an understanding of the routes open to us and of the pitfalls, and being able to apply knowledge to achieve our end and select appropriate ends.

Key idea

Morality depends on freedom. If people are not free, the possibility of making moral choices is denied.

Word watch

autonomous

? Key question

If everything is predestined, how can anyone be morally responsible for his or her actions?

Word watch

unconscious

Predestination

The Judaeo-Christian view, expressed in Genesis in the Bible, is that human beings are free to choose between good and evil. We are created as free, autonomous agents, responsible for our actions. However, some Christians have believed, and still believe, that God has already decided who will be saved and who will not. This idea is called predestination and originates in the words of St Paul: 'And so those whom God set apart, he called; and those he called, he put right with himself, and he shared his glory with them' (Romans 8:30). Predestination suggests that we do not have free will.

Hard determinism

Hard determinism is the view that all events are totally predetermined by other events. Freedom of choice is therefore an illusion. We are all slaves to past causes and ultimately have no control over our actions. According to hard determinism, factors like our environment, heredity, unconscious impulses, defence mechanisms and other influences, determine the way we act. Hard determinism can come in different forms:

- theistic – predestination by an omnipotent God
- fatalistic – 'what will be, will be'
- behaviourist – psychological conditioning.

Hard determinists argue that we may believe that we have free will and are able to choose any number of options, but in reality our choices are determined by factors outside our control. We might spend hours pondering about what to do and make a decision believing that we have freely done so, but, say determinists, our decision was inevitable because of all the underlying causes.

The main problem with hard determinism is that if I am not free and responsible for my actions, how can I be held responsible for my actions?

Are we ultimately slaves to past causes with no control over our destinies?

Libertarianism

Libertarianism is the view that we are free to act and are morally responsible for our actions. We are not made to act by any outside sources. Libertarians argue that when we act we are actually *choosing* to act in a particular way. We think of ourselves as free agents and have a sense of making decisions. For example, even if

I am brought up by a family of criminals and genetically/socially disposed to a life of crime, moral intuition can make me question what I am doing.

Libertarianism has its problems. How do we know that our moral judgements are not dependent on any outside source? How can we determine exactly what the influences from our environment or our upbringing are?

❛ Quotable quote

'Either it is an accident that I choose to act as I do, or it is not. If it is an accident, then it is merely a matter of chance that I did not choose otherwise; and if it is merely a matter of chance that I did not choose otherwise, it is surely irrational to hold me morally responsible for choosing as I did. But if it is not an accident that I choose to do one thing rather than another, then presumably there is some causal explanation of my choice; and in that case we are led back to determinism.'

A.J. Ayer, *Philosophical Essays* (1959) ❜

Discussion

Is my 'voluntary' action at any moment completely determined by:

1 my character as it has been partly inherited (biological dispositions)

and/or

2 my circumstances and the external influences acting on me at that moment?

Could the action I am just about to do be calculated by someone who knows my character and the forces acting upon me? Or is there always an incalculable element to behaviour?

Soft determinism

'Soft' determinism (compatibilism) is an attempt to combine the insights of 'libertarianism' with those of 'hard' determinism. According to soft determinism, freedom means being able to do what one wants to do without external coercion or interference from anyone else. What one wants, as expressed by one's personality or character, is determined by external events; for example, **genetics**, culture, upbringing; but as long as one is able to act consistently with the choices he or she makes, he or she is free. The main problem with soft determinism is that it ignores the fact that inner, unconscious coercive forces (for example, compulsions) can also sometimes determine our actions.

Hot tip

Remember that a belief in genuine free will is central to religious notions of decision-making and responsibility; hard determinism makes it impossible to believe in free will.

Hot tip

In your exam you will need to show an understanding of soft determinism, hard determinism and libertarianism, and also how soft determinism can be seen as an attempt to combine the major insights of the other two.

Key idea

Key idea

'Soft' determinism (compatibilism) is an attempt to combine the insights of 'libertarianism' with those of 'hard' determinism.

Key idea

Soft determinism is the claim that a deterministic account of human behaviour (every action is caused by previous events) does not necessarily rule out the idea of a person being responsible for his or her actions.

Word watch

superego
taboos

 Think it through

1 Discuss in pairs what a determinist and a libertarian would make of the following situations and decide whether or not the people concerned are morally to blame.

(a) A German, terrified of Hitler's Secret Police, hands over some hiding Jews.

(b) A desperate suicide bomber, who has lost his home and family, blows himself up in a crowded street where his enemies live.

(c) After days of torture a captured soldier gives away secrets that will result in the arrest and possible death of his comrades.

(d) A girl, after drinking huge quantities of alcohol, allows herself to be seduced by a man she has only just met.

(e) A homeless person prostitutes her/himself to get some money.

(f) A man knowingly infects a prostitute with a sexually transmitted disease.

(g) A local politician makes a dreadful economic decision, resulting in the loss of hundreds of jobs.

(h) A motorist is unaware that he has broken the speed limit.

(i) A man is blackmailed into committing a terrible crime.

(j) An alcoholic is caught stealing a bottle of vodka.

(k) A sex addict accesses porn daily from the Internet.

(l) A bomber pilot bombs a village that contains both civilians and 'terrorists'.

Freudianism

Until Sigmund Freud (1856–1939) started delving into the unconscious, most moral philosophers assumed that we are always in control of our thought processes and that the choices we make are ours. However, Freud's theory is that we are programmed by instinctive psychic structures in the unconscious mind, which exert powerful pressures upon us to fulfil our basic desires.

According to **Freudianism**, the superego is part of the unconscious mind that has internalized societal and parental taboos and is similar to the authoritarian conscience (see pp. 63–64). It is like an inner voice reminding us of the social norms acquired through childhood. Freud said that we need this voice in order to exist in a law-abiding society. For Freud, being moral may not accord with our real natures at all, and to base a moral system on what we essentially are is impossible.

Freud's most radical modern disciple, Jacques Lacan (1901–81), took Freud's ideas on the absence of an essentially moral self even further. He said that the 'self' itself is a fiction – nothing more than a linguistic construct. Since language exists as a structure before the individual enters into it, then the whole notion of human identity is untenable. In this way, self-knowledge or moral choices cannot be 'ours'.

Web quest

See lecture notes on free will and determinism by Norman Swartz, information on free will and determinism at the Catholic website and a slide show on the dilemma of free will and determinism by visiting www.heinemann.co.uk/hotlinks and clicking on this section.

Review

Autonomy: a person's capacity to choose freely and direct his/her own life.

Hard determinism: all events are totally predetermined by other events. Freedom of choice is an illusion.

Libertarianism: we are free to act and are morally responsible for those actions.

Soft determinism (compatibilism): like hard determinism, it acknowledges that human actions have causes, but allows for free actions when the actions are caused by one's choices rather than external forces.

Predestination: everything we do is predetermined and so we do not have free will.

Freudianism: we are programmed by instinctive psychic structures in the unconscious mind – the superego reminding us of the social norms acquired through childhood.

Exam questions

1 (a) Explain the views of those who believe that we have no freedom to make moral decisions. (33 marks)

(b) To what extent might a determinist question the punishment of offenders? (17 marks) (OCR, June 2001)

2 (a) Explain how 'soft' determinism can be seen as an attempt to combine the insights of 'libertarianism' with those of 'hard' determinism. (20 marks)

(b) 'A religious approach to ethics cannot be sustained given the insights of "hard determinism".' Outline the arguments that support this view and assess how successful they are. (30 marks) (AQA, June 2002)

3 (a) Explain the difference between 'hard' and 'soft' determinism. (33 marks)

(b) 'I cannot be blamed for my behaviour; it's in my genes!' Discuss this statement in relation to sexual relationships. (17 marks) (OCR, January 2001)

4 Is it all relative?

> 'If we'd been born where they were born and taught what they were taught, we would believe what they believe.'
>
> A sign outside a church in Northern Ireland

Word watch

absolutism
relativism
universal

Objectives

In this chapter you will explore two very different ethical approaches to reality – **absolutism** and **relativism**. For absolutists, universal moral standards apply equally to everyone at all times. Relativists are less sure that everything is certain and argue that circumstances arise that make exceptions to any rule. These two approaches determine the way that individuals and communities see the 'rest of the world'.

But are moral absolutes merely principles created by humans to make society workable? Or are they enduring principles expressed to us by some transcendent or godlike authority? Efforts to resolve this conundrum have perplexed and sometimes inflamed our best minds for centuries. In this chapter you will explore relativism and absolutism by looking at:

- the claims, strengths and weaknesses of relativism and absolutism
- St Thomas Aquinas's natural law theory and its applications to sexual ethics
- the theories of **Marxism** and **postmodernism**.

Word watch

Marxism
postmodernism

Key questions

1 Is 'truth' different for different people?

2 Are there situations when an action might be right and other situations when the same action might be wrong?

3 Are things that are true for you necessarily true for me?

4 Is one culture or religion's view of morality as good as that of another culture or religion?

5 Are there some actions that are always right?

6 Are there certain moral rules that exist for all times and for all places?

7 Is each individual equally good so long as each person does what he or she believes in?

8 Do we invent our ethical absolutes in order to make society workable?

9 Are enduring principles expressed to us by some transcendent or godlike authority?

Think it through

The nomadic Masai of East Africa practise polygamy and wife-lending between men of the same age group. Some Westerners practise open marriages, whereby spouses engage other spouses in shared and open sexual relations. Christians practise monogamy. Is any one way morally better or morally worse than another?

Relativism

Relativism is the theory that the truth is different for different people. Someone might say to you, 'Come on, say what you think, there *are* no right or wrong opinions.' This statement is relativist – relativism is the philosophy that denies absolutes. There are different kinds of relativism:

- metaphysical relativism is the claim that there are no absolutes in reality
- epistemological relativism is the idea that there are no absolutes in knowledge
- ethical relativism is the denial of moral absolutes.

Ethical relativism

In this book we are concerned with *ethical* relativism. There are two types of ethical relativism:

- **descriptive ethical relativism** claims it is a matter of fact that different people have different moral beliefs, but takes no stand on whether those beliefs are valid or not
- **normative ethical relativism** claims that each culture's, or group's, beliefs are appropriate within that culture, and that it is impossible to judge another culture's values from the outside.

Varieties of ethical relativism

Ethical relativism

This theory states that morality is relative to the norms of one's culture. An action is therefore right or wrong depending on the moral norms of the society in which it is practised. By the same token, the same action may be morally right in one society but morally wrong in another.

Key question

If we accept that different cultures have different values and beliefs, can we still judge these cultures' value systems?

For the ethical relativist, there are no universal moral standards – standards that can be universally applied to all peoples at all times. The only moral standards against which a society's practices can be judged are its own. If ethical relativism is correct, there can be no common framework for resolving moral disputes or for reaching agreement on ethical matters among members of different societies.

Individual ethical relativism

This theory states that right and wrong can be different for each individual. Ethical judgements are only expressions of individual feelings or opinions. Because everyone has different moral views, and will make different moral judgements under the same circumstances, there is no point in trying to find a common moral standard.

Cultural ethical relativism

This theory states that right and wrong are whatever each society or culture *says* or *believes* is right and wrong. Different cultures have different moral standards, and it is simply a prejudice of our own cultural perspective to find fault with different cultural views. So, although one can justifiably condemn the actions of a person that are inconsistent with the moral beliefs of that person's culture, condemnation of the actions of a person of a different culture are not justified if those actions are consistent with the moral beliefs of that culture.

Cultural ethical relativism supports the claim that we should respect the beliefs and practices of other cultures, and that we should prevent our own cultural beliefs from being the basis for unfair assessments of these cultures. A modern relativist, J.L. Mackie, argues that the differences in ethical values, expressed in different places and at different times, is evidence that no moral absolutes exist.

❛ — Quotable quote

Anthropologist William Graham Sumner dramatically expresses the notion of ethical relativism thus:

'The "right" way is the way which the ancestors used and which has been handed down. The tradition is its own warrant. It is not held subject to verification by experience. The notion of right is in the folkways. It is not outside of them, of independent origin, and brought to test them. In the folkways, whatever is, is right. This is because they are traditional and therefore contain in themselves the authority of the ancestral ghosts. When we come to the folkways we are at the end of our analysis.'

Folkways (1906) ❜

Analysis of cultural relativism

Cultural relativism is the reasonable idea that certain social, economic, cultural and political practices are inherent to particular groups and that the abrupt, artificial introduction of alien influences can be disruptive. In practise, however, cultural relativism is often employed by ruling elites as a pretext for opposing reform movements that threaten their power or status. Therefore, calls for the respect of basic human rights are dismissed by politically motivated relativists as culturally insensitive or socially impracticable. Such claims often conceal crude anti-foreign nationalism.

Discussion

Consider the following statements.

Because different cultures have different moral codes, there is no **objective** moral truth.

The conclusion 'no objective moral truth' does not logically follow from the premise 'different cultures have different moral codes'.

Think it through

Imagine you are a cultural relativist. Try to construct an argument to convince an absolutist that there are no absolute truths in ethics. How would you answer their criticisms and examples such as young African girls being mutilated during the practice of female circumcision?

Discussion

1 Does 'morality' itself change if a culture or a society changes its mind; for example, in one era slavery is right and in the next era it is wrong?

2 What if society disagrees about a moral issue? What proportion of society does it take to make something right or wrong?

3 Is it plausible that each culture or society is equally good or bad? Are we really no better than the ancient Romans, whose idea of entertainment was throwing Christians to the lions?

4 Is each individual equally good so long as each person does what he or she believes in?

5 What is the difference between doing what is right and doing what you feel like?

Criticism of relativism

The main reason why people support relativism is that they believe we should tolerate different beliefs and even different behaviour. While this could be seen as a worthy idea, it does have its problems.

• Relativism must not be confused with tolerance. While we can agree that other cultures have different values, if these values are intolerable (for example, they

Word watch

objective

are persecuting a minority group), should we remain tolerant? Some people think that the belief that there are generally valid moral standards is the basis for imposing one person's moral beliefs on another who might believe other things about morality. But imposing one person's moral beliefs on another is only wrong if the belief is really wrong! Tolerance is itself a moral principle.

Key question

If a relative belief were adopted universally, would relativism itself become an absolute moral code?

- If the rightness or wrongness of an action depends on a society's norms, then it follows that one should obey the norms of one's society. To deviate from those norms would therefore be to act immorally. If I am a member of a society or group, for example, the Ku Klux Klan, which believes that racism is morally permissible, then I should accept those practices as morally right. However, such a view promotes social conformity and leaves no room for moral reform or improvement within a society.

A member of the Ku Klux Klan – a racist group in America who believe in white supremacy. Should we tolerate all actions that are acceptable to particular groups?

- Cultural relativists argue that people should respect the beliefs and traditions of other cultures, even if they do not agree with them. Ironically, however, cultural relativism actually undermines any moral basis upon which one might justify this claim. If the people of a given culture believe that it is acceptable to destroy another culture, should there be justification for respecting them?

- Critics of cultural relativism point out that there have never existed cultures with *totally* different values. No society has ever condemned honesty, courage, co-operation, wisdom, and self-control, or praised lying, theft, murder and rape. While the moral practices of societies may differ, the fundamental moral principles underlying these practices tend to be very similar. For example, in some societies, killing one's parents after they reached a certain age was common practice, stemming from the belief that people were better off in the afterlife if they entered it while still physically active and vigorous. While such a practice would be condemned in our society, we would agree with these societies on the underlying moral principle – the duty to care for parents.

Societies, then, may differ in their application of fundamental moral principles but tend to agree on fundamental ethical principles. In his book *Elements of Moral Philosophy* (1986), James Rachels argues that there are a common set of values that are universal and are necessary for social harmony:

- care for children
- tell the truth
- do not murder.

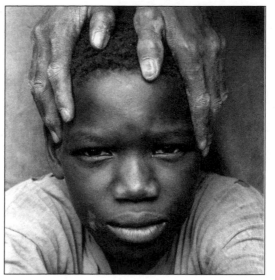

Is caring for children a universal value?

Why believe relativist theories?

- There is huge disagreement about right and wrong; for example, the abortion debate.
- There is little confidence that this disagreement will ever go away.
- It is often very hard to know what is right or wrong.
- Situations vary so much from place to place and time to time that it is difficult to believe that right and wrong stay the same regardless of such differences.

Sometimes people embrace relativism as a reaction against traditional moral beliefs they regard as oppressive, 'fundamentalist' or old fashioned. Certainly some people hold moral beliefs that, from a more enlightened point of view, are clearly wrong; for example, supporting slavery. But the rejection of ethical relativism does not imply that traditional moral beliefs should be accepted just because they are traditional.

Some people adopt relativism because they sense that, given the complexity of contemporary moral issues, there are no absolute answers. There are many different views on euthanasia, abortion, war, genetic engineering and so on, all supported by what appear to be convincing arguments. It is easy to conclude that no 'truth' can be found. However, most important issues are resolved only after much debate and analysis, and the complexity of these issues suggest it will take time to resolve.

The current tendency of moral **scepticism** is perhaps because people have lost sight of the fact that many moral issues that were hotly debated in the past have been settled in ways that no reasonable person would object to today; for example, slavery, women's rights, religious freedom.

Another reason why people have adopted ethical relativism is that if one rejects relativism, then the only recognized alternative view is to accept a position that they find unacceptable, commonly known as absolutism (the view that a certain set of moral rules apply in all relevant cases).

Word watch

scepticism

Word watch

absolutism

Rejecting ethical relativism, however, does not require the acceptance of moral absolutism, although it does imply the acceptance of a broader position commonly known as *moral objectivism* or *moral realism*. This view simply claims that normative judgements can be justified on objective (non-relativistic) grounds, but that a moral objectivist is not necessarily committed to the claim that moral standards are absolute. In this way, common moral standards can be understood to apply in different ways, depending on the circumstances of particular moral situations.

Discussion

In pairs, discuss the following scenario.

A student in an RE class announced that she was a relativist. The teacher responded, 'Fine. Oh, but by the way, I'm going to fail you on your latest essay.'

'That's not fair!' the student protested.

'Oh, really?' replied the teacher. 'I thought you were a relativist. Do you mean to tell me that you think there is a *standard of fairness*? Please, tell me about it.'

In threes – using the information and the arguments in this chapter – construct a three-way debate between a relativist, an absolutist and a critic of relativism.

Think it through

1 Situation: Hairophobia is a country that contains two distinct cultural groups: the noreds and the gings. The *noreds* make up 90 per cent of the population, the *gings* the remaining 10 per cent. There is a long history of suspicion and hatred against the gings. According to *nored* cultural history, the *noreds* are a superior race.

You are a *ging*. One day a *ging* assassinates a *nored* leader and the fragile truce between the *noreds* and *gings* disintegrates. A new law is passed to round up all *gings* and put them in concentration camps where the *gings* are subjected to slave labour and medical experimentation.

2 Implications: The actions of the *noreds* are consistent with their cultural beliefs – so how would an ethical relativist view the situation?

Would a cultural relativist be right in maintaining that nobody has a moral basis upon which to complain about the actions of the *noreds*?

Hot tip

If an exam question asks for an explanation of moral relativism, you can do this by referring to situation ethics (see Chapter 10) or social contract theory (see Chapter 11, part 2) or utilitarianism (see Chapter 9). When evaluating moral relativism, mention how it can give scope for compassion and common sense, and also allow the individual to focus on a particular situation – as against some of the criticisms of moral relativism.

One example of the application of moral relativism, the just war theory (see Chapter 15), can be mentioned as a feature of a relativist approach to questions about war, as against moral absolutist ideas of pacifism (see Chapter 15).

Evaluation of relativism

The common reasons offered for adopting ethical relativism are, on close examination, quite unconvincing, and in practise it is quite difficult for any reasonable person to adopt the view consistently.

' — Quotable quote

'Those are my principles. If you don't like them I have others.'

Groucho Marx (1890–1977), comedian

Most philosophers reject ethical relativism. As a theory for justifying moral practices and beliefs, ethical relativism fails to recognize that some societies have better reasons for holding their views than others. But even if the theory of ethical relativism is rejected, it must be acknowledged that the idea raises important issues. Ethical relativism reminds us that different societies have different moral beliefs and that our beliefs are deeply influenced by culture. It also encourages us to explore the reasons underlying beliefs that differ from our own, while challenging us to examine our reasons for the beliefs and values we hold and how they are part of the cultural norm.

Ethical absolutism

Ethical absolutism is the theory that there are moral principles that are always and everywhere applicable.

Absolutists believe that right and wrong are based on constant objective moral principles, fashioned by a divine reality establishing moral order in the universe.

To the absolutist, right and wrong is viewed in much the same way as a scientist views nature: there is a truth out there waiting to be discovered – once discovered, everything else falls into place.

Absolutists believe that the moral quality of an act is inherent in the quality of the act itself, *regardless of the consequences* that result from the act.

This is a deontological view of ethics – certain rules have inherent worth in themselves and are not justified by other considerations. The rules may be the commandments of God, the **natural law** of the universe, or the tried and tested laws of one's culture.

Absolutists believe that the reasons for the moral value of actions are based upon principles – or a code of laws – that are a recognized standard for moral conduct. Good consequences flow from good actions (those that follow the code of laws). Bad consequences flow from bad actions (those that **violate** the code of laws). Good actions are not good just because good results follow from them; good actions are *inherently* good because they reflect **absolute** truth.

Key idea

If an absolutist believes that life begins at conception, it becomes obvious to him or her that abortion is the taking of a human life and is therefore wrong.

Word watch

inherent
natural law
violate
absolute

Key idea

Absolutists believe that the moral quality of an act is inherent in the quality of the act itself, regardless of the consequences that result from the act.

Hot tip

If an exam question asks for an analysis of the main features of moral absolutism you can refer to both religious absolutism (for example, divine command theory; see pp. 50–54) and non-religious absolutism (for example, Kantian ethics; see Chapter 8).

Key idea: the golden rule

If we look at some teachings from the sacred scriptures of the world religions, we find some 'core principles'. Despite differences in cultural beliefs and customs, underlying ethical principles – arising at different periods of history – are identical.

'Do for others what you want them to do for you: this is the meaning of the Law of Moses and of the teachings of the prophets.'

Gospel of Matthew: Christian tradition

'Do not to others what ye do not wish
Done to yourself; and wish for others too
What ye desire and long for, for yourself
This is the whole of the dharma.'

Mahabharata: Hindu tradition

'What is hateful to you, do not do to your neighbour;
that is the entire Torah; the rest is commentary.'

Talmud: Jewish tradition

'Since to others, to each one for himself, the self is dear, therefore let him who desires his own advantage not harm another.'

Udana-Varqa: Buddhist tradition

'None of you truly believes until he wishes for his brother what he wishes for himself.'

Hadith: Islamic tradition

'If thine eyes be turned toward justice, choose thou for thy neighbour that which thou choosest for thyself.'

Kalimat-i-Firdawsiyyih: Baha'i tradition

Plato's Forms

In Book 6 of his *Republic* (360 BCE), Plato (428–347 BCE) explains how the universe is divided into two realms: the visible realm of material things and the intelligible realm of the Forms. Mathematics inspired Plato's view of the Forms. When we look, for example, at mathematical relations, such as $1 + 1 = 2$, they seem to be timeless concepts that never change and apply everywhere in the universe. Humans do not invent numbers and humans cannot alter them. Plato explained the eternal character of mathematics by stating that they are abstract entities that exist in the spirit-like realm of the Forms. Plato saw Goodness, Justice, Truth and Beauty as Forms, existing as objects, never changing, and the standard by which all things should be judged.

If values are not objects, how can they be objective?

The twentieth-century philosopher G.E. Moore suggested that values might be *objective properties* of acts or people. For instance, being six feet tall is not an object, but a property that some people have and on which there is objective agreement. In the same way, Moore argued that being good, or doing the right thing, might be properties that certain people or actions have and on which there is objective agreement. While we can measure people to prove how tall they are, we cannot 'measure' abortion to see whether it is ethically acceptable or not. So if goodness is a property, it is not one that science recognizes. Moore agreed. He said that we know what is good or bad, right or wrong, by a power called intuition.

Subjectivism

If objectivism is false, must we be relativists after all? No! The opposite of objectivism is not relativism but **subjectivism**. Subjectivism is the theory that ethics is fundamentally subjective, or a matter of feeling.

Is it possible to believe in a universal kind of subjectivism? The eighteenth-century Scottish philosopher David Hume (1711–76) argued that all people have the same basic feelings about good and bad: they approve of things that are useful or enjoyable and they disapprove of things that are useless or unpleasant. Hume argued that this is subjective because it is purely a matter of feeling, but it is not relative, because every sane person feels the same way unless he or she is biased.

Hume believed that asking whether something is morally or ethically good is like asking whether it is rough or smooth. Roughness is not a property recognized by science – it is purely a matter of how something feels to the touch. Still, things are either rough or smooth. Insane people and people with damaged hands might not be able to tell them apart, but every normal person can. Similarly, insane people or morally crippled people might not see that murder is wrong, but every normal person can.

Criticism of moral/ethical absolutism

Moral or ethical absolutism can be used to legitimize one powerful culture imposing its moral values on all others by claiming it possesses moral absolutes. In the seventeenth century, European settlers in Africa and the Americas imposed their own moral truth on the tribal cultures, often justifying wholesale slaughter, slavery and the environmental destruction of lands held to be sacred, by maintaining that they had 'absolute moral knowledge' about how these people *ought* to live.

In defence of ethical absolutism, many people today would not want to interfere with other moral belief systems. They argue that although customs and practices vary, the underlying beliefs are the same. For instance, the sacrificial religion of the Aztecs in Central America suggests a belief that ritualistic death is for the ultimate long-term heavenly good of the victims involved. The sanctioning of the murder of innocents for any other reason is not morally acceptable.

For more on Moore see pp. 15–16.

Word watch

subjectivism
subjective

Key idea

Subjectivism is not the same as relativism.

What are the dangers of religious and ethical absolutism?

Think it through

Can you think of practices in different cultures which illustrate that beneath the forms of practice lies the essence of moral knowledge?

Postmodernism

Postmodernist thinkers are sceptical about the existence of some kind of objective reality. They argue that there is no supreme principle that can tell us which ethical system is the best or the truest one – we live in a relativistic universe where there are only *human* truths and *human* ethics. They argue that this lack of moral certainty makes it impossible to condemn societies whose moral belief systems we find totally repugnant. In a postmodern world we are free to shop around for any set of moral values we feel are appropriate, but there are no signposts: we each have to decide for ourselves.

Postmodernist thinkers like Jean-François Lyotard (b. 1924) and Jacques Derrida (b. 1930) claim that reason is itself a fiction because it is a human, linguistic construct, not a transcendent entity. They argue that our worship of reason has led to much suffering and to the dangerous political 'certainties' of large totalitarian regimes holding on to the objectivity of their utopian visions.

Marxism

Karl Marx (1818–83), the German philosopher and thinker behind Marxism, argued that morality is simply ideology in disguise and that it exists to serve the interests of the ruling classes. Underlying society's beliefs about everything is a sole factor: economics. Marx argued that capitalism has survived so successfully because the ruling classes have monopolized education, religion, the law and ideas about morality. Only after a revolution – when everyone is free of imposed and therefore illusory morality – will human beings be liberated from the shackles of conditioning, exploitation and alienation.

Post-Marxist writers like Herbert Marcuse (1898–1979) and Michel Foucault (1926–84) have examined how the spectacle of consumerism hypnotizes us into accepting the absolute 'morality' that supports capitalism, consumerism, profit not principle, and the monolithic power of multinational corporations.

Word watch

exploitation
alienation
monolithic

Web quest

'If we have chosen the position in life in which we can most of all work for mankind, no burdens can bow us down, because they are sacrifices for the benefit of all; then we shall experience no petty, limited, selfish joy, but our happiness will belong to millions, our deeds will live on quietly but perpetually at work, and over our ashes will be shed the hot tears of noble people.'

Karl Marx, letter to his father (1837)

'Religion is the sigh of the oppressed creature, the heart of a heartless world, and the soul of soulless conditions. It is the opium of the people.'

Karl Marx, *Critique of Hegel's Philosophy of Right* (1844)

For more information on Karl Marx visit www.heinemann.co.uk/hotlinks and click on this section.

Natural law theory

The **natural law theory** states that everything is created for a particular function and that fulfilling this purpose is the good to which everything should aim.

To be moral, then, according to natural law, has to do with the *function* of a human being. But what is my function? Why am I here? What must I do? Who am I? Anything that is good or bad is so because it *functions,* well or badly, and if we could discover the function of human beings, we would understand how the words 'good' or 'bad' could be applied to them.

In his book *Nicomachean Ethics* (350 BCE) , Aristotle taught that the proper function of human beings is *to reason* and that being moral was reasoning well. By reasoning well, Aristotle argued, people would have a successful, fulfilled and harmonious life.

Word watch

natural law theory

To find out more about Aristotle's ethics see pp. 111–113.

St Thomas Aquinas and natural law

The most famous exponent of this absolutist view of ethics was St Thomas Aquinas (1225–74) – the greatest of all scholastic philosophers. Aquinas argued that the world was created and as such has God's ultimate purpose as its final end or good. According to Aquinas human beings survive physical death and, ultimately, the purpose of human existence does not lie just in this life. However, we have been endowed with reason and freedom and can choose to follow 'natural law', the rational understanding and following of God's final purpose.

For Aquinas, this purpose was to reproduce, to learn, to live harmoniously in society and to worship God. By using reason, men and women discover God's intention and the purpose of human existence, thus arriving at the principles of natural law, which describe not only how things *are*, but also specify how things *ought* to be. Things are as they ought to be when they are fulfilling their natural purpose, and unnatural when they are not. Moral laws, therefore, have their source in natural law – some ways of behaving are natural but some are unnatural and morally wrong. Aquinas argued that:

- each person is born with a particular purpose to fulfil in his or her life and human nature was created by God
- there is a link between happiness and virtuous behaviour
- reason can guide people in developing virtue
- morality is not based on commands from God but on reason – 'the moral life is the life according to reason' (*Summa Theologica*, 1265)
- there is an 'ideal' human nature that we all can potentially achieve
- '**sin**' is falling short of this ideal (the good), literally meaning 'missing the mark' (as in archery). People often miss the mark because they confuse apparent good with the ideal (for example, drinking alcohol may make me feel more sociable – apparent good – but the ideal would be feeling self-confident and sociable without having to alter my body chemically)
- although an act may be good in itself (for example, giving to charity), it may come from a bad intention (giving to charity so you can boast about it).

Word watch

sin

Think it through

Imagine it was proved beyond doubt that we survived physical death. Would your behaviour change at all? Would your aims in life be changed? What would your new aims be?

Criticism of natural law

Modern science has presented a worldview that makes little or no reference to purposes or values. All life has its particular characteristics not because it is the way it *ought* to be, but because it is *the way it is*, dictated by factors like natural selection, evolution and the laws of cause and effect. 'Natural laws' are the laws of biology, chemistry and physics; morality and values have nothing to do with the natural order. Although this viewpoint has permeated Western thinking over the last 300 years, modern nuclear physics, by discovering that even the smallest atom is part of an intrinsically complex, law-conforming and meaningful universe, challenges a mechanistic and materialistic view of reality.

Natural law and sexual ethics

Religious thinkers have traditionally opposed sexual practices not aimed at procreation and condemned them because they do not fulfil the 'natural' purpose of sex.

Gay rights protestors challenge the traditional natural law approach to sexual ethics

This way of thinking about sex dates back to St Augustine in the sixth century and traditionally has been the basis of Christian thinking about sex. But, is *what is* the case and *what ought* to be the case logically different? For example, sex does produce babies, but this does not necessarily mean that people *ought* to have sex *only* for this purpose.

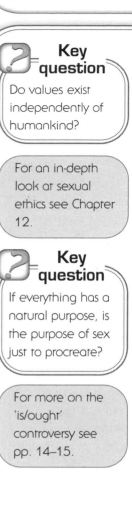

Key question

Do values exist independently of humankind?

For an in-depth look at sexual ethics see Chapter 12.

Key question

If everything has a natural purpose, is the purpose of sex just to procreate?

For more on the 'is/ought' controversy see pp. 14–15.

Think it through

Jot down some ideas in response to the following questions before discussing your findings with the class.

1 If we woke up tomorrow and murder suddenly seemed right to everyone, then would it actually be right?

2 Explain the view that there are objective moral truths.

3 What are the strengths and weaknesses of relativism and absolutism?

4 Explain the 'is/ought' controversy (see pp. 14–15) in terms of sexual ethics.

Hot tip

In answering questions on issues like abortion, euthanasia, suicide and sexual ethics from a Christian perspective the natural law approach to ethics is central. Basically, this is the idea that morality is embodied in 'natural laws' created by God and reflecting God's plan for creation, which, according to the biblical book of Genesis, 'is good'. These divine laws are the ones that humans as God's creation ought to follow.

Review

Relativists:
- Believe that morality is relative to the norms of one's culture.
- An action is right or wrong depending on the moral norms of the society in which it is practised.
- There are no objective eternal moral principles; morals are subjective.

Absolutists:
- Believe that there *are* objective eternal moral principles that are applicable everywhere.
- Good actions are not good just because good results follow from them; good actions are *inherently* good because they reflect absolute truth.

Natural law theory:
- Is an absolutist theory.
- Being moral has to do with the *function* of a human being. Anything that is good or bad is so because it *functions* well or badly.
- St Thomas Aquinas: eternal laws are given by God and are understood by human reason.

Evaluation:
- Relativism explains the diverse values that different people have and supports diverse expressions of beliefs and values.
- Absolutism, in contrast, can give clear moral guidelines for everyone everywhere to adopt, but it can, too, appear intolerant of cultural diversity.

Exam questions

1 (a) Explain the differences between a relative morality and an absolute morality. (33 marks)

(b) How useful is a relative morality in dealing with issues surrounding genetic engineering? (17 marks) (OCR, January 2001)

2 (a) Explain what is meant by 'moral relativism'. (33 marks)

(b) Assess the strengths and weaknesses of moral relativism. (17 marks) (OCR, June 2002)

RELIGION AND ETHICS
5 Religion and morality

> 'Is the holy approved by the gods because it's holy, or is it holy because it's approved?'
>
> Plato, *The Last Days of Socrates* (c. 360 BCE)

Do moral guidelines exist outside the human mind, or are they contrivances of the mind?

Objectives

Is an act right because God commands it, or does God command it because it is right? Key areas of enquiry include the following:

- the ethical teachings of India and Ancient Greece – comparisons and contrasts
- the strengths and weaknesses of **divine command theory**
- the meaning of the Euthyphro dilemma.

Key questions

1 When did humans begin discussing ethics?

2 What is the ethical life?

3 Do you have to be religious to be ethical?

4 What is the truth? Where does it come from? Do moral guidelines exist outside the human mind, or are they contrivances of the mind?

5 Does ethical thought come from God? If not, where does it come from?

6 Could God command a wrong act?

Ethics before the Greeks

When did human beings start thinking about and discussing ethics? In a modern Western society it sometimes appears as though philosophy, science and ethics were unknown before the Classical period in Greece, around the fifth to third centuries before Christ. In fact, everything that was necessary for civilization had been developed thousands of years before the Greeks by the ancient civilizations of Iraq, India, Egypt and China. Irrigation, agriculture, stock-breeding, pottery, weaving, architecture, mining, metalwork, ocean-going ships, writing, painting, sculpture, poetry, dance and the martial arts, mathematics, astronomy, surveying, philosophy, science and medicine had all been employed for thousands of years.

Key question

How might belief in the soul, God and an afterlife affect people's moral behaviour in this life?

Egyptian ethics

The ancient world did not develop ethics as we know it, as its approach to ethics was prescriptive (see p. 13) and absolute (see p. 37). For the great civilizations of Egypt, the existence of God and the divine world was accepted without question. The after-death fate of human beings was thought to be decided by the purity and goodness of their conduct during their lifetime.

For the people of Egypt, the supreme truth was reflected in the principle of Maat, the divine order of **justice** that underlies the visible universe. The role of individuals was to purify themselves and serve the divine in this life so that after death they might live with God in an astral heaven for all eternity. After judgement, evil people would be destroyed in the underworld while good people would attain an immortal body.

Indian ethics

Word watch

dharma

In India this principle of universal moral order, called **dharma**, is to be found in the operation of natural law and in the laws of morality. According to traditional Indian thought, all actions have consequences. As we sow, so shall we reap. If we act with harmful or selfish intent, not only will others be hurt, but we too will suffer in the long run. Acting with benevolent intent, on the other hand, not only helps others but also purifies our hearts and brings us closer to God.

Indian philosophy sees Brahman, the universal godhead, as the ground of being, without form, unconditioned, unborn, beyond death, time and space. This is the one Being, the only thing that can truly be said to exist, and all beings are like sparks of this spiritual fire. All things are interrelated, mutually dependent and arising together. As universal consciousness, the light of awareness appears in all things, veiled by the darkness of this world. According to Indian ethics, our task is to penetrate through the darkness of Maya, the magical illusion of God's play, to escape from the bondage of our desires and to achieve **enlightenment**. The great spiritual teachers of India such as Krishna, Buddha and Guru Nanak taught a path to salvation through meditation and prayer, through good thoughts and kind acts, and the beginning of the path was found in ethical conduct. Virtues like truthfulness, non-violence and compassion are prescribed in order to purify the mind and make it fit for religious practice, and to bring society into harmony with the universal law.

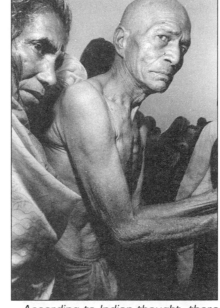

According to Indian thought, there is a universal moral order

The temple schools

The temple schools of India, Iraq and Egypt were the source of all scientific and spiritual knowledge in the ancient world, but depended on faith in the teachers and the teaching. There was little room for questioning or disbelief. Religious faith was easier in the ancient world when living prophets experienced God and taught the truths of his revelation, but by the Classical era it seemed as if the gods no longer spoke to humankind.

Moses, according to the Bible, experienced God directly, but by the time of the second temple (around 500 BCE) God was silent. In Greece the gods of Mount Olympus no longer spoke to the people and so philosophers began to question religious belief itself. If the gods did not exist, or were so capricious as not to be trusted, then human beings were alone in the universe and had to work out their own salvation.

In the ancient world suffering was seen as a necessary part of our purification from the effects of our past actions; what was 'good' was what brought us closer to God, even if that meant losing everything we hold dear in this world; what was 'evil' was what separated us from God.

On the other hand, in the Classical world, people began to think *that what was 'good' was what was pleasant and what was painful was evil*, and this attitude has

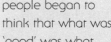 **Key idea**

In the Classical world people began to think that what was 'good' was what was pleasant and what was painful was evil. Indian philosophy teaches that this view is illusory, for we cannot achieve lasting satisfaction just through the pursuit of pleasure.

Word watch

capricious

Key question

Is 'good' always pleasant and 'bad' always unpleasant?

Key fact

The movement of sophism began around the fifth century BCE in Greece led by a group of philosophers who were paid to use rhetoric. Sophists made a living by speaking and teaching about what they knew, relying upon wisdom tested and gained by experience.

Word watch

teleos

remained to this day in the assumptions of our society. But according to Indian philosophy, this view is deeply mistaken, for we have identified with an illusion that we think we can achieve lasting satisfaction through pleasure, wealth and power.

The Greeks
Socrates

In the fifth century BCE the sophists taught that all human judgement is subjective and we can never fully understand objective values. Socrates (c. 470–399 BCE) disagreed and his ideas are represented in the dialogues of his pupil Plato (428–347 BCE). Socrates argued that people will be virtuous if they know what virtue is. Ignorance leads to evil and wrongdoing. Socrates argued that virtue is knowledge and the search for knowledge was the highest and noblest of all pursuits.

Athens became the classroom of Socrates. He went about asking questions of authorities and of the man in the street in order to arrive at political and ethical truths. He questioned groups of his students as a means of instruction, to make them think a problem through to its logical conclusion. His dialectic method, or method of investigating problems through discussions, came to be known as the 'Socratic Method'. Socrates pretended that he knew no answers and feigned ignorance to learn from others in order to reveal the truth or expose the error of their answers. He argued that each life has a purpose (*teleos*) and that we have a 'real self' inside us – something essential that is truly and deeply 'I'. Morality, treating others well, is the key to truth. Although moral knowledge is attainable through discussion, Socrates stressed that morality is not the sort of knowledge that can actually be taught. Real knowledge is about 'essences' of things like 'justice' that all individuals have to discover for themselves in everyday life experiences.

Some of Socrates' ideas challenged the conventional norms of Athens of the time, particularly his view that it is better to be wronged than to wrong someone else. Perhaps most strange to the ears of the Athenian rulers was his vision of a state ruled *not by politicians but by philosophers*.

Discussion

Consider and discuss the following Socratic virtues:

'Intellectual eagerness ... the ability to learn easily ... good memories ... determination ... fondness for hard work ... ready to go through an elaborate course of study ... feels no indignation when its (his/her) own ignorance is shown ... a free man (or woman) ought not to learn anything under duress ... be able to bring together the disconnected subjects they've studied.'

Plato, *Republic* (360 BCE)

Plato

In his greatest work, *Republic* (360 BCE), Plato (428–347 BCE) argued that good is the essential element of reality; evil does not exist. It is merely an imperfect reflection of the real, which is good. In *Dialogues* (c. 360 BCE) he argues that human virtue lies in our ability to perform our proper *function* in the world. The human soul has three elements, each possessing a specific virtue:

- Intellect: the virtue of intellect is wisdom and understanding about the meaning of life.
- Will: the virtue of will is courage; the capacity to act and to be.
- Emotion: the virtue of emotion is self-control in speech and behaviour.

For Plato, the ultimate virtue is justice, a sublime state which sees the three elements of the soul working together in harmony: the intellect sovereign, followed by the will and then the emotions. The 'just' person is someone whose life is balanced in this way.

Key idea

For Plato, the 'just person' is someone who develops and balances his or her intellect, will and behaviour.

Aristotle

Aristotle (384–322 BCE), philosopher, scientist and pupil of Plato, gave a systematic account of ethics in *Nichomachean Ethics* (350 BCE), the heart of which is his account of moral virtues in Book 2. Aristotle's ethics are called '**virtue ethics**' because the virtues or qualities of character are at the heart of his arguments. The foundation of morality is the development of good character traits, or virtues, so a person is good if he has virtues and lacks vices.

For more on Aristotle's virtue ethics see Chapter 11, part 1.

Does ethics depend on religion?

Humanists and atheists see no connection between religion and ethics. They argue that it is possible to be ethical without being religious. Popular thinking, however, understands ethics and religion as being inseparable, a view shared by Muslims, Christians, Hindus, Jews, Buddhists, Sikhs and Baha'is. It is not unusual for religious leaders to be regarded as moral 'experts' and be invited to sit on ethics committees, especially those concerned with medical ethics. Because religious leaders are the spokespeople for religion, it is assumed that they must be spokespeople for morality, too. But should they necessarily be? In discussing the proposed connection, or lack of it, between religion and ethics, we will focus on one religion, Christianity.

❛ Quotable quote

'A little philosophy inclineth man's mind to atheism, but depth in philosophy bringeth men's minds about to religion.'

Francis Bacon, *The Advancement of Learning* (1605)

Think it through

(a) Read the following extract of a speech by the Archbishop of Canterbury, Rowan Williams. (b) What does it tell you about the role of religious leaders as spokespeople? (c) In your opinion, should religious leaders get involved in debates about contemporary moral issues? (d) Discuss Rowan Williams's ideas in class.

'Why should we do what the government tells us? It's a question that takes us into some unexpectedly complicated areas; it raises issues about the unspoken contracts people feel exist between themselves and their rulers. You need to be reasonably confident that your system of government is worth supporting overall if you are prepared to go along with what it tells you in some particular areas where you may not feel completely convinced or are frankly not convinced at all. What happens, though, when the state no longer seems to have the power to keep its side of the bargain? In the twenty-first century, the cracks in the structure get more and more visible. Intercontinental missile technology designed to carry weapons of mass destruction

makes nonsense of traditional ideas of defending your territory; you have to rely on strategic means, above all deterrent counter threats, when things look menacing. Then there is the way in which capital is now able to move where it pleases in the world, ignoring frontier controls. No national economy can protect itself completely, and so no nation state government can guarantee employment levels in the old way. Government has to negotiate favourable deals with fickle and mobile investors who can always afford to look for new and more profitable locations and outlets at will.'

Rowan Williams, Archbishop of Canterbury, *The Richard Dimbleby Lecture 2002*

The divine command theory

Much of western thought has been influenced by theism. Theism is the view that God is unlimited with regard to knowledge (**omniscient**), power (**omnipotent**), extension (**omnipresent**), and moral perfection, and is the creator and sustainer of the universe.

The divine command theory – dominant in theism – is the theory that an act is morally right if it has been commanded by God and morally wrong if God has forbidden it. Right and wrong become an objective matter. Ethics, therefore, is not merely a matter of custom or personal feelings but relates to a 'higher good'.

For Christians, God's purpose for humankind has been revealed through the Holy Spirit, the Holy Scriptures, the Church, the Prophets, and through natural reason. These sources teach that God has promulgated laws which, if followed, allow people to live in harmony with themselves and with others. In the Judaeo-Christian tradition the most famous of these laws are the Ten Commandments.

Word watch

theism
omniscient
omnipotent
omnipresent
divine command theory

God requires something of humankind and stands ready to reward obedience and punish violation. Biblical writers do not view ethics *naturalistically*, that is, rooted in human nature or in the social environment, or *abstractly* in terms of some generalizations about human values, but *theologically* as rooted in the nature and activity of God. As a consequence, our relation to God is thought to be of vital importance, not simply for ethics, but within ethical theory itself.

> **' ═ Quotable quote ═**
>
> *'If you have no God then your moral code is that of society. If society is turned upside down, so is your moral code.'*
>
> Jung Chang, writer quoted in *Independent on Sunday*, September 1995 **"**

> **☝ ═ Discussion ═**
>
> *'A consequence of divine command theory is that, if there is no God, nothing is morally forbidden, nothing is morally obligatory, and everything is morally permitted.'*
>
> Philip Quinn, *The Primacy of God's Will in Christian Ethics* (1992)
>
> *'Everything is permissible if God does not exist, and as a result, man is forlorn, because neither within him nor without does he find anything to cling to.'*
>
> Jean-Paul Sartre (1905–80), French philosopher

The Euthyphro dilemma

The Euthyphro dilemma is found in Plato's *The Last Days of Socrates* and concerns Socrates' discussion with a young man, Euthyphro. Socrates is on the way to the courthouse to face prosecution for apparently corrupting the youth of Athens with his wisdom. Outside the courthouse he meets a young man called Euthyphro who is there to prosecute his father for allowing a 'prisoner' to die. Euthyphro believes that his actions are holy, so Socrates challenges him to state what he thinks holiness is. Euthyphro's answer is that 'what is agreeable to the gods is holy and what is not agreeable is unholy'.

Socrates, however, notes that disagreements arise among the gods so there can be no universal definition of holiness (what is agreeable) among them. Euthyphro argues that although they disagree on many things, all the gods would agree that killing a man is wrong (unholy). But Socrates wants evidence for this claim and it is here that the Euthyphro dilemma is stated: 'is the holy approved by the gods because it's holy, or is it holy because it's approved?'

Hot tip

The Euthyphro dilemma became one of the most famous questions in the history of philosophy. The twentieth-century British philosopher Antony Flew believed that 'one good test of a person's aptitude for philosophy is to discover whether he can grasp its force and point'. It is important that you spend some time trying to 'grasp its force and point'!

Key question

Is conduct right because the gods command it, or do the gods command it because it is right?

Think it through

See if you can grasp Euthyphro's dilemma by discussing it with a partner.

STOP ARGUING!

Do as we say!

'is the holy approved by the gods because it's holy, or is it holy because it's approved?'

Plato, *The Last Days of Socrates* (c. 360 BCE)

Word watch

omniscience

If we agree that God's laws are absolute – for example, the reason we must not lie is because God commands it – we have a problem! We could ask why God does not command laws that allow cruel actions as well as good actions. If he commanded that we lie, then lying, not truthfulness, would be regarded as being acceptable behaviour. Socrates argues that God commands right behaviour because it *is* right and God's commands are the result of his omniscience and infinite wisdom. God is good and only commands what is good. If God is good, he can only command what is right.

However, the above argument assumes that there is a standard of goodness *independent* of God. God is no longer the ultimate standard of morality. We are saying that God sees that truthfulness is right, yet this is very different from his *making* it right. The idea of rightness exists prior to and independent of God's command. So if we want to know why we should try and be truthful, the reply 'Because God commands it' will not take us very far. We can still ask, 'But why does God command it?' and the answer to that question will give us the underlying reasons why truthfulness is a good thing. However, the divine command theory states that God would never command anything evil because God is benevolent (all-loving).

Think it through

A father can be loving but sometimes he might decide to 'be cruel to be kind'. Try to think of some examples!

Who decides what is good? If it is God who decides what is good, then presumably he could call lying good, and it would be. But who wants a God like that? If it is not God – since he has to obey a higher law just as we do – then he is not supreme because laws exist independently of him. Who wants a God like that?

Theists would argue that goodness is not something *external* to God, but rather something with which he is fully *identified*. Goodness is what the word 'God' means. He could no more cease to be good than he could cease to be God. In the Hebrew Bible, for example, God is constantly celebrated in terms of loving kindness and merciful compassion. This goodness does not mean that God cannot also be just, and he is sometimes portrayed in religious literature as a fierce judge, but never inconsistent in his loving nature either:

'The Lord is loving and merciful, slow to become angry and full of constant love … Your kingdom is founded on righteousness and justice.'

(Psalms 145: 8, 89: 14).

' — **Quotable quote**

'It is certain that the mortality or immortality of the soul must make an entire difference to morality. And yet philosophers have constructed their ethics independently of this.'

Blaise Pascal (1623–62), French philosopher

Criticism of the divine command theory

- It assumes that a God exists who issues commands. This is very difficult to prove to somebody who refuses to believe in God. The history of philosophy contains numerous attempts to prove that a personal God exists, but it is safe to say that each of these 'proofs' is controversial.
- Even assuming that God exists, there are the problems associated with human understanding and ignorance in finding out what God's commands exactly are.
- If the Bible is the Word of God, we still have the problem of interpreting it. Different people interpret the Bible in different ways.
- Why should we obey a supreme moral governor in the first place? Surely threats of reward or punishment are not good moral reasons for obedience? Don't we have a right, indeed a duty, to decide for ourselves what is right and wrong? Would a 'good' God be a punishing God?
- Moral judgements arise from human reason, which we are able to understand because God has made us rational beings. However, because the natural law theory sees the ultimate recourse to moral decisions and actions as reason, this means that the religious believer has no special access to moral truth. The believer and the non-believer are in exactly the same position. God made everyone, not just believers, rational.

Hot tip

In analysing whether religious theories of ethics can be justified you can refer to Euthyphro's dilemma.

Key question

Are ethical principles independent of human experience or are they human creations?

'But above all else we must impress on our memory the overriding rule that whatever God has revealed to us must be accepted as more certain than anything else. And although the light of reason may, with the utmost clarity and evidence, appear to suggest something different, we must still put our entire faith in divine authority rather than in our own judgement.'

René Descartes, *Principles of Philosophy* (1644)

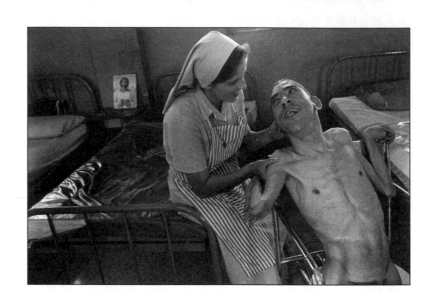

Consider how this Cuban nun might answer the question 'Is conduct right because God commands it, or does God command it because it is right?'

Web quest

Through the ages, religious philosophers have chosen between one of two options presented in the Euthyphro dilemma. Visit www.heinemann.co.uk/hotlinks and click on this section to use the links in *The Internet Encyclopedia of Religion* and find out the views of (a) St Thomas Aquinas, (b) David Hume, and (c) William Ockham.

Summary

- It seems that no satisfactory answer can be given to the dilemma: *is an act right because God commands it, or does God command it because it is right?*
- If an act is right simply because God commands it, then its being right is merely **arbitrary**. God could arbitrarily command a person to murder his or her child (as in the biblical story of Abraham and his son Isaac) and that would supposedly make it right. But would it?
- On the other hand, if God commands an act because it is right, then is there a standard of rightness that exists independent of God's commands? It might be, say, the principle of utility (see p. 89). If so, then we could discover this

principle without knowing God's commands. God's commands, therefore, are not necessarily a prerequisite for living a moral life.

- The various arguments about the connection between religion and ethics point to a common conclusion. Right and wrong are not to be defined in terms of God's will; morality is a matter of reason and **conscience**, not religious faith; and religious considerations do not always provide definite solutions to the specific moral problems that confront us.

- However, this conclusion does not undermine the validity of religion, but illustrates that the discipline known as 'ethics' can remain independent. For believers and non-believers alike, making a moral judgement is a matter of listening to one's reason.

Review

Indian ethics: understands the principle of a universal moral order called dharma. All actions have consequences. As we sow, so shall we reap – if we act with harmful or selfish intent, then not only will other people be hurt, but we also will suffer in the long run.

The Greeks: Socrates, Plato and Aristotle used reason to try to understand what a good and virtuous life is.

The divine command theory: an act is morally right if it has been commanded by God and morally wrong if God has forbidden it. Right and wrong become an objective matter. Ethics, therefore, is not merely a matter of custom or personal feelings but relates to a 'higher good'.

The Euthyphro dilemma: *Is conduct right because the gods command it, or do the gods command it because it is right?* If God's laws are absolute, why does God not command laws that allow cruel actions as well as good actions? If God is good, can he only command what is right? Is there a standard of goodness *independent* of God?

Exam questions

1 **(a)** Explain with examples, Aquinas' 'natural law' ethical theory. (15 marks)
   (b) Consider how far this theory is compatible with a religious approach to making moral decisions. (15 marks) (WJEC, January 2001)

2 **(a)** Examine the reasons for the view that morality is based upon religion. (10 marks)
   (b) Examine and consider the view that morality is independent of religion. (10 marks) (EDEXCEL, June 2001)

3 **(a)** Explain how the principles of natural law might be applied to the argument that every woman has the right to a child. (33 marks)
   (b) To what extent could a believer in the natural law theory accept foetal research? (17 marks) (OCR, June 2001)

See pp. 145–147.

6 Conscience

'Conscience is the inner voice that warns us that someone might be looking.'

H.L. Mencken (1880–1956), American journalist

Word watch

conscience

Objectives

'Conscience doesn't keep you from doing anything wrong; just from enjoying it', said King Stanislas I of Poland (1764–95). So what is consience? In this chapter you will explore the following questions:

- the difficulties of defining real conscience?
- different philosophers' views of conscience?
- arguments for and against using conscience as a guide for moral decision-making?

Word watch

sanctioned

Key questions

1 Is conscience always a suitable moral guide?

2 Can conscience be weak, variable, misinformed and even defective sometimes?

3 Is it possible to commit evil acts **sanctioned** by 'conscience'?

4 Is it right to go with what we really feel to be right even when others disagree with us?

5 Is conscience something that has been installed in us, or is it something we learn?

6 Are there situations when we should go against conscience?

7 Is conscience evidence of the existence of God?

8 Is conscience a product of evolution – a mechanism that was developed in order that human beings might survive their violent and destructive nature?

9 Is conscience simply a voice that knows what it has been taught to know; therefore, it is no more accurate in ethical situations than the teaching it has received?

Introduction

The Oxford Dictionary defines conscience as 'a moral sense of right and wrong, especially as felt by a person and affecting behaviour (*my conscience will not allow me to do that*) or an inner feeling as to the goodness or otherwise of one's behaviour (*my conscience is clear; has a guilty conscience*)'. Thus we have the idea that conscience both reflects on and directs behaviour.

There is perhaps no nobler statement than the one that goes something like 'I shall act according to my conscience.'

Everyday use of the term 'conscience' refers to an inward principle, which decides as to the character of one's own actions, warning against and condemning actions that are wrong, and approving and prompting us to right actions. It is seen as a sort of moral faculty capable of making us pass judgement on ourselves.

Think it through

In pairs, try to think of examples of (a) people who have upheld the principle of justice, like Nelson Mandela, despite every kind of pressure to relinquish what they knew and believed in, and (b) any situations when you made decisions according to your conscience that were unpopular.

Web quest

Visit the Nobel e-Museum to find out more about the lives of some of the greatest men and women of the last 100 years and find out more about prisoners of conscience and the work of Amnesty International by visiting www.heinemann.co.uk/hotlinks and clicking on this section.

Since the Nazi atrocities towards the Jews were discovered at the end of World War II (1939–45), people have wondered how so many could collectively have engaged in such atrocities. The death camps in which Jews were systematically tortured and killed were efficiently organized and managed by well-trained administrative personnel. The Germans who ran the death camps seemed to be ordinary 'decent' citizens, with consciences no different from those of any of us. How could they have blinded themselves to the clear injustice of what they were doing? More generally, what motivates the unethical acts of ordinarily decent people?

Key idea

Conscience both reflects on and directs behaviour.

Word watch

moral faculty

Key fact

The Old Testament prophets acted and spoke according to their conscience when they denounced and predicted society's collapse because of greed and corruption. Jesus of Nazareth was sentenced to death and crucified for speaking out according to his conscience.

'The only tyrant I accept in this world is the still voice within ... in matters of conscience, the law of the majority has no place.'

Mohandas Gandhi (1869–1948), political and spiritual leader

Think it through

1 Apparently motivated by conscience, people have actually harmed others. The French philosopher Blaise Pascal (1623–62) reminds us, 'Men never do evil so fully and so happily as when they do it for conscience's sake.' So what is 'conscience'? Consider the idea that there is hardly any act of cruelty or indifference that has not been sanctioned by conscience. What implications does this have for ethical thought? Or can conscience somehow be 'blocked' or 'ignored' allowing acts of cruelty and indifference?

2 Between 1939 and 1945, horrific medical research projects took place in Nazi concentration camps. Thousands of men, women and children were subjected to forced experiments that broke all the rules and norms of medical research. Experiments involved freezing people alive, dissecting them alive, slowly burning them, and others too brutal to tell – in the name of the advancement of medical knowledge to see what the human body was capable of. About 200 Nazi doctors participated in this work, none more infamous than the Auschwitz camp doctor, Josef Mengele (1911–79) who performed his experiments on camp inmates, particularly those with any physical deformity. After the war he escaped to South America and died in Brazil in 1979.

Imagine Mengele had been caught and brought to trial for crimes against humanity. You are one of the judges whose turn it is to cross examine him. What sorts of questions would you ask him? Consider how Mengele might justify his experiments.

Jewish view

For followers of Judaism, the presence of conscience in us is a testimony that human beings are more than just animals and illustrates that we are created in the image of God. A conscience causes humans to think about their actions, as they seek approval from their own hearts. It is not a substitute for what God has revealed; to provide maximum guidance it must be instructed in what God has taught. The conscience can become corrupted if the person insists on acting against what he/she has been taught to be right and good.

Think it through

1 What do you think are the implications of the Jewish view of conscience?

2 How might a survivor of the Holocaust have treated Mengele?

3 In what ways do you think conscience can become 'corrupted'?

Christian views
St Jerome

St Jerome (347–420 CE), one of the early Christian 'Fathers of the Church', spoke about the innate power capable of distinguishing good from evil as the 'spark of conscience ... by which we discern that we sin'. It later became usual for Christian thinkers to use the term conscience (*conscientia*) for the ability to distinguish good from bad at the level of particular actions.

Quotable quote

'The safest course is to do nothing against one's conscience. With this secret, we can enjoy life and have no fear from death.'

Voltaire (1694–1778), French philosopher

St Augustine of Hippo

St Augustine of Hippo (334–420 CE) saw conscience as a tool (an innate faculty) for observing God's moral law as inscribed in the human heart. His account of conscience is closely related to many ancient mystical traditions, including the writings of Plotinus (204–69 CE) and Origen (185–255 CE), in the idea of moral purification. According to St Augustine, God endows each human being with a conscience whereby he or she may know the moral law. However, this knowledge by itself is insufficient. Virtue requires that the will should also be turned towards the good. God's **grace** illuminates the soul by a revelation of God's goodness, which *induces* virtue as the soul becomes charged with love for God's perfection. It is only by grace that the soul flies away from the world.

Word watch

grace

❝ ══ Quotable quote ══════

'I do not understand what I do; for I don't do what I would like to do, but instead I do what I hate … For even though the desire to do good is in me, I am not able to do it. I don't do the good I want to do; instead, I do the evil that I do not want to do.'

St Paul, Romans 7:15–19

❞

St Thomas Aquinas: conscience is the power of reason

Aquinas (1225–74) regarded conscience as equivalent to 'right' reason (*recta ratio*). He argued that ultimately the moral life is the life 'according to reason'. Rather than being an inner voice that tells us what to do, Aquinas believed that conscience is 'reason making right decisions'. In his great work *Summa Theologica* (1265), Aquinas said that acting reasonably and acting as a Christian are one and the same thing:

'To disparage the dictate of reason is equivalent to condemning the word of God … Conscience is the dictate of reason … he who acts against his conscience always sins.'

Although conscience was seen to reveal the moral law, medieval thought interpreted moral law in two different ways:

- conscience is a form of knowledge that enables a person to examine and discern states of affairs that constitute moral facts in the same way as the scientific method examines facts that make up science
- conscience is a way of coming to know and understand what God wills, rather like consulting a textbook to discover something.

Joseph Butler: intuitive conscience

The Anglican priest and theologian Joseph Butler (1692–1752) argued that conscience was the final moral decision-maker. Butler argued that we are driven either by self-love or by **benevolence** (love of others) and conscience guides us away from self-love towards concern for others. Conscience is an intuitive faculty – 'the rule of right' within ourselves. It is our 'natural guide' given to us by God. As such it must always be obeyed, absolutely. In his *Fifteen Sermons upon Human Nature* (1726), Butler writes:

'Conscience does not only offer itself to show us the way we should walk in, but it likewise carries its own authority with it, that is our natural guide, the guide assigned to us by the Author of our nature.'

'There is a principle of reflection in men by which they distinguish between approval and disapproval of their own actions … this principle … is conscience.'

Butler's theory does not allow for the possibility that conscience is weak, variable, misinformed and even defective. What if an 'intuitive conscience' ('I intuitively know I should act in this way'), obeyed without question, is used to justify all sorts of evil acts? How is it possible to know exactly what my conscience is?

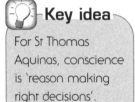
Key idea

For St Thomas Aquinas, conscience is 'reason making right decisions'.

Word watch

intuitive

John MacQuarrie: the struggle to be

Modern theologian John MacQuarrie (b. 1919) distinguishes three kinds of conscience:

- conscience 'wrestling with some particular decision'
- conscience as a more generalized knowledge of right and wrong (*synderesis*)
- conscience as a special and fundamental mode of self-awareness, the awareness of 'how it is with oneself'.

MacQuarrie argues that the basic function of conscience is 'to disclose us to ourselves' and that as well as disclosing things it is also a call or summons. Although conscience is commonly thought of as commanding us *to do* certain things, the fundamental command of conscience is *to be — what we seek to do in any particular situation depends on what we seek to be*. Sometimes authentic conscience may come into conflict with conventional morality. For example, conventional morality accepted slavery, but William Wilberforce (1759–1833) and Abraham Lincoln (1809–65) acted according to conscience and worked for its abolition. Before the second Gulf War in 2003 Robin Cook, a former Foreign Secretary, resigned from the British government because his conscience would not allow him to be part of a government that invaded Iraq in an 'unjust war'.

Overview of Christian views

Traditionally, Christian ethics has justified moral judgements by the use of reason, and conscience has been the name given to the power of that reason brought to bear on moral issues. It is 'conscience that must always be obeyed'. However, no claim is made that conscience is infallible or will necessarily provide certainty. The teaching has traditionally been accompanied by the call for the development of an informed conscience by living in the Christian community and making use of tradition, scripture and spirit in sensitizing and developing an awareness of conscience. However, some critics argue that the moral faculty (conscience) has only a limited range of operations and on many matters we 'have no conscience'. Moreover, it can vary considerably from person to person and culture to culture, seeming to depend on cultural conditioning or moral training (see relativism in Chapter 4).

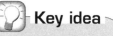

Key idea

John MacQuarrie argues that the fundamental command of conscience is *to be*. What we seek to do in any particular situation depends on what we seek to be.

Key idea

Believers and non-believers approaching moral decision-making may come up with similar conclusions. However, when it comes to theorizing about how they arrived at a similar position, they may disagree. The believer may regard the results of this inquiry as revealing God's will – whereas the non-believer asserts that his or her decision was dependent on his or her own reasoning alone.

Discussion

'*If one trains one's conscience, it will kiss us as it bites.*'

Friedrich Nietzsche, *Beyond Good and Evil* (1886)

Is conscience a sound moral guide?

Given all these ideas, can we be sure that conscience can guide us? St Paul understood conscience as 'the voice of God … written on the heart' (Romans 2:15). So acting on one's conscience is an act of moral **integrity** reflecting one's deepest conviction. Aquinas believed that it was wrong to go against one's conscience, as it speaks to the heart and provides one with a profound sense of right and wrong coming from God. Christian churches have in general accepted this view, but some philosophers have urged caution when considering whether conscience is a moral guide.

Michel Montaigne

Michel Montaigne (1533–92), a French thinker, wrote in *Essays of Custom* (1574):

'Laws of conscience, which we say are born of nature, are born of custom. Each man, holding in inward veneration the opinions and the behaviour approved and accepted around him, cannot break loose from them without remorse, or apply himself to them without self satisfaction.'

Henry David Thoreau

Henry Thoreau (1817–62), an American writer, wrote in *Journal* (1845):

'The conscience really does not, and ought not to monopolize the whole of our lives, any more than the heart or the head. It is as liable to disease as any other part. I have seen some whose consciences, owing undoubtedly to former indulgence, had grown to be as irritable as spoilt children, and at length gave them no peace.'

Key fact

Thoreau was jailed briefly for refusing to pay a tax in support of a war in Mexico.

Jean-Jacques Rousseau

Jean-Jacques Rousseau (1712–78), a French philosopher, wrote in *Emile* (1762):

'I need only consult myself with regard to what I wish to do; what I feel to be right is right, what I feel to be wrong is wrong; conscience is the best casuist; and it is only when we haggle with conscience that we have recourse to the subtleties of argument.'

Immanuel Kant

The German philosopher Immanuel Kant (1724–1804) wrote in *Groundwork to the Metaphysic of Morals* (1785):

'Conscience is not a thing to be acquired, and it is not a duty to acquire it; but every man, as a mortal being, has it originally within him. The duty here is only to cultivate our conscience, to quicken our attention to the voice of the internal judge, and to use all means to secure obedience to it, and is thus our indirect duty.'

Søren Kierkegaard

Søren Kierkegaard (1813–55), a Danish philosopher, wrote in *Works of Love* (1847):

'A man could not have anything upon his conscience if God did not exist, for the relationship between the individual and God, the God-relationship, is the conscience, and that is why it is so terrible to have even the least thing upon one's conscience, because one is immediately conscious of the infinite weight of God.'

Martin Luther King

Martin Luther King (1929–68) wrote in *From Strength to Love* (1963):

'I submit that an individual who breaks a law that conscience tells him is unjust, and who willingly accepts the penalty of imprisonment in order to arouse the conscience of the community over its injustice, is in reality expressing the highest respect for the law.'

*Martin Luther King arrested at a **civil rights** march in Montgomery, Alabama*

Hot tip

If a question on conscience comes up in your exam, remember to highlight the idea that conscience is the product of cultural and/or genetic influences set against the idea that conscience has a divine origin. Remember, also, to analyse whether or not conscience is a sound moral guide.

In one of his speeches King said:

'Cowardice asks the question — is it safe?
Expediency asks the question — is it politic?
Vanity asks the question — is it popular?
But conscience asks the question — is it right?
And there comes a time when one must take a position that is neither safe, nor politic, nor popular; but one must take it because it is right.'

Erich Fromm

Erich Fromm (1900–80) was a German psychoanalyst who escaped from Nazi Germany when the fascists came to power in 1933. Fromm distinguished two types of conscience, each with its own characteristics.

1   Authoritarian conscience: Fromm argued that we are born into a world influenced by external authorities — parents, police, politicians, bosses, bureaucrats, teachers, religious leaders. The laws and conditions that these

authorities impose on us *become part of ourselves*. They become *internalized*. Conscience becomes, therefore, a very effective way for those with power and authority to control people. A good authoritarian conscience produces a feeling of well-being and security. The guilty conscience produces fear and insecurity because going against authority implies that you will be punished. Guilt can reduce our power and make us more submissive to that authority. Fromm argued that we feel good from feelings such as submission and obedience as a result of the authoritarian conscience.

2 Humanistic conscience: Fromm defines this as the 'real' conscience, a conscience that judges our functions as human beings. He saw our conscience as our real selves, which tells us how to live properly and to become who we truly are.

On February 15th 2003 an estimated one million people marched through London protesting against the imminent invasion of Iraq. Was this an act of collective conscience?

Authority tends to do all in its power to break our will. But many children are not born to be broken. Some will refuse to conform. At some stage they will stand up to, and struggle against, authority. Thus, fighting for their freedom to be themselves, humanistic conscience or real conscience arises. They begin to break free from external authority. They are now capable of judging their 'functions as human beings' and have knowledge of their respective 'success or failure in the art of living'. Humanistic conscience, then, is 'a reaction of ourselves to ourselves; the voice of our true selves' guiding us as we become what we potentially are. In true conscience, therefore, we preserve the knowledge of our aim in life and of the principles we have discovered ourselves, as well as those we have learned from others. We are able to live with integrity.

Friedrich Nietzsche

Friedrich Nietzsche (1844–1900) was one of the most influential philosophers of the nineteenth century and one of the German language's most brilliant prose writers. In *On the Genealogy of Morals* (1887), Nietzsche sought to unmask the root motives that underlie traditional Western religion, morality and philosophy. His ideas exerted considerable influence over many aspects of culture in the twentieth century.

Nietzsche attacked the dominant morality in the modern Western world, which derived from Judaism and Christianity. He detested the idea of morality being validated by religion. He believed that the destruction of Judaeo-Christian morality would make room for something better. Nietzsche gives a central place to deciding what sort of person you want to be and then going on to create yourself by the 'will to power'.

Nietzsche utterly rejected **altruism** and argued that the idea of loving your neighbour is a disguise for mediocrity. People too weak to override others disguise their weakness as moral virtue, 'the bad conscience is an illness' and the man Nietzsche admires will overcome 'bad conscience', the mark of 'slave morality', and learn to dominate others. In *On the Genealogy of Morals*, Nietzsche writes:

'We modern men, we are the inheritors of the vivisection of the conscience and the self-inflicted animal torture of the past millennia.'

Think it through

1 How do you think Erich Fromm would have interpreted the actions of men like Josef Mengele?

2 Erich Fromm concluded that 'at the bottom of every neurosis is a parent'. In pairs, discuss Fromm's ideas.

3 If authoritarian conscience is based upon a very rigid and powerful authority, the development of humanistic conscience can be almost entirely suppressed. A person then becomes completely dependent on external powers and ceases to feel responsible for his or her own existence. All that matters, then, is the approval or disapproval by these powers – which can be a parent or even friends. Can you think of cases when you have done something wrong but only feel guilty because of 'what you think others might think'?

4 Compare and contrast the views of Montaigne, Thoreau, Rousseau, Kant, Kierkegaard, King, Fromm and Nietzsche on conscience.

Review

Is conscience a sound moral guide?

- **St Jerome:** the innate power capable of distinguishing good from evil is the 'spark of conscience'.

- **St Thomas Aquinas:** conscience is equivalent to 'right' reason – ultimately the moral life is the life 'according to reason'. Rather than being an inner voice that tells us what to do, conscience is 'reason making right decisions'.

- **Joseph Butler:** conscience is an intuitive faculty – 'the rule of right' within ourselves, a 'natural guide' given to us by God. However, conscience can be weak, variable, misinformed and even defective. What if an 'intuitive conscience', obeyed without question, is used to justify all sorts of evil acts?

- **Blaise Pascal:** 'Men never do evil so fully and so happily as when they do it for conscience's sake.'

- **Michel Montaigne:** conscience is a product of our conditioning.

- **Henry Thoreau:** conscience is capable of corruption – 'liable to disease'.

- **Jean-Jacques Rousseau:** conscience *can* be a sound ethical guide.

- **Immanuel Kant:** everyone has conscience originally within.

- **Søren Kierkegaard:** 'It is so terrible to have even the least thing upon one's conscience, because one is immediately conscious of the infinite weight of God.'

- **Martin Luther King:** 'Conscience asks the question – is it right?'

- **Erich Fromm:** laws that authorities impose on us become *internalized*. 'Good' conscience is consciousness of pleasing the external (and internal) authority. On the other hand, humanistic conscience is the voice of our true selves' guiding us as we become what we potentially are.

- **Friedrich Nietzsche:** conventional conscience is 'bad conscience' – the mark of 'slave morality'.

Exam questions

1 **(a)** Give an account of *two* ways of understanding conscience. (33 marks)
   (b) 'Conscience is not a reliable guide for making moral decisions.' Discuss. (17 marks) (OCR, January 2001)

2 **(a)** What are the characteristics of 'conscience'? (14 marks)
   (b) Comment on the claim that 'conscience' allows people the freedom to behave as they wish. (6 marks) (EDEXCEL, June 2001)

3 **(a)** Give an account of the view that conscience is 'the voice of God'. (33 marks)
   (b) On what grounds might conscientious objectors defend their attitude to war? (17 marks) (OCR, June 2001)

For more on conscientious objection see p. 168

7 Egoism

Word watch

altruists
egoists

Objectives

In this chapter you will address a fundamental question in ethics: how do I reconcile self-interest and morality? How can I act so that my desire to maximize my own pleasure does not conflict with doing the right thing? You will explore:

- The meaning and consequences of universal, psychological and personal **ethical egoism**.
- The meaning and consequences of **egoism** as a means to the common good – Adam Smith's, Thomas Hobbes's and Joseph Butler's views.

Word watch

self-interest
universal
ethical egoism
egoism
common good

Introduction

Egoism is a teleological theory of ethics (see p. 76) that sets as its goal the benefit, pleasure or greatest good of oneself alone. It is contrasted with altruism – which is not strictly self-interested but includes in its goal the interests of others.

Word watch

teleological

Key questions

1 Are we all driven ultimately by self-interest?

2 Is it always wrong to act in your own self-interest?

3 Can egoism provide an ethic by which society can live harmoniously or would it lead to chaos?

Varieties of egoism

There are different ways in which the theory of egoism can be presented.

Universal ethical egoism

This is the theory that everyone ought to act in his or her own self-interest. *My act is right if it is in my self-interest and wrong if it is not in my self-interest. Your act is right if it is in your self-interest and wrong if it is not.*

Universal ethical egoism involves a contradiction (although this theoretical contradiction is not always easy to spot). Suppose Terry and Mary are arguing. As a practising universal ethical egoist, I tell Terry to win (since that is in my self-interest so as to prevent him falling out with me too), but I also then tell Mary that she should win (for the same reasons). But they cannot *both* win, so there is something odd about this advice. Nevertheless, it is not formally self-contradictory to tell them both to try to win.

Personal ethical egoism

Personal ethical egoism is another version of universal ethical egoism: *I ought to do those actions that most benefit me*, but I have nothing to say about your actions. This is not really an ethical theory, but is more like a personal philosophy of life.

Individual ethical egoism

This is yet another version: you and I both ought to do what is in my self-interest. This view involves a strange asymmetry: *you ought always to help me, but I should never help you, unless that benefits me.*

Word watch

contradiction

Word watch

self-contradictory

 Key idea

Egoist theories of ethics basically argue that we ought to do what is in our own self-interest.

Discussion

'The very vicious — those who live a life of aggression against others — whether through physical violence or through psychological manipulation, are also radically lacking in the willingness to be the autonomous agents of their own lives and establish an independent relationship to reality … For the more they aggress and scheme against others, the less they live lives of their own; and the more they succeed in rationalizing their behaviour to themselves, the less they see a reason to make lives of their own. Their callous attitude toward others' well-being is reflected in a like attitude toward themselves, an attitude of indifference to their moral selves, their characters. Thus, they rob themselves not only of the pleasures of living lives of their own, but also of the pleasures of friendship.'

Neera Badhwar, 'Altruism as self interest', *Altruism* (1993)

Word watch

autonomous agents

Psychological egoism

None of these views should be confused with **psychological egoism**, which holds that everyone will ultimately do what is in their self-interest. Psychological egoists argue that all humans, deep-down, are egoists in so far as our behaviour is always aimed at what we believe is our greatest good. This is actually not an ethical theory but a description and claim about how people act.

Psychological egoism seizes on the idea that people are motivated by self-interest — and because they are, they ought to pursue their own good as effectively as they can. Note the step in this argument from a psychological generalization taken as 'fact' (that is, 'people are motivated by self-interest') to an ethical 'ought'; from a description to a prescriptive obligation. For this reason, it can be considered a doubtful logical **inference**. Ethical egoists, however, would defend this move as being a recognition of the psychological condition of humanity. But can there ever be direct evidence for this other than the interpretation of motivation?

Word watch

inference

Psychological egoism is a descriptive claim about human nature. Since the claim is universal (that is, all acts are motivated by self-interest), it could be proven false by a single counter-example.

Egoism as a means to the common good

Some writers suggest we should all focus our resources on satisfying our own interests, rather than those of others. Society will then be more efficient and this will better serve the interests of all.

Key fact

Adam Smith was a Scottish political economist and philosopher. His *Inquiry into the Nature and Causes of the Wealth of Nations* (1776) was written during the years of strife between Britain and its colonies. It was published the same year as the American 'Declaration of Independence'.

Adam Smith

According to the economist and leading advocate of 'free trade' Adam Smith (1723–90), such a view leads to the idea that if each business person pursues his or her own interest as he or she conceives of it, then the interest of everyone is promoted.

Adam Smith's theory of economics established capitalism as an economic system. Smith believed man to be basically self-interested, though capable of relating to others through sympathy. Smith's theory of economics developed from his ideas regarding the proper relations among men. As people had a right to the product of their own work, they also had a right to keep or trade it as they saw fit.

Thus, through capitalism and free trade, each transaction benefits each participant, while no one trades value for non-value and no one demands what belongs to another because people can sympathize with others.

American moral philosopher Kurt Baier, in *The Moral Point of View* (1958), challenges this view. Baier argues that practical reasoning that takes into account both individual and social considerations is the appropriate method for deciding 'what is the best thing to do' in particular circumstances. Thus we are moral because it is rational to be so, even when our private interests are outweighed by the welfare of others.

Apart from positing an invisible hand guiding capitalism and the market processes, the common good egoist makes the mistake of thinking that if everyone promotes his or her own interest, then everyone else's interests are somehow promoted too. Clearly, this is a **fallacy**, for the interests of different individuals or classes or nations may, and under certain conditions

Consider how egoism as a means to the common good has not worked for this child in Guatemala City, living and working in a rubbish tip

(of which the scarcity of resources is the most obvious) do, conflict. Then the interest of one is to the detriment of the other.

❝ — Quotable quote

'It is not from the benevolence of the butcher, the brewer, or the baker that we expect our dinner, but from their regard to their own interest.'

Adam Smith *Inquiry into the Nature and Causes of the Wealth of Nations* (1776)

Discussion

1 'What rich nations can also afford to do – what they cannot help doing – is to distribute the benefits of wealth ever more widely. Adam Smith noticed economic growth's possible ills, but he firmly believed in its happy effects ... A bicycle, a radio, a package of aspirin, some pork with their rice, shoes rather than sandals: for these things, villagers worldwide are delighted to shatter what has been glamourized as "the world we have lost". Good riddance, they say with Smith.'

David Frum, 'Adam Smith, the Sensible Philosopher', in *The New Criterion* (March 1996)

2 'Consider the fact that the GDP (gross domestic product) of the poorest 48 nations (that is, a quarter of the world's countries) is less than the wealth of the world's three richest people combined. In today's global economy, Adam Smith's view that business people should be unimpeded by legal or self-imposed moral constraint to promote their own good thus promoting the good of others, is utterly unconvincing and inevitably immoral.'

3 'For a number of decades our colleges have been teaching a serious fallacy. This fallacy is that our present system of political organisation is capitalism. This is not true. What we are calling capitalism in our schools and in our media is not capitalism. We abandoned free enterprise long ago in the aftermath of World War I in favour of Mussolini's "corporatism"; that is, economic facism, where Big Business and Big Finance combine to exploit the people with monopolized prices and corrupted dollars.'

Nelson Hultberg, *Economic Fascism and Tax Slavery* (2003)

Word watch

GDP – gross domestic product

Key fact

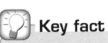

All over the world, disparities between rich and poor, even in the wealthiest of nations, is rising sharply. Fewer people are becoming increasingly well off while a disproportionately larger population are also becoming even poorer.

Web quest

To find out more about the common good and the causes of world poverty visit www.heinemann.co.uk/hotlinks and click on this section.

Quotable quote

'Egoists are self-centred, inconsiderate, unfeeling, unprincipled, ruthless self-aggrandizers, pursuers of the good things in life whatever the cost to others, people who think only about themselves or, if about others, then merely as means to their own ends.'

Kurt Baier, *A Companion to Ethics* (1991)

Think it through

Compare and contrast the different types of egoism and evaluate whether they can serve as useful theories of ethics.

Are we ultimately driven by self-interest?

Psychological egoists argue that any act, no matter how selfless and altruistic it might seem, is actually motivated by some selfish desire (for example, a desire to be liked, for reward, avoidance of guilt, personal happiness). If I gave money to a homeless man, for example, I might feel happy afterwards. But is that happiness the motive for my action or just a result of it? Does the psychological egoist fail to distinguish the beneficial consequences of an action from the self-interested motivation? Why would it make me happy to see the man get a warm drink if I did not already have some prior concern for his best interest? Would that not be altruism?

Followers of the world's faiths would argue that history is ennobled by examples of people who have unceasingly and unselfishly worked for the good of others. The egoist again may counter this by saying that unselfish acts may still ultimately be in these people's own interest and may provide them with a great deal

of satisfaction or ego-fulfilment. Buddhists, Christians and Muslims would suggest that this is a cynical view of human nature and one that fails to take into account Buddha, Jesus and Muhammad's lives — exemplary figures of heroic proportions who *emptied* themselves of self-love and served others.

In his book *Leviathan* (1651), the English political philosopher Thomas Hobbes (1588–1679) argued that every action we perform, no matter how charitable or benevolent, is done for reasons that are ultimately self-serving. For example, when I donate to charity, I am actually taking delight in demonstrating my power. Hobbes argued that any account of human action — including morality — must be consistent with the fact that we are all ultimately self-serving.

He speculates how selfish people would behave in a state of nature, before the formation of any government. People, he argues, are essentially equal, both mentally and physically, in so far as even the weakest person has the strength to kill the strongest. Given our equal standing, Hobbes observes how situations make us naturally prone to quarrelling and conflict.

Word watch

self-serving

Discussion

Discuss Hobbes' idea that there are three natural causes of quarrel among people:

- competition for limited supplies of material possessions
- distrust of one another
- glory in so far as people remain hostile to preserve their reputation.

Hobbes concludes that the natural condition of humans is a state of *perpetual war of all against all*, where no morality exists, and everyone lives in constant fear — 'the life of people, solitary, poor, nasty, brutish, and short' (*Leviathan*, 1651).

However, Hobbes observes that people can engage in a **social contract** with one another. For example, I agree to give up my right to steal from you, if you give up your right to steal from me. We have then transferred these rights to each other and thereby become obligated to not steal from each other. From selfish reasons alone, we are both motivated to transfer these and other rights mutually, since this will end the dreaded state of war between us.

For more on social contract see Chapter 11, part 2

❛ Quotable quote

'For the laws of nature (justice, equity, modesty, mercy, and, in sum, doing to others as we would be done to) of themselves, without the terror of some power, to cause them to be observed, are contrary to our natural passions, that carry us to partiality, pride, revenge and the like.'

Thomas Hobbes, *Leviathan* (1651)

Criticism of Hobbes's theory

* It is uncertain whether people who are fundamentally equal in the state of nature would be motivated to attack each other.
* If I am motivated only by self-interest, I would have reasons to break rules occasionally when breaking them served my interests. A social contract will obligate me to follow moral rules only to the point where it is necessary to keep society together. But by keeping society together, am I not protecting my own self-interests, too?
* Bishop Joseph Butler (1692–1752) argued that while people do actually desire their own inner happiness in general, motivation is tied in specific cases to particular external objects (*Fifteen Sermons upon Human Nature*, 1726). For example, I do not want food for the sake of my own happiness, but because I am hungry and need it to go on working, to go on serving others. Therefore, my desire for food is not self-contained and solely egotistical. This is the difference, according to Butler, between 'true self-love' and 'unnatural or debauched self-love'. True self-love does not conflict with loving people or things for their own sake: friendship, marriage and parenthood help us develop non-egotistical motivations to such an extent that people often sacrifice their own interests for those they love. We desire their well-being as much and sometimes more than our own.
* Despite Hobbes's analysis, it must also be recognized that despite greed, self-interest and apathy, many people have not turned their backs on helping others. What about people who dedicate their lives in service to others? Thomas Hobbes's view that egoism left to itself would lead to chaos, led him to argue that if society were not to be brutal and nasty, it would need

Key question

How can we love others if we do not love ourselves?

Word watch

debauched

enlightened, self-interested, benevolent monarchs in charge. But surely such rulers, like their subjects, are ultimately polluted by egoism?

Think it through

1 Consider whether you agree with Hobbes that in our natural state 'life is nasty and brutish'.

2 Consider whether life would be fairer and more peaceful if 'benevolent monarchs', rather than self-interested politicians, ran the world.

A Christian view of egoism

For many Christians, Jesus' parable of the Good Samaritan sums up the actions of a morally mature person, one who acts not out of egoistic motivation. Compassion for someone in need motivated the Samaritan's behaviour – he went to the aid of an injured person. The Samaritan was inconvenienced by this altruistic act. He was, the story tells us, on a journey. He rendered practical, rational help, binding up the injured man's wounds, and then took the further step of acting responsibly by 'lifting him on to his mount, carried him to the inn and looked after him'. The innkeeper was then asked to look after the injured person until the Samaritan's return. Because the helper was a Samaritan and the injured person a Jew (at a time when great animosity existed between these people), the Samaritan showed a high degree of moral autonomy by going to his aid.

- While a legitimate psychological self-interest is assumed in the Bible, this is balanced by ethical concern for others: 'Love your neighbour as you love yourself.'
- For Christians, everyone is a member of the whole, related by a common humanity living in *relationship* to others and to God.
- The doctrine of human depravity must be balanced by the doctrine of Common Grace, that is, God in his goodness restrains the evil possibilities inherent in a degenerative egoism, maintaining a degree of order in nature and society.
- The highest end for the Christian is not egoistic, but 'to seek first the kingdom of God'. The highest motivation is love for God and love for neighbour.

Word watch

Common Grace
degenerative

Quotable quote

'He therefore who loves men, ought to love them either because they are righteous, or that they may become righteous. For so also he ought to love himself, either because he is righteous, or that he may become righteous; for in this way he loves his neighbour as himself without any risk.'

St Augustine, *On the Trinity* (410)

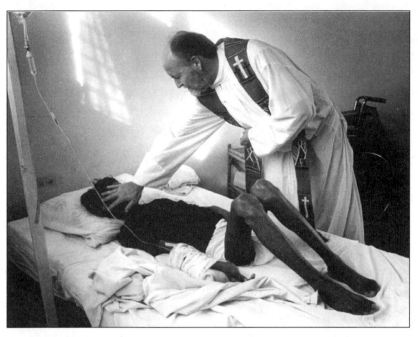

The last rites to an AIDS patient – are egoists right in saying that acts are always motivated by self-interest?

Review

Universal ethical egoism: everyone ought to act in his or her own self-interest.

Personal ethical egoism: another version of universal ethical egoism: *I ought to do those actions that most benefit me*, but I have nothing to say about your actions.

Individual ethical egoism: another version of universal ethical egoism: you and I both ought to do what is in my self-interest.

Egoism as a means to the common good: by focusing our resources on satisfying our own interests, rather than those of others, ultimately everyone will be better off. This is a fallacy, for the interests of different individuals or classes or nations may, and do, conflict. Therefore, the interest of one is the detriment of the other.

Psychological egoism: everyone will ultimately do what is in his or her own self-interest. This is actually not an ethical theory but is a description and claim about how people act.

Psychological egoists: no matter how selfless and altruistic we might seem, we are actually motivated by some selfish desire. Since this claim is universal (that is, all acts are motivated by self-interest), it could be proven false by a single counter-example.

Thomas Hobbes: in the absence of a social condition, every action we perform, no matter how charitable or benevolent, is done for reasons that are ultimately self-serving.

Christian criticism of egoism: we are all interdependent and cannot live without *relationship* to others. The highest end for the Christian is not egoistic, but love for God and love for neighbour.

ETHICAL THEORY

We all have to think about work and career choices. In order to arrive at a conclusion about which actions and choices lead to a successful life for you and for others it is useful to understand some principles of action. The next four chapters look at different ethical theories.

Moral reasoning is like a prism that can shine light onto dilemmas. Which light is shone will depend upon the person you are, but the more theories of ethics are understood, the more options there are about which light to shine.

Two approaches to ethics

Most philosophers argue that there are two systems for determining what is right or good. The ways in which 'right' and 'good' affect a course of action is the primary difference between two of the most common ethical systems.

Teleological theories: right is defined as that which maximizes what is good or minimizes what is harmful for the greatest number of people. The focus is on the consequences, or end. One example is **utilitarianism** (see Chapter 9), which advocates maximizing the amount of 'good' for the largest group. Good is defined by the results of the chosen action or by following a rule that enhances the most favourable outcome. Critics point out that a utilitarian philosophy can lead to behaviours that are clearly unacceptable. Imagine a town where people enjoy watching public hangings so much that the guilt or innocence of the one hanged is unimportant. A key problem with this system is who decides what is beneficial or harmful for whom?

Deontological theories: what is right and good are separated – one is independent of the other. Right is not defined in terms of what is good; producing a favourable outcome is not the goal. Doing right means avoiding actions said to be wrong by some external standard. For instance, if lying is wrong, then telling a lie to a person is wrong, even if the lie would prevent a death. With deontological theories, certain things are inherently right or wrong, as often defined by religious tenets or professional codes of behaviour. The Ten Commandments are an example of an external set of rules. So, for deontologists, the important thing is not the result or the consequences of an action, but the action itself. In the next chapter we will explore the most influential deontological theory as argued by Immanuel Kant.

Think it through

A politician has to make a decision about a 'terrorist' who is in police custody. The 'terrorist' is suspected of having information that could result in the death of innocent people, but he refuses to talk. The police argue that the only way they will get the 'terrorist' to reveal his information is to torture him. The politician argues that torture is always wrong, no matter what the consequences. Consider which viewpoint is teleological and which viewpoint is deontological.

8 Kantian ethics

> *'Two things fill the mind with ever new and increasing wonder and awe ... the starry heaven above and the moral law within.'*
>
> Immanuel Kant, *Critique of Practical Reason* (1788)

Objectives

This chapter explores a key idea in ethics, namely that we are not morally obligated to seek the best overall outcome by our actions, but rather that we are obligated to perform those actions that accord with our moral **duty**. The main focuses of this area of enquiry are:

- the deontological theory of ethics
- Immanuel Kant's theory of the **categorical imperative**, moral law, good will and duty, and the application of his ideas
- the strength and weaknesses of **Kantian ethics**.

? Key questions

1 Are actions more important than consequences?
2 Is morality about doing one's duty?
3 Are moral statements true in all circumstances?
4 Are we ever justified in treating other people as a **means** to an end?
5 Is it ever morally permissible to lie?
6 Should we treat another badly if they treat us badly?

Hot tip

In your examination paper there will be questions about a whole range of ethical issues. The key to success will be your ability to apply the ethical theories explored in this book to these issues. The theories explored in these chapters do not of course provide automatic solutions to specific contemporary moral issues. They will, however, help you to identify the important ethical considerations. In the end, we must deliberate on moral issues for ourselves, keeping a careful eye on both the facts and the ethical considerations involved.

The categorical imperative of Immanuel Kant

In *Groundwork to the Metaphysic of Morals* (1797), the German philosopher Immanuel Kant (1724–1804) argued that morality is a matter of following absolute rules – rules that admit no exceptions and appeal not to religious considerations but to reason.

> **❛ — Quotable quote**
>
> *'Opinions alter, manners change, creeds rise and fall, but the moral law is written on the tablets of eternity.'*
>
> Lord Acton, *Inaugural Lecture on the Study of History* (Cambridge, 1895) **❜**

The hypothetical imperative

Immanuel Kant observed that the word 'ought' is often used non-morally; for example, 'If you want to become a better artist or guitarist, you *ought* to practice'; 'If I want to learn more about ethics, I *ought* to study this book.' We have a certain wish and, recognizing that a certain course of action would help us fulfil this wish, we follow this course of action. Kant called this the **hypothetical imperative**; telling us what we *ought* to do if we want to fulfil our wishes.

The categorical imperative

In contrast, Immanuel Kant observed that moral obligations do not depend on particular wishes or desires. The form of a moral obligation is not 'If you want something, you ought to do such-and-such.' Instead, moral requirements are categorical, that is, 'You ought to do such-and-such' regardless of your particular wishes and desires.

Hypothetical 'oughts' are easy to understand – we merely choose the means necessary to achieve the ends we desire. They are possible because human beings have wishes and desires. Categorical 'oughts', however, are possible because we have reason – which is binding on rational agents *simply because they are rational*. But why? Kant argues that categorical oughts are derived from a principle, called the categorical imperative (sometimes called the **formula of universal law**, or formula of the **kingdom of ends**).

This states:

'Act only according to that maxim by which you can at the same time will that it should become a universal law.'

Word watch

hypothetical imperative

Word watch

categorical imperative

Word watch

rational agents
kingdom of ends
maxim

Discussion

- Before acting, ask yourself what rule you would be following if you were to do this action (the 'maxim').

- Then ask whether you would be willing for that rule to be followed by everyone all the time and in all places (making it a 'universal law').

- If the maxim can be universalized, then do it. If it cannot, then do not.

Think it through

A friend who is appearing on a television quiz show asks you to sit in the audience and cough at particular key moments during the multiple choice questions to help him win the top prize of a million pounds. He promises to split his winnings with you.

Before deciding what to do, ask yourself what rule you would be following if you were to sit in the audience and help your friend. Then ask yourself whether you would be willing for that rule to be followed by everyone all the time and in all places. If that 'rule' can be universalized, should you do it? If it cannot, then should you refrain from doing it?

Quotable quotes

'So act that your principle of action might safely be made a law for the whole world.'

'Always recognize that human individuals are ends and do not use them as means to your end.'

Immanuel Kant (1724–1804)

Lying though your teeth!

Immanuel Kant illustrated the categorical imperative with the example of telling lies. His reasoning went something like this: a man is so poor that even if he borrows money he will not be able to repay the loan. The debt collectors are threatening action. The man asks himself whether he should borrow money from his friend to get the debt collectors to leave him alone, knowing that he will not be able to repay his friend. If he were to go down this path and borrow money, his maxim would be: 'Whenever you need a loan, promise to repay it, even though you know you cannot do so.'

Now, could this maxim become a universal law? No, says Kant. If it did, people would no longer believe each other and nobody would lend money. Such a maxim, therefore, would be self-defeating.

Key idea

Only those actions that conform to rules that could be adopted by all people at all times (that is, universally) are moral.

Key idea

You should do only those actions that conform to rules that you could will to be adopted universally (at all times and at all places). If you were to lie, you would be following the rule 'It is permissible to lie.' This rule could not be adopted universally, because it would be self-defeating: people would stop believing one another, whether you lied or told the truth. Therefore you should not lie.

Kant argued that *lying* was always wrong. We would not reasonably want lying to become a universal law – people would quickly learn not to trust anybody and there would be chaos. If a lie is to become successful, people must believe that others are telling the truth; so the success of a lie depends on there not being a 'universal law' permitting it.

Crime and punishment

To clarify Immanuel Kant's ideas, it is useful to look at the issue of crime and punishment. Traditionally, punishment of an evil deed has been justified as paying back the offender – they deserve to be treated badly in return: 'An eye for an eye, a tooth for a tooth.' This is called **retributivism**.

Thinkers like Jeremy Bentham (1748–1832), a utilitarian philosopher (see Chapter 9), argued that retributivism is unsatisfactory, as it demanded the infliction of suffering without any compensatory gain in happiness, and ultimately would increase, not decrease, the amount of suffering in the world. So punishment is only acceptable if:

1   it can be shown that it prevents people taking part in criminal activities (that is, 'the theory of deterrence')

2   it can help rehabilitate wrongdoers so that they will not take part in further criminal activities and will re-enter society as law-abiding citizens (that is, 'the theory of reform').

Kant disagreed! He argued that such theories are incompatible with human dignity because they *use people as a means to an end*.

As for rehabilitation – trying to mould people into behaving according to our own codes – Kant argues that it is a violation of the rights of autonomous people capable of deciding for themselves what sort of people they are or will become. We have the right to 'pay them back' but not to manipulate their personalities.

Kant argued, therefore, that:

1   punishment should be in proportion to the crime committed ('If you strike another, you strike yourself; if you kill another, you kill yourself').

2   punishment is a matter of *justice* – if the guilty are not punished, justice is not being done.

3   because rational beings are responsible for their actions, they are accountable for what they do. When a rational being decides to treat people in a certain way, he or she decrees that in his or her judgement *this is the way people are to be treated* (universalism). If he or she treats another badly, and we treat him or her badly in return, we are complying with the choice he or she has made, for, in Kant's words, 'His own evil deed draws the punishment upon himself.'

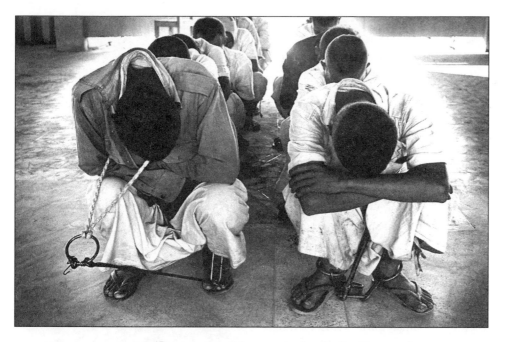

'One man ought never to be dealt with merely as a means subservient to the purpose of another.' [Immanuel Kant]

Think it through

Consider the following in pairs before reporting your findings back to the rest of the class.

1 Imagine Liam is fleeing from a murderer. He tells you that he is going home to hide. The murderer appears. The murderer wants to know where Liam went. If you tell the truth, the murderer will find Liam and kill him. Sometimes, in the hustle and bustle of life, some rules cannot be applied universally.

2 There are obviously many rules which Kant thought were 'absolute'. But what if two 'absolutes' are in conflict? For example, a man believes in two absolute principles: (a) 'It is wrong to lie', and (b) 'It is wrong to permit the murder of innocent people.' Suppose he lives in Nazi Germany and gives a group of persecuted Jews a hiding place. The Nazis ask him if he has any Jewish people living in his house. Should he lie or tell the truth and see them sent to their deaths?

3 Considering the ways in which we make choices, the complex situations we can find ourselves in and the different influences that affect our behaviour, do we always act on reason alone?

4 Imagine a war situation: a brutal platoon invades a village where a guerilla fighter is hiding. They threaten to kill everyone in the village unless the guerilla fighter reveals himself. The guerilla fighter is fighting a just war (see Chapter 15) and has the support of everyone in the village, who hate the invading army. The guerilla fighter is faced with an extreme ethical decision to make. Should he reveal himself and in consequence save the village, or should he escape to fight another day to rid his country of these brutal invaders? Consider whether a deontologist would disagree with the maxim 'It is better that one man die than a whole village be destroyed.' But is he right?

❝ — Quotable quote

'Act so you treat humanity, whether in your own person or in that of another, always as an end and never as a means also.'

Immanuel Kant, *Groundwork to the Metaphysic of Morals* (1785) ❞

Respect is due!

Immanuel Kant argued that human beings occupy a special place in creation and have 'an intrinsic worth, that is, dignity' that makes humankind valuable 'above all price'. Other animals, by contrast, have value only in so far as they serve human purposes. According to Kant, people can *use* animals any way they please. We do not even have a 'direct duty' to refrain from torturing them – although Kant thought it wrong, especially as it was far more likely that 'he who is cruel to animals becomes hard also in his dealings with men'. Kant believed that human beings, on the other hand, could never be 'used' as a means to an end.

'But so far as animals are concerned, we have no direct duties. Animals … are there merely as a means to an end. The end is man.' (Immanuel Kant, *Lectures on Ethics*, 1779)

Word watch

intrinsic worth

For more on animal rights see Chapter 14.

Hot tip

Find out how Kantian ethics might be applied to anthropocentric (human centred) approaches to the environment (look at Chapter 14).

Furthering the ends of others

Immanuel Kant argued that we have an *intrinsic* worth and dignity because we are rational agents; that is, free agents capable of making decisions, setting targets and guiding our conduct by reason. Kant argued that if we did not exist, the moral dimension of life on Earth would disappear. Rational beings embody the moral law itself and so inhabit a universe in which even 'things' have value. The human value system is therefore absolute and incomparable, and as such, we have value 'beyond all price', and must be treated 'always as an end and never as a means only'.

Therefore we have a duty to treat others well; respect their rights; treat everyone as equal; promote the welfare of others; never manipulate others or use them to achieve our own purposes (no matter how good those purposes may be). We should, in Kant's own words, 'try as far as we can, to further the ends of others'.

'Human beings have a value beyond price'

Hot tip

Kantian ethics can be applied to all ethical issues you have to study. For example, you could be asked how useful Kantian ethics are for drawing conclusions about the 'right to life' (think voluntary euthanasia, abortion and/or suicide). A balanced discussion is expected in your essay (that is, the strengths and weaknesses of Kantian ethics when applied to these issues). For example, (1) Abortion: does abortion violate the principle that agents are to be treated as ends not means? Can the right to abortion be universalized? (2) Embryo research (see Chapter 13): should the society considering embryo research be concerned with hypothetical outcomes (for example, treatment of genetically determined diseases) or with the application of the categorical imperative. Would embryo research violate the principle that agents (that is, the embryo in this case) are treated as ends not means? How might 'a woman's right to choose' conflict with her duty to be rational?

Key question

To what extent can it be concluded that religious ethics tend to be deontological?

God: the Moral Governor

In *The Critique of Pure Reason* (1781), Immanuel Kant argued that since human reason is limited, it is incapable of discovering God by reason alone, for God is infinite and transcends all things. He rejected, therefore, the traditional arguments for God's existence; although he also argued that God can be discovered by observing how *obligation* dominates all our lives (for example, I *ought* to be kinder to my pet; I *should* practise the piano; I *must* do my homework). This sense of *ought*, *should*, *must* is universal (we all do it!) and since we do not invent it (or often even want it!), it must come from another source, which religion calls God – the Supreme Moral Authority, who speaks through human conscience.

This argument – the *Moral Argument for God's Existence* – is not without its problems. How can we *prove* that God is the Moral Governor of the universe and the sovereign authority of moral obligation? Different cultures have different views on what is right and wrong, suggesting that 'the voice of God' is sometimes more dependent on cultural conditioning than on an absolute moral law (see Chapter 4).

Kant believed that to act morally is akin to being 'holy', and because philosophy is based on reason alone, it has supremacy over theology. He reinterpreted the claims of Christianity so that they expressed a call to moral righteousness, with Jesus being interpreted as 'The Holy One', the perfect exemplar of the morally good life – Jesus, in Kant's system, 'compared with our idea of moral perfection'.

Duty

For Kant, the highest form of good is good will. To have a good will is to do one's duty. Kant thought that morality rarely has anything to do with happiness and is all to do with duty. Kant argued that ordinary people are correct to believe that morality is essentially about sticking to a set of compulsory rules. He aimed to give philosophical justification to this belief. He argued, formidably, that to be moral we have to imagine ourselves on the receiving end of other people's decisions and universalize from there.

Think it through

Kant's system has been criticized for not allowing exceptions to the rule and for failing to address conflicts between moral rules. For example, two moral rules might be: 'I have a duty to be conscientious in my work' and 'I will not engage in any work that harms others.' A conflict might arise if the computer firm I work for asks me to develop a programme to spy on people's emails. In pairs, try to think of similar situations where moral rules come into conflict.

The kingdom of ends

Kant argues that it is never right to treat people as mere means to an end.

We are always *ends in ourselves*, and because of this we are all *holy*. For Kant, human reason is the key and by making laws for ourselves based on reason we become 'law-abiding members of a kingdom of ends' – a community in which the laws adopted by all the individuals will be in harmony, with disagreements sorted out by reasoned argument.

It is never right to treat people as mere means to an end

If we compare Jesus' ethical teachings with Kant's categorical imperative ('Act only on that maxim whereby thou canst at the same time will that it should become a universal law'), we find agreement in that both value the ultimate dignity and worth of all people irrespective of class, colour, race, age or gender.

For Kant all human beings, 'exalted beyond all price'.

Rights

Kant's theories have helped shape our legal system and our sense of moral law. Certain political conclusions follow from Kant's ethical theories. Kantian ethics require individual liberty, since each member of a society should be as free as possible to choose for himself or herself. Each member of a community, too, should consider himself or herself a member of the *moral community* – a community shared by others with equal moral rights and equal moral responsibilities.

Kant focused on the individual's right to choose for himself or herself. What distinguishes human beings from other animals or other objects is their dignity based on their ability to choose freely what they will do with their lives, and humans have a fundamental moral right to have these choices respected. People are not objects to be manipulated; it is a violation of human dignity to use people in ways they do not freely choose. Of course, many different but related rights exist besides this basic one; for example, the right to truth; the right of privacy; the right not to be injured; the right to what is agreed.

Web quest

People are not objects to be manipulated according to Kantian ethics. But given the power of the media moghuls in today's world, are we really being informed about what is going on? Write an essay using some Kantian ideas on The Right to the Truth. Visit www.heinemann.co.uk/hotlinks and click on this section for information that will help you in your deliberations.

Kant argued that the moral status of an action is not determined by its consequences. We are not morally obligated to seek the best overall outcome by our actions, but rather we are obligated to perform those actions that accord with our moral duty – the fundamental demand that we should treat others, and ourselves, in a manner consistent with human dignity and worth.

Key idea

In spite of its daunting title, Immanuel Kant's *Groundwork to the Metaphysic of Morals* (1785) is a short book. It has, however, had a tremendous influence on ethical thought and the broad framework of Kant's approach to ethics is still widely used today as a guide to ethical discussion.

Review

Teleology: what you achieve by your action determines the moral status of that action (consequences); justification for recognizing certain rights and duties is dependent upon their utility (usefulness) in achieving a maximization of value.

Deontology: what you do in your action and the nature of the action itself determines its moral status; rights and duties are justifiable regardless of consequential values. So rights and duties are 'fundamental', 'inalienable'.

Maxim: the principle according to which the subject acts. What the moral agent is doing or intends to do is expressed as his or her maxim.

Imperative: the objective principle valid for every rational being; the principle by which a rational agent ought to act.

Hypothetical imperative: an imperative that represents the practical action as means to something else that is willed or desired.

Categorical imperative: an imperative that represents an action as necessary of itself without reference to another end. Categorical imperatives represent our moral duty.

Word watch

moral agents

- A permissible act is one that could rationally be recommended to **moral agents** (everyone). These permissible acts then are universalizable.
- Thus, if a moral agent cannot rationally and consistently universalize his or her maxim (so that it applies to all moral agents), it is a categorical imperative that one ought *not* to act upon that maxim.
- Universal law formulation: I should never act except in such a way that I can also will that my maxim become a universal law.

Exam questions

1 (a) Describe Kant's theory of duty as the basis for morality. (33 marks)
   (b) How satisfactory is his theory for practical purposes? (17 marks) (OCR, January 2002)

2 (a) Identify and explain the central principles of Kant's ethical theory. (20 marks)
   (b) 'Given the demand for organ transplantation, the organs of individuals should be automatically available for use after their death.' Explain what objections a religious believer might raise in response to this claim and assess how far such objections are valid. (20 marks) (AQA, May 2002)

3 (a) Clarify the key features of a deontological theory of ethics. (20 marks)
   (b) To what extent, if any, do the weaknesses outweigh the strengths of this theory? (20 marks) (EDEXCEL, June 2002)

9 Utilitarianism

> 'Actions are right to the degree that they tend to promote the greatest good for the greatest number.'
>
> John Stuart Mill, *Utilitarianism* (1861)

Word watch

utilitarianism

Objectives

In this chapter you will learn about the best-known teleological theory of ethics – one that concentrates on consequences – namely, utilitarianism. You will explore:

- utilitarian theory – including the utility principle, hedonic (utility) **calculus** and act and **rule utilitarianism**
- the strengths and weaknesses of utilitarian approaches to ethics, including Christian responses.

Word watch

teleological
utility
hedonic calculus
act utilitarianism
rule utilitarianism

Key questions

1. What makes an action good or bad – the action itself or the consequences of that action?

2. Do the ends always justify the means?

3. Are consequences all that matter?

4. Does the 'good' of the many outweigh the 'good' of the few or the 'good' of a single individual?

5. By keeping to the rules, do we always produce the greatest good for the greatest numbers?

6. Is ethical decision-making ultimately concerned with balancing possible costs against possible benefits?

Word watch

consequences
ends
means

Deontological and teleological theories

Deontological theories (see previous chapter) maintain that the important thing is not the result or consequences of an action, but the action itself. If an action is wrong in and of itself, then do not do it. Teleological theories, on the other hand, understand the rightness or wrongness of actions by looking at the *consequences* of that action. For a teleological thinker, the end justifies the means. The rightness of an action is determined by the end it produces; for example, lying may be right if it results in a good end.

Jeremy Bentham

The most influential teleological theory is utilitarianism. In its simplest form, utilitarianism can best be summed up by the phrase 'the greatest happiness for the greatest number'. This is sometimes called the greatest happiness principle (GHP).

Utilitarianism was devised by Jeremy Bentham (1748–1832), an English thinker who worked on legal reform and who wrote *The Principles of Morals and Legislation* (1789). Bentham's theory can be divided into three parts:

1 **Hedonistic** utilitarianism: Bentham can be called a hedonist (*hēdonē* is Greek for pleasure). He argued that ultimately human beings are motivated by pleasure and pain – Bentham saw seeking pleasure and avoiding pain as a moral fact – pleasure is the sole good and pain the sole evil. This type of utilitarianism is called hedonistic utilitarianism.

The question 'what things are good?' is not necessarily the same question as 'What actions are right?' Utilitarianism answers the second question by referring back to the first one. Right actions are the ones that produce the most good.

Hedonism has always been an attractive theory because it expresses the idea that things are good or bad only on account of the way they make us feel.

However, there are serious flaws to hedonism. Hedonism misunderstands the nature of happiness. Happiness is not something that is always *recognized* as good and sought for its own sake, with other factors appreciated only as a means of bringing happiness about. Instead, happiness is a *response* we have. Setting out after happiness is very different from deciding what to do to make us happy and then deliberately doing it.

Today there are few philosophers who would call themselves hedonists. Those sympathetic to utilitarianism have tried to formulate their view without adopting a hedonistic account of good and evil. The English philosopher G.E. Moore (see pp. 15–16) tried to compile a short list of things to be regarded as good in themselves, that is, intrinsic goods such as pleasure, love, friendship and aesthetic enjoyment; and right actions are those that create such things.

2 The principle of utility: the rightness or wrongness of an action is determined by its 'utility' or usefulness — the amount of pleasure or pain caused by the action. In other words, 'An action is right if it produces the greatest good for the greatest number.' The greatest good is therefore the greatest pleasure or happiness and the least pain or unhappiness for the majority. Good, seen in this way, is the maximization of pleasure and the minimization of pain.

3 The utility, or hedonic, calculus: according to Bentham, it is possible to give specific content to ideas about right and wrong by reference to the *amount* of pleasure and pain involved in situations. This is a quantitative principle. To determine which actions lead to the most pleasure and the least pain, Bentham proposed the '**hedonic calculus**', which takes the following criteria into account:

- duration — how long does it last?
- intensity — how intense is it?
- remoteness — how near is it?
- certainty — how sure are we that it will come?
- purity — how free from pain is it?
- richness — how much will it lead to more pleasure?
- extent — how widely does it cover?

Think it through

One criticism of Bentham's calculation is that in real-life situations we may not have time to calculate the right action and his hedonic calculus is too complicated. In pairs, use Bentham's calculus to decide the best course of action in the following situations.

1 You are a surgeon with the money for one transplant operation, but there are four patients who would benefit from the donor organ. They are a brilliant scientist working on a cure for cancer, a fifteen-year-old girl, a father of two small children, and a single mother with one child. To whom would you give the operation? How do you decide which person benefits the most? Give reasons for your choice.

2 A four-year-old girl has a life-threatening kidney illness and has only a limited chance of survival if she has a kidney transplant. An organ becomes available. The transplant can go ahead. However, this is the little girl's second operation. The first one was unsuccessful because the organ was rejected. The operations cost as much to perform as a hundred routine operations for children – all of which have an almost 100 per cent chance of success. The girl's second operation has little chance of success because the child is very sick. There comes a time when doctors have to write off a patient's chance of survival when that person just cannot be healed. Should doctors write off the child in this case? Are they right to perform the transplant, or should the money be used for other purposes more likely to succeed?

Key question

Are actions always right if they promote the greatest good for the greatest number?

Word watch

quantitative

Key idea

Utilitarians maintain that actions are to be judged right or wrong solely by virtue of their consequences – right actions are those that have the best consequences.

John Stuart Mill

John Stuart Mill (1806–73) – regarded by some as the leading British philosopher of the nineteenth century – was a Member of Parliament and an advocate of women's rights. Mill agreed with Bentham in emphasizing that a person's well-being is of the utmost importance and that happiness is most effectively achieved when people are free to pursue their own ends (subject to rules that protect the common good of others).

> It is better to be Socrates unsatisfied than a pig satisfied.

Although Mill agreed with the utility principle – the greatest good for the greatest number – he was concerned that one person's 'pleasure' could be entirely overlooked if the majority were to gain pleasure from a particular action. For example, a prisoner is tortured for information that might save 100 men. All well and good for the 100 men, but no pleasure for the tortured! In other words, Mill saw the utility principle as purely quantitative. To address this difficulty Mill focused on qualitative pleasures and developed a system of 'higher' and 'lower' pleasures, preferring the 'higher' ones to the 'lower' ones. According to Mill, to pursue pleasures of the intellect were 'higher' than, say, the pursuit of pleasures of the body – drugs, sex and rock 'n' roll.

Act utilitarianism

According to act utilitarians, the principle of utility must be directly applied to each situation – it is the value of the consequences of the particular act that counts when determining whether the act is right.

When faced with a moral choice, a person must decide what action will lead to the greatest good in that particular situation. For example, if stealing will create the greatest pleasure, then I should steal. If, in the next situation, stealing will bring about a less pleasurable result than not stealing, then I should not steal.

To summarize, consequences are all that matters.

- Actions are to be judged right or wrong solely by virtue of their consequences. Right actions are simply those that have the best consequences.
- In assessing consequences, the only thing that matters is the amount of happiness or unhappiness that is caused. Right actions are those that produce the greatest balance of happiness over unhappiness.
- In calculating happiness or unhappiness, no one's happiness is to be counted as more important than another's. Each person's welfare is equally important.

Word watch

quantitative
qualitative

Key idea

Act utilitarianism implies that each individual action is to be evaluated by reference to its own particular consequences.

Think it through

In pairs, apply the utilitarian principle – actions are right to the degree that they tend to promote the greatest good for the greatest number – to the following situations.

1 Building a new dam will create hundreds of new jobs, but protestors argue that long-term consequences for the environment would be catastrophic.

2 A genetically modified crop is engineered in a desperately poor country to survive herbicides and increase food production, but critics argue that there is a possibility that it could cross-breed and transfer its weedkiller resistant genes from the crops into weeds and thus cause superweeds ultimately destroying the whole ecosystem.

For more on environmental ethics see Chapter 14.

Criticism of utilitarianism

Although utilitarianism seems to be a very flexible approach to decision-making, it can be criticized on the following grounds.

• If the value of the consequences of the particular act is great enough, any crime could be justified – a crime could even be seen as a moral obligation.

Discussion

The American dropping of atomic bombs on two Japanese cities in 1945 may have ended World War II in the east, but these acts also resulted in tens of thousands of immediate deaths and agony for survivors and succeeding generations. Was it worth it?

'*The moral debate about the use of the bombs is about two central issues. Could the war have been stopped by other means? And, if there were no alternative ways of stopping the war, would this justify dropping the bombs? Maybe the Japanese government could have been told of the bomb. They could have been given photographs and other evidence from the test already carried out in New Mexico. They could have been invited, quietly through diplomatic channels, to send representatives, including physicists, to a demonstration of the bomb. In the light of what happened to the people of Hiroshima and Nagasaki, the thought is unavoidable that such an approach should have been tried.*'

Jonathan Glover, *Humanity: A Moral History of the Twentieth Century* (2001)

- We hardly ever have the time and the knowledge to predict the consequences of an act, assess its value, and make comparisons with alternative acts. For example, we have a choice on how to spend our money. We know that if we give all our money to charity and thus generate the greatest happiness among the greatest number of the poor, then most of our leisure activities would cease because we would have no money to spend on them. In the long run, would this necessarily lead to good consequences for everyone? The people who receive our charity may be happier, but the football clubs, cinemas, pizza houses, clubs and bars may have to make employees redundant.

- Utilitarianism claims that only consequences matter. The most fundamental idea underlying the theory is that in deciding whether an action is right *we should look at what will happen as a result of doing it*. If other factors are important in determining what is right, then utilitarianism falls down as a theory. The most serious anti-utilitarian arguments attack the theory at just this point, arguing that various other considerations, in addition to utility, are important in determining whether actions are right.

Think it through

Utilitarianism can sometimes be incompatible with justice. Justice requires that we treat people fairly according to their individual needs and merits. How effective is the following criticism of utilitarianism by the modern philosopher D.D. Raphael in this extract from his book *Moral Philosophy* (1981)?

'Imagine that the happiness of the whole human race were to be immeasurably increased – poverty eliminated, brotherhood achieved, disease conquered ... but the condition is that one man, his life mysteriously prolonged, is to be kept involuntarily in a state of continuous and agonizing torture. According to the utilitarian criterion, which measures the rightness of an act by its results, it would seem that the argument is justified ... the net balance of the utilitarian moral scale would have to point in the direction of maximum happiness and away from the eternal agony of the single suffering man. But most people who consider the proposed bargain feel that there is something terribly wrong with it.'

- Utilitarianism is at odds with the idea that people's *rights* should not be trampled on merely because one anticipates good results. This is an extremely important idea and explains why a great many philosophers have rejected utilitarianism, as other rights are at issue – the right of freedom of religion, to free speech, or even the right to life itself. It may sometimes appear that good purposes are served from time to time by ignoring these rights, but rights should not be set aside so easily.

- Suppose you have promised a friend that you will teach her to play the guitar. When the time comes to go and help her, you would rather stay at home and watch television. What should you do? Does a *small* gain in utility overcome the obligation imposed by the fact that you promised? Because of its exclusive concern with consequences, utilitarianism looks to what *will happen* as a result of our actions and fails to accept the fact that the *past* is also important. The fact that you promised to help your friend is a fact about the past, not the future. Therefore, utilitarianism may be seen as an inadequate moral theory because it ignores 'backward-looking reasons and considerations'.

Rule utilitarianism

Utilitarians admit there are problems with their theory and some have tried to save the theory by giving it a new formulation. The problem is that act utilitarianism implies that each action is to be evaluated by reference to its own particular consequences. If, on a certain occasion, you are tempted to steal, it is the consequences that determine whether it is right or wrong. This is the point that causes all the trouble – even though we know that stealing has bad consequences, sometimes stealing might have positive consequences. Rule utilitarianism modifies the theory so that individual actions are no longer judged by the principle of utility. Instead, rules will be established and individual acts can be judged right or wrong by reference to rules.

A rule utilitarian would ask, 'What general rules of conduct tend to promote the greatest happiness?' Suppose we imagine two societies, one in which the rule 'do not steal' is followed and one in which this rule is not followed. In which society are people likely to be better off? Clearly, from the point of view of utility, the first society is preferable. Similar arguments can be used to establish rules against cruelty, lying and so on. By following such rules, a general universal welfare is established. Having appealed to the principle of utility to establish the rules, we do not have to invoke the principle again to determine the rightness of particular actions. Individual actions are justified simply by appealing to the already-established rules. In this way, rule utilitarians do not violate our ordinary ideas of justice and personal rights.

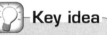

Hot tip

It will be a good opportunity at this point for you to compare and look at these criticisms in the light of Kantian ethics in the previous chapter.

Key idea

Rule utilitarianism: individual actions are no longer judged by the principle of utility. Rather, rules applying to the principle of utility are established so that individual acts can be judged right or wrong by reference to the rules.

Think it through

A country is taken over by a murderous dictator. A man follows the rule that he must always stand up for human rights. He goes into hiding and begins working with others to save his country from the dictator. However, his political involvement results in the death of his family at the hands of the state police. By not breaking his rule, have the man's actions led to the greatest good for the greatest number?

Hot tip

You can apply utilitarianism to a range of ethical issues. For example, you could apply the hedonic calculus to environmental issues (see Chapter 14) – it could be argued from a utilitarian perspective that current human happiness and interests (particularly in less developed countries) should take preference over hypothetical future generations. Reference could also be made to the application of the hedonic calculus to the issue of conserving natural resources; for example, the criteria of 'certainty' and 'remoteness' may be used to argue against taking the interests of future generations into account. It must also be remembered that other criteria in the hedonic calculus may be used to argue for the protection of natural resources; for example, the 'extent' of the people affected by future environmental losses. The hedonic calculus can also be applied to genetic engineering (see Chapter 13) – the possible benefits as well as the risks should be examined; for example, potential removal of genetic diseases, improvements for food production, ability to improve human lifestyle and longevity, and so on.

R.M. Hare

R.M. Hare (1919–2002) (see p. 19) argued that although a great gulf is thought to separate utilitarianism and Kantianism, they actually have significant common ground in the injunction to take everyone's ends as seriously as one's own.

Hare argues that the **universalizability** of moral judgements (see pp. 78–80) coupled with general facts about human beings and the human condition, implies a two-level form of utilitarianism. He claims that this version answers the standard objections to utilitarianism better than any other version. Hare's version of utilitarianism draws upon both act and rule versions for his resulting two-level analysis of moral thinking. This involves the claim that people are capable of two types of moral deliberation, illustrated by two extreme characters.

In *Moral Thinking: Its Levels, Method, and Point* (1981), Hare introduces 'the archangel' and 'the prole'. The archangel is a character who can think critically and make rational decisions using the act utilitarian principle directly. These archangels have 'superhuman powers of thought, superhuman knowledge, and no human weaknesses'. They do not suffer from partiality, either to self or to friends and family.

'When presented with a novel situation, the "archangel" will be able at once to scan all its properties, including the consequences of alternative actions, and frame a universal principle

Word watch

injunction

Key fact

A 'prole' is a 'proletarian' – the lowest socio-economic class of a society.

(perhaps a very specific one) which he can accept for action in that situation, no matter what role he himself were to play in it.'

The rule-utilitarian 'prole', on the other hand, thinks intuitively and acts according to rule-like dispositions. 'Proles' are 'totally incapable of critical thinking (let alone safe or sound critical thinking)'. They have all the human weaknesses, including partiality, lacked by the archangel and to an extreme degree.

Prole   Archangel

In real life, Hare maintains, we are capable of, and need, both – though we are not very good at the archangel-type reasoning. Which we use, and when, depends upon circumstances and our individual abilities.

For more on intuitionism see pp. 19–20.

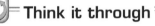

Think it through

1 What are the problems with Hare's distinctions? Could 'intuitive' thinking be used to justify any act such as sexual oppression or racism? Are there dangers in stereotyping 'proles' and 'archangels'?

2 Think about examples from your own life, or the life of others when (a) the archangel predominates, and (b) when the prole predominates. Do you agree with Hare that the right combination of these could lead to the greatest happiness?

3 What are your views on the idea that the happiness of the whole human race is increased on condition that one man, his life mysteriously prolonged, is kept involuntarily in a state of continuous and agonizing torture? What difficulties might this cause to (a) utilitarianism, and (b) to a deontologist?

4 Why might the fact that we can seldom predict the future prove to be a problem for utilitarians?

5 Are there some 'pleasures' that can turn out bad and some 'pain' that may turn out to be good? Think of some examples. How might these examples cause difficulties for utilitarians?

Hot tip

Questions about utilitarian perspectives on issues are frequently asked in the examination. Practise applying utilitarian principles to these issues. Think about consequences; possible benefits vs possible costs; rules vs acts; social justice vs individuality; quality and quantity of pleasure.

' — Quotable quote

'I maintain that if the discoveries of Newton could not have been made known except by sacrificing the lives of one, a dozen, a hundred or more men, Newton would have had the right, would indeed have been duty bound ... to eliminate the dozen or the hundred for the sake of making his discoveries known to the whole of humanity ... But if such a one is forced for the sake of his idea to step over a corpse or wade through blood, he can, I maintain, find within himself, in his conscience, a sanction for wading through blood. That depends on the idea and its dimensions, of course.'

Raskalnikov in Fyodor Dostoyevsky's *Crime and Punishment* (1866)

Benefits of utilitarianism

Utilitarianism has been a popular theory and continues to be widely accepted and applied today, even though it has been challenged by a number of arguments. These 'anti-utilitarian' arguments are so convincing that some philosophers have concluded that utilitarianism must be abandoned. However, many thinkers refuse to let the theory go. According to modern utilitarians, the anti-utilitarian arguments show that the classical theory needs only to be *modified* into a more satisfactory form; they argue that the basic concept of utilitarianism is correct and should therefore be preserved. The benefits of utilitarianism are as follows.

- It seems 'common sense' to consider the consequences of our actions when deciding what to do.
- It is reasonable to equate morality with the pursuit of happiness and the avoidance of pain.
- It offers a democratic and balanced morality that promotes the general welfare and happiness of everyone.

Christian responses

For Christians, the life and teachings of Jesus are the essence of Christian morality. Christians believe that they only have to look to the example of Jesus to find out how best to live. Some of the most challenging of Jesus' teachings are to be found in the Sermon on the Mount (Matthew 5–7), which focus on ethical conduct in our daily life and how it affects our destiny in the next life. Jesus teaches that it is not just the outer rules and laws that must be obeyed but the inner spirit of the law. Jesus' teachings are more than a set of rules but a challenge to the inner world of deeper motivation and intent.

In chapter 7, Jesus describes the essence of moral behaviour: 'Do for others what you want them to do for you,' known as the **Golden Rule** (see p. 38).

John Stuart Mill believed that his utilitarian ethic had caught the very spirit of the golden rule – to treat others as we would want them to treat us. However, for Christians to love one's neighbour as if he or she were oneself, is not to treat him or her as one of many. Utilitarians define 'justice' as treating 'similar cases similarly', whereas the Christian ethical approach is to treat similar cases dissimilarly. In other words, a Christian should, if necessary, be willing to sacrifice his or her own ego for the good of others.

6 — Quotable quote

'When a Christian meets with an armed robber he cannot return his blows, lest in defending his life he should stain his love toward his neighbour. The verdict on this is plain and clear in the books of the Gospel … What robber is more hateful than the persecutor who came to kill Christ? But Christ would not be defended by the wounds of the persecutor, for he willed to heal all by his wounds.'

St Ambrose, *The Duties of the Clergy* (391)

Christian ethics differs from utilitarianism in the importance each gives to the question '*Whose* good'? While utilitarians answer this question with '*What* is the good?', Christian ethics answer it with '*Whose* is the good?' For utilitarians, love is subordinate to justice, whereas for Christians, selfless love (*agape*) is at the heart of all ethical behaviour.

This difference is highlighted in the events around the trial of Jesus before Caiaphas, as recorded in John's Gospel (chapter 18). Jesus and Caiaphas act from totally different ethical principles, even though they might have spoken the same words: 'It was better that one man should die for all the people' (John 18:14). But Caiaphas applied this principle to the other person, whereas Jesus applied it to himself. Caiaphas was concerned to maintain an existing social order, whereas Jesus' concerns were to challenge it.

While utilitarianism aims to create a just social order and community, this is not always sufficient for bringing in an isolated or hostile individual into that community. Christians believe that only love can penetrate the barriers that often exist between people. It is *relationship* that is ultimately important and only by loving others for their own sake can true community come into being.

Web quest

Find out more about utilitarianism and Peter Singer, 'the world's most controversial utilitarian philosopher', by visiting www.heinemann.co.uk/hotlinks and clicking on this section. Choose an article from 'Writings by Peter Singer' and analyse his views on ethics in the world today.

Review

Deontological theories: concentrate on actions.

Teleological theories: concentrate on consequences – the end justifies the means.

Jeremy Bentham:

- Devised the utilitarian theory. In its simplest form, utilitarianism can be summed up by the phrase 'the greatest happiness for the greatest number'.
- Ultimately, human beings are motivated by pleasure and pain – hedonistic utilitarianism.
- The principle of utility: the rightness or wrongness of an action is determined by its 'utility' or usefulness – the amount of pleasure or pain caused by the action. In other words, 'An action is right if it produces the greatest good for the greatest number.'
- The hedonic calculus: weighs up pain and pleasure based on duration, intensity, remoteness, certainty, purity, richness, extent.

Hedonism:

- Happiness is the ultimate good and unhappiness the ultimate evil.

John Stuart Mill:

- The well-being of an individual is of the utmost importance – happiness is most effectively achieved when people are free to pursue their own ends – subject to rules that protect the common good of everyone.
- Focused on qualitative pleasures and developed a system of 'higher' and 'lower' pleasures, preferring the 'higher' ones (mind/intellect) to the 'lower' ones (physical pleasures).

Act utilitarianism:

- Act utilitarians maintain that a good action is one that leads to the greatest good in any given situation.
- Act utilitarians are flexible, taking into account individual situations at a given moment.
- However, act utilitarianism can potentially justify any act – criminal or cruel. It is also impractical to suggest that we can measure every moral choice in every situation.

Rule utilitarianism:

- Rule utilitarianism tried to overcome these difficulties by maintaining that a rule is morally right if the consequences of adopting that rule are generally more favourable than unfavourable to everyone.
- So rule utilitarians establish the best overall rule by determining the course of action that, if followed by everyone, leads to the best result.

Exam questions

1   (a) Explain, with examples, the ethical theory of utilitarianism. (15 marks)
    (b) Assess how far this theory is compatible with the traditional morality of any one major world religion. (5 marks) (WJEC, June 2001)
2   (a) Describe the main strengths of a utilitarian ethical system. (33 marks)
    (b) To what extent is utilitarianism a useful method of making decisions about abortion? (17 marks) (OCR, January 2001)
3   (a) Describe the main strengths and weaknesses of utilitarianism. (33 marks)
    (b) Evaluate a utilitarian approach to genetic engineering. (17 marks) (OCR, June 2002)

10 Situation ethics

'The law of love is the ultimate law because it is the negation of law.'

Paul Tillich, theologian, *Systematic Theology* (1951)

Objectives

No one situation or moral dilemma is exactly the same. In this chapter you will learn about one theory of ethics that claims to allow for a practical and flexible approach to decision-making. The focuses of study will be:

- the legalistic and **antinomian** forms of ethical decision-making
- the theory of **situation ethics**
- the strengths and weaknesses of situation ethics
- an exploration of 'love' and the **agapeistic calculus**
- some general criticisms of Christian ethics.

❛ ═ Quotable quote ═

'There is only one ultimate and invariable duty and its formula is, "Thou shalt love thy neighbour as thyself." How to do this is another question, but this is the whole of moral duty.'

William Temple (1881–1944), Archbishop of Canterbury ❜

Introduction

In 1963 an Anglican theologian, Joseph Fletcher (1905–91), offered a radical departure from the natural law approach to ethics. In *Situation Ethics: The New Morality* (1966), Fletcher challenged the method of ethics whereby a rule or principle is applied to a situation. In the foreword, Fletcher wrote:

'Let an anecdote set the tone. A friend of mine arrived in St Louis just as a presidential campaign was ending, and the cab driver, not being above the battle, volunteered his testimony. "I and my father and grandfather before me have always been straight-ticket Republicans." "Ah," said my friend, who is himself a Republican, "I take it that means you will vote for senator So-and-So." "No," said the driver, "there are times when a man has to push his principles aside and do the right thing."'

Before looking at Fletcher's theory in detail, it must first of all be noted that Fletcher rejected two other forms of ethical decision-making.

Word watch

antinomian
agapeistic calculus

⋀⋀⋀ Hot tip

Situation ethics is an interesting theory when applied to ethical issues and it will be worth your while thinking of issues surrounding abortion, euthanasia, environmental ethics, war and peace and sexual ethics while exploring this chapter.

🔅 Key fact

Joseph Fletcher was an Episcopal priest, a member of the Euthanasia Educational Counsel, and an advocate for planned parenthood. He was a supporter of both euthanasia and abortion.

1 The legalistic approach to ethics

Legalistic ethics has a set of prefabricated moral rules, laws or regulations. Decisions are made by appealing to these rules, laws and regulations. The legalist codifies rules, adds them to existing laws, takes into account exceptions and special factors and tries to codify rules to cover these. The legalist seeks to apply moral rules and laws to real-life situations and creates a whole system of rules, sub-rules and regulations. This approach to ethics, according to Fletcher, can produce a kind of textbook morality that means people simply check the manual to decide what is right or wrong. The laws of Scripture do not give *specific* guidance for dealing with various modern ethical dilemmas and, according to Fletcher, it is unsatisfactory to apply general rules to contemporary moral issues.

OK, what does the textbook say about sex and love?

2 The antinomian approach to ethics

The term 'antinomian' means 'against law'. This approach argues that the situation itself will show us what we ought to do. Each decision and each occasion is totally unique. Making a moral decision is a matter of spontaneity. The right thing to do is dependent on things like intuition, or waiting for that 'inner voice' to guide us. Fletcher argues that such an approach leads to moral anarchy – everyone claiming their intuition or 'inner voice' is right or falling into disagreement with those who have experienced a 'different voice.

For more on intuitionism and its weaknesses see pp. 19–20.

Word watch

legalism

Think it through

Fletcher rejected two forms of ethical decision-making – **legalism** and antinomianism.

1 What, according to Fletcher, are the problems of a 'textbook morality' – simply checking a 'manual of morality' to decide what is right or wrong?

2 Can you think of situations when it is not possible to 'look up the answer' to a moral dilemma?

3 What, according to Fletcher, are the problems of relying on intuition or an 'inner voice' to decide the most ethical course of action in any given situation?

4 Can you think of situations when it is impossible to rely on intuition?

Fletcher's situational approach

Fletcher argued that the most efficient way of coming to an ethical decision is the situationist approach. A situationist enters into a moral dilemma with the ethics and principles of his or her particular tradition, but is prepared to set these laws and principles aside in the situation if love seems better served by doing so.

Fletcher founded his model upon a statement found in the New Testament: 'God is Love' (1 John 4: 8). He argued that the only moral principle that could be applied to all situations is *to do whatever is the most loving thing*. There is only one duty and that is to love 'your neighbour as yourself' (the agapeistic calculus).

This requirement is *not a law* stating what *should* be done in any particular situation but *rather an attitude* that informs moral choice. Situation ethics, therefore, *has no concern for following an absolute moral law nor for the consequences of a decision*. For Fletcher, any course of action should have practical working results that are ultimately judged by the criterion of love. He rejects words like 'absolute', arguing that different circumstances more often than not throw up exceptions and Christians are meant *to love people, not prohibitions*.

‘ — Quotable quote

'Jesus said nothing about birth control, large or small families, childlessness, homosexuality, masturbation, fornication, pre-marital intercourse, sterilization, artificial insemination, abortion, sex foreplay, petting and courtship. Whether any form of sex (hetero, homo or auto) is good or evil depends on whether love is fully served.'

Joseph Fletcher, *Situation Ethics: The New Morality* (1966)

— Think it through

A fire is uncontrollably destroying a house. Inside it are my elderly father and a skilled surgeon. I have time to enter the house and rescue one of them but not enough time to rescue both. Which one *should* I rescue? Notice the question! Not who do I *want* to rescue but who *should* I rescue?

According to situationists we should work out what is the most loving thing to do in any situation we find ourselves in. We should not act on impulse, intuition or feelings alone. We should also think carefully about what is ethical. Obviously it would be most loving to rescue both people in the building but this is impossible. So we must decide which of the people we will help. Consider whether we should help the person whose need is greater. Is the right action the one that helps the greatest number in the long run? Or should we save the person who is most valuable? In pairs, consider how a situationist would approach this dilemma.

❝ ━ Quotable quote ━━━━━━━━━━━━━━━━━━━━

'The "Summary of the Law" given by Jesus is the only binding absolute moral law: "You shall love the Lord your God with all your heart, and with all your soul, and with all your mind. This is the first and great commandment. The second is like it, you shall love your neighbour as yourself. On these two commandments depend all other laws and the prophets."'

'According to this view, love of God, neighbour, and self, is the only absolute law which ought never to be broken. Other laws are to be put into action to the extent that they bring about the best possible love in each situation, in terms of both individual morality and social justice. Never should the other commandments be set aside lightly, but only when and if love is better served.'

Richard Nolan, *Is There a Gay Lifestyle?* (2002)

━━━━━━━━━━━━━━━━━━━━━━━━━━━━━━━━━━ ❞

The four propositions

Fletcher sets out four presuppositions before setting out his theory in full.

Personalism: the situationist puts people first, while the legalist puts law first.

Positivism: situation ethics depends on Christians freely choosing that God is love, so giving first place to Christian love.

Pragmatism: any theory of ethics must be practical and work towards the end that is love.

Relativism: there are no fixed rules and so situation ethics is relativistic. This does not mean anarchy but that all decisions must be relative to Christian love. Situation ethics 'relativizes the absolute, it does not absolute the relative' (*Situation Ethics: the New Morality*, 1966).

Word watch

personalism
positivism
pragmatism
relativism

A street child in Mexico City carrying his friend whose crutches were stolen the night before while he slept

The six principles

For Fletcher, there are six fundamental principles of situation ethics.

First Proposition: '*Only one thing is intrinsically good, namely love, nothing else at all.*' In other words, actions are good if they help people and bad if they hurt people.

Second Proposition: '*The ruling norm of Christian decision is love, nothing else.*' Jesus replaced the strict Jewish Law with the principle of love.

Third Proposition: '*Love and justice are the same, for justice is love distributed, nothing else.*'

Fourth Proposition: '*Love wills the neighbour's good, whether we like him or not.*'

Fifth Proposition: '*Only the end justifies the means, nothing else.*' In other words, the end must be the most loving result. When confronted by an ethical dilemma, one must consider the most loving result.

Sixth Proposition: '*Love's decisions are made situationally, not prescriptively.*' Jesus teaches that it is not just the outer rules and laws that must be obeyed but the inner spirit of the law: Jesus' teachings are more than a set of commandments; they are a challenge to the inner world of deeper motivation and intent.

Some major ethical principles that derive from the agapeistic calculus

Respect: human beings should be treated as subjects, not objects. The life of each person is of significance. Exploitation of anyone violates love.

Autonomy: human beings deserve liberty to make judgements and decisions about their own lives.

Beneficence: do good. For Christians, 'Love your neighbour as you love yourself.'

Non-maleficence: do no harm and prevent harm being done.

Justice: human beings ought to be provided with what is fair and what is deserved.

Honesty: telling the truth is essential to promote and maintain respect for persons and for autonomy.

Discussion

'*In determining whether a man is a good man, one does not ask what he believes or what he hopes, but what he loves.*'

St Thomas Aquinas (1224–74), theologian

'*In reality, the love which is based on emotions of sympathy or affection is self-love; for it is the love of preference, of choice, and the standard of preference of choice is the self.*'

Rudolf Bultmann (1884–1976), theologian

'*All you need is love.*'

John Lennon (1940–80) and Paul McCartney (b. 1942), songwriters

Key fact

Situation Ethics actually dates back to the early Christian era. St Augustine of Hippo (354–430 CE) was one of the first to articulate this theory, claiming a basis in Jesus' teaching when telling his congregation – and troops – to 'love and do what you will'. Because the protection of Hippo was seen as a loving motive, this included killing barbarians attacking the city. The biblical commandment not to murder could have lead to the fall of Hippo as passive soldiers and citizens stood by. A 'situational approach', however, allowed them to defend themselves.

Word watch

autonomy
beneficence
non-maleficence

Evaluating situation ethics

Advantages of situation ethics

Situation ethics is a practical and flexible approach to ethics. Acknowledging the complexities of life, it can break free from hard-line legalistic perspectives and deadlocked moral dilemmas. This highlights one of the key strengths of situation ethics – because it sees the motive as all important, it is not vulnerable to the impossible situations that the unchangeable following of rules can lead to.

Situation ethics appears to be more in line with Jesus' teachings whereby love is more important than law. Jesus broke the law when the situation demanded it for reasons of love. Jesus' ethics are centred around love: 'Do for others what you want them to do for you' (Matthew 7:12); 'Love one another, as I love you' (John 15:12). Some Christians argue that the churches have failed to see this and have concentrated too much on prescriptive laws and prohibitions.

Quotable quote

'The Situationist avoids words like "never" and "perfect" and "always" and "complete" as he avoids the plague, as he avoids "absolutely".'

Joseph Fletcher, *Situation Ethics: The New Morality* (1966)

Criticism of situation ethics

- The situationist's 'love' is purely subjective. She or he *decides* what love is in any given context. Bert Thompson, in *The Effects of Situation Ethics upon Moral Values* (1988), notes that Fletcher has defined 'love' in no fewer than a dozen ways. According to Thompson, situation ethics removes God from the throne as the moral sovereign of the universe and substitutes man in his place, ignoring the biblical view that mere mortals are void of sufficient wisdom to guide their earthly activity:

'Lord, I know that no one is the master of his own destiny, no person has control over his life'

Jeremiah 10:23

- The situationist assumes that his or her own actions, driven by love, are capable of moral sensitivity and wisdom – this is the vice of subjectivism. What criteria have we to show us that the situationist is right? Objective morality might disagree with his or her 'sensitivity'.
- Situation ethics contends that there are no rules except the rule to love. But what if, in a certain situation, one decides that love is not the appropriate course of action? According to the situationist, there are no absolutes – except that one absolutely must love in all situations! But what is the standard by which this claim is defended?
- Situation ethics, by rejecting legalism, assumes that 'love' is some sort of cure-all for all moral problems. This is like suggesting that there will be no rules

except 'fairness' in a football game between Rangers and Celtic. But fairness according to *whose* judgement? Celtic supporters? Rangers supporters? The sports writers? TV pundits?

I don't know, let's ask the Celtic fans what they think.

That's not fair!

- Situationism assumes a sort of infallible omniscience that is able always precisely to predict what the most 'loving' course of action is. For instance, the theory implies that lying, adultery or murder could be 'moral' if done, in certain situations, within the context of love. Yet who is able to foretell the consequences of such acts and so determine, in advance, what is the most 'loving' thing to do?

- Often people interpret situations according to their own point of view and there is a danger that people claiming to act in 'the name of love' may in fact be acting from selfish motives.

- A situational ethic breaks up the moral life into separate acts and denies the reality of a unitary personal self that grows and deepens through its successive experiences. We are more than just functional beings and our lives are more than just a succession of compartmentalized experiences.

- Where does one draw the boundaries around 'a situation'? Real situations usually involve more than the emotions of the principal actors in the immediate drama. There are others to be considered too.

Think it through

1 During the first years of Christianity, thousands of Christians were martyred for their faith. If situation ethics is valid, why could those saints not have lied and pretended they did not follow their faith? Could they have rationalized that the preservation of their lives would grant them more time in which to proclaim the Gospel?

2 Think of occasions when you would have acted differently than you would now. Discuss your example with a friend. What does this suggest about learning through experience?

3 Think of some actions that do not necessarily become good just because they are done from a loving motive.

4 Natural law theorists argue that an individualistic and subjective appeal to actions may actually conflict with the will of God. Think of some examples.

Hot tip

Sometimes exam questions ask for an evaluation of 'religious theories of ethics'. In your answer include the divine command theory, natural law and situation ethics.

Word watch

situationism
omniscience

Hot tip

Sometimes an exam question demands that you compare and contrast different ethical theories. Compare situation ethics (Chapter 10) with utiltarianism (Chapter 9), Kantian ethics (Chapter 8) and natural law pp. 41–44.

Web quest

1 Explain Fletcher's theory of situation ethics, and assess the strengths and weaknesses of his view by visiting www.heinemann.co.uk/hotlinks and using the article in *Student Central*.

2 Does the agapeistic calculus always work as an ethical theory?

Quotable quote

'The situationist enters into every decision-making situation fully armed with the ethical maxims of his community and its heritage, and he treats them with respect as illuminators of his problems. Just the same, he is prepared in any situation to compromise them or set them aside in the situation if love seems better served by doing so.'

Joseph Fletcher, *Situation Ethics: The New Morality* (1966)

Quotable quote

'Your neighbour-love is your bad love of yourselves. Ye flee unto your neighbour from yourselves and would fain make a virtue thereof! But I fathom your "unselfishness" … You cannot stand yourselves and you do not love yourselves sufficiently.'

Friedrich Nietzsche, *Beyond Good and Evil* (1886)

Quotable quote

'The law of love is the ultimate law because it is the negation of law; it is absolute because it concerns everything concrete … The absolutism of love is its power to go into the concrete situation.'

Paul Tillich (1886–1968), theologian

Discussion: criticism of Christian ethics

'Christian ethics breed intolerance'

Historically there is much evidence (for example, the Crusades and the Inquisition) to support this criticism. Different churches have persecuted each other as well as people of other faiths, and the activities of some missionaries has left much to be desired, especially those that assume that only Christian teachings can lead to 'good'. Ludwig Feuerbach (1804–1872), the nineteenth-century thinker, wrote:

'Wherever morality is based on theology, wherever right is dependent on divine authority, the most immoral, unjust, infamous things can be justified and established.'

'Christian ethics are built on fear – a system of reward or punishment'

Traditionally, churches have taught that immoral behaviour is punished in the torments of 'hell and damnation', frightening people to conform out of fear.

'So in saying that things are not good by any rule of goodness, but sheerly by the grace of God, it seems to me that one destroys, without realizing it, all the love of God and his glory. For why praise him for what he has done if he would be equally praiseworthy in doing exactly the contrary?'

Leibniz, *Discourse on Metaphysics* (1686)

'Christian ethics are repressive'

Sometimes Christian ethics are viewed as a set of 'do nots', interpreted in a life-denying way, making them appear restrictive and curtailing individual autonomy and freedom. Bertrand Russell (1872–1970), the twentieth-century English philosopher, described the effects of repressive ethics thus:

'We are heirs to the conscience – vivisection and self-crucifixion of 2000 years.'

'Christian ethics make people weak'

Some critics of Christian ethics argue that they disempower people, leading them to stock moral reactions and preventing them from learning from their own experiences and mistakes.

The Prussian philosopher Friedrich Nietzsche (1844–1900) despised Christian values. Christianity, Nietzsche argued, had led to a systematic devaluation of this world in favour of the next and thus to a false spirituality. Nietzsche declared that 'God is dead'. Christians, according to Nietzsche, exalt the virtues of the weak, the humble, the poor, the oppressed, not because they love these people but because of their own psychological dysfunctions – their hidden hatred of strength, their fear of life, and their complacency, vanity and pride.

For more on Nietzsche see p. 65.

Word watch

philios
storge
eros
agape

Word watch

conditional and
unconditional love

Think it through

Love is ...

The Greeks (see pp. 48–49) had four meanings.

Philios: love of friends; a deeply connecting brotherly or sisterly love. *Philios* is rooted in the social need of every human being.

Storge: instinctual love. Storge begins to 'love' for the sake of loving. It is not as conditional as *philios* love. A new mother loves her child instinctively.

Eros: sexual affection, passion or desire. The word *eros* is better known to us (think 'erotic!') than the other three Greek words. This is the 'love' and the word that our society often confuses with 'lust'.

Agape: self-giving love, tolerance and respect towards all people. For Christians, *agape* is God's love: perfect, total, unconditional and eternal. St Paul's definition of agape is found in 1 Corinthians 13: 1–13:

I may be able to speak the languages of angels, but if I have no love, my speech is no more than a noisy gong or a clanging bell. I may have the gift of inspired preaching; I may have all knowledge and understand all secrets; I may have all the faith needed to move mountains — but if I have no love, I am nothing. I may give away everything I have, and even give up my body to be burnt — but if I have no love, this does no good.

Love is patient and kind; it is not jealous or conceited or proud; love is not ill-mannered or selfish or irritable; love does not keep a record of wrongs; love is not happy with evil, but is happy with the truth. Love never gives up; and its faith, hope, and patience never fail.

Love is eternal. There are inspired messages, but they are temporary; there are gifts of speaking in strange tongues, but they will cease; there is knowledge, but it will pass. For our gifts of knowledge and of inspired messages are only partial; but when what is perfect comes, then what is partial will disappear.

When I was a child, my speech, feelings, and thinking were all those of a child; now that I have grown up, I have no more use for childish ways. What we see now is like a dim image in a mirror; then we shall see face to face. What I know now is only partial; then it will be complete — as complete as God's knowledge of me.

Meanwhile these three remain: faith, hope, and love; and the greatest of these is love.

1 Give examples of 'love' conveying (a) altruistic concern, (b) mindless obsession, (c) deep affection, (d) the desire for manipulative possession, (e) jealous ownership, (f) friendship, and (g) simple lust.

2 Explain which Greek word relates to each of these.

3 Consider whether *philios*, *storge*, *eros* and *agape* are all independent of one another or are they dependent, at all, on each other?

4 Which of these definitions is most relevant to situation ethics?

Review

Legalistic ethics: a set of prefabricated moral rules, laws or regulations. Decisions are made by appealing to these rules, laws and regulations.

Antinomian approach to ethics: 'antinomian' means 'against law'. Making a moral decision is a matter of spontaneity. The right thing to do is dependent on things like intuition or waiting for that 'inner voice' to guide us.

Joseph Fletcher's approach: the most efficient way of coming to an ethical decision is the situationist approach. A situationist enters into a moral dilemma with the ethics and principles of his or her particular tradition but is prepared to set these laws and principles aside in the situation if love seems better served by doing so.

The agapeistic calculus: the only moral principle that could be applied to all situations is *to do whatever is the most loving thing*. There is only one duty and that is to 'love your neighbour as yourself'.

The four working principles: personalism, positivism, pragmatism and relativism.

The six fundamental principles: only love is intrinsically good, the ruling norm of Christian decision-making is love, love and justice are the same, love wills the neighbour's good whether we like him or not, only the end justifies the means and love's decisions are made situationally not prescriptively.

Evaluating situation ethics: Situationists believe that situation ethics is consistent with the teachings of Jesus as outlined in the Gospels – a practical theory that takes into account the complexities of decision-making in life and allows for flexible adaption to particular situations rather than being constrained by laws. Situation ethics is too individualistic and too subjective; people are not always morally sensitive enough; egoistic motives could still appear; some actions do not necessarily become good just because they are done from a loving motive; consequences are not always easy to determine.

Criticism of Christian ethics:
- Christian ethics breed intolerance (Ludwig Feuerbach).
- Christian ethics are built on fear, a system of reward or punishment (Leibniz).
- Christian ethics are repressive (Bertrand Russell).
- Christian ethics make people weak (Friedrich Nietzsche).

Exam questions

1 (a) Explain the principles of 'situation ethics'. (15 marks)
   (b) Assess how far the application of 'situation ethics' offers satisfactory moral guidance to someone thinking of committing adultery. (15 marks) (WJEC, January 2001)
2 (a) Explain how a religious ethic might take the situation into account before recommending action. (33 marks)
   (b) 'Utilitarianism helps us to focus on quality of life rather than length of life.' Discuss. (17 marks) (OCR, June 2002)

11 Virtue theory and social contract theory

> 'We are what we repeatedly do.'
>
> Aristotle (384–322 BCE), *Nicomachean Ethics* (350 BCE)

Part 1: Virtue theory

Objectives

All the ethical theories in this book attempt to work out the right thing to do. For example, according to natural law, the right thing to do is that which is in accordance with the purpose of what it is to be human. Kant understood the right thing to do in terms of duty; utilitarians, in terms of the greatest good for the greatest number; relativists, that there are no moral laws; others, that moral statements are simply either emotional expressions or 'intuitions'. In the first part of this chapter you will learn about virtue ethics – a theory that rejects these views and argues that rather than trying to work out the right thing to do we should concentrate on *how* we can become better people. The main focuses of enquiry will be:

- the meaning of excess and deficient virtues. The **golden mean** and the relationship between *doing* and *being*
- the contribution of Aristotle and Alasdair MacIntyre to virtue theory
- the strengths and weaknesses of virtue theory.

Key questions

1 Are we what we repeatedly do? Is excellence a habit or an act? Do we become brave by doing brave acts?

2 Is there more to morality than appearing to do what is good or right?

3 What virtues are dominant in a predominantly secular society?

4 Can practising virtues make you a better person?

5 Do character traits change as people develop? Do we risk losing our proficiency in these areas if we stop practising? Do we need a more character-free way of assessing our conduct?

6 Can virtues be taught?

7 Who is virtuous? How do we tell – by some external criterion such as visible indications? Are these indications a real guarantee that the person's inner being is virtuous?

The Greeks

Historically, virtue theory is the oldest normative tradition in Western philosophy, having its roots in ancient Greek civilization. Epic stories like Homer's *The Odyssey* (c. 800 BCE) repeatedly explores virtue or greatness (***aretē***) – the moral achievement of realizing your greatest potential as a human being.

Aristotle

Aristotle (384–322 BCE) gave the most influential and systematic account of virtue theory in Book 2 of his *Nichomachean Ethics* (350 BCE). For Aristotle, the foundation of morality is the development of good character traits or virtues, so a person is good if he or she has virtues and lacks vices.

The mean

Aristotle argues that moral virtues occur at a mean (midpoint) between extreme character traits (or vices). For example, in response to the natural emotion of fear, we should develop the virtue of courage. If we develop an excessive character trait by curbing fear too much, then we are said to be rash, which is a **vice**. If, at the other extreme, we develop a deficient character trait by curbing fear too little, then we are said to be cowardly, which is also a vice. The virtue of courage, then, lies at the mean between the excessive extreme of rashness and the deficient extreme of cowardice. Most moral virtues – not just courage – are to be understood as falling at the mean between two accompanying vices.

Vice of deficiency	Virtuous mean	Vice of excess
Cowardice	Courage	Rashness
Insensibility	Temperance	Intemperance
Illiberality	Liberality	Prodigality
Pettiness	Munificence	Vulgarity
Humble-mindedness	High-mindedness	Vaingloriousness
Want of ambition	Right ambition	Overambition
Spiritlessness	Good temper	Irascibility
Surliness	Friendly civility	Obsequiousness
Ironical depreciation	Sincerity	Boastfulness
Boorishness	Wittiness	Buffoonery
Shamelessness	Modesty	Bashfulness
Callousness	Just resentment	Spitefulness

For more on Greek philosophy see pp. 48–49.

Key idea

A virtue is a characteristic habit of excellence of the soul that aligns a person in accordance to right reason and to a proper human end (*teleos*) of happiness. A virtue has both individual and social dimensions and perfects one's nature. Plato believed that the quest for truth consisted of understanding the ideal nature of virtues such as justice and courage.

Word watch

the mean

Word watch

insensibility
illiberality
temperance
liberality
munificence
vaingloriousness
irascibility
obsequiousness

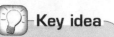

Key idea

The golden mean: moral virtue that is always the mean, a middle way between excess and deficiency.

Think it through

Aristotle concludes that it is difficult to live the virtuous life, primarily because it is often difficult to find the mean between the extremes. Do you agree? Can you come up with your own example of a deficiency, mean and excess?

Quotable quote

'We are what we repeatedly do. Excellence, then, is not an act, but a habit ... Moral excellence comes about as a result of habit. We become just by doing just acts, temperate by doing temperate acts, brave by doing brave acts.'

Aristotle, *Nicomachean Ethics* (350 BCE)

The cardinal virtues

By the late Middle Ages, Aristotle's virtue theory was the definitive account of morality, especially in so far as it was endorsed by the medieval philosopher St Thomas Aquinas.

In medieval discussions, the particular virtues described by Aristotle and the ancient Greeks became known as the **cardinal virtues**. They are called cardinal (Latin: *cardo*, 'hinge') virtues because they are the 'hinges' on which all moral virtues depend.

1 **Prudence:** also known as practical wisdom, is the capacity to deliberate well about what is good and advantageous for one's self in practical affairs.

2 **Justice:** is a social as well as an individual virtue. It is the excellence of the soul that distributes each according to his merits and a characteristic that enables the individual to direct his will appropriately to relate properly to others.

3 **Courage:** also known as fortitude, is a characteristic that enables the individual to regulate pain and strive towards the mean between cowardice and recklessness.

4 **Temperance:** a form of self-control; a characteristic that enables individuals to strive towards the mean between insensitivity and self-indulgence.

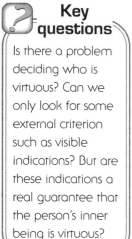

Key questions

Is there a problem deciding who is virtuous? Can we only look for some external criterion such as visible indications? But are these indications a real guarantee that the person's inner being is virtuous?

Web quest

Apply at least one of the cardinal virtues to the world's worst industrial accident at Bhopal. Visit www.heinemann.co.uk/hotlinks and click on this section to use the Sambhavna Trust's 'Bhopal Medical Appeal' for further information. Write a report of (a) what happened at Bhopal, (b) the consequences of the accident, and (c) the action, or lack of it, taken by Union Carbide.

The demise of virtue theory

With the rise of the Scientific Revolution, the influence of Aristotle and Aquinas's virtue theory declined. In the seventeenth century the Dutch philosopher Hugo Grotius (1583–1645) criticized Aristotle's doctrine of the mean as failing to explain adequately basic moral concepts such as truthfulness and justice. He argued that someone does not necessarily have special moral insight simply because he is virtuous; instead, morality is fixed in natural laws that can be rationally perceived by all. By the twentieth century, theories such as Kantian ethics and utilitarianism were popular – supplanting the character-trait emphasis of virtue theory.

Alasdair MacIntyre

The British philosopher Alasdair MacIntyre (b. 1929) re-examined the beliefs of the ancient Greeks concerning virtues. He was so impressed with what he found – and so alarmed that this kind of ethical explanation had been so overlooked by modern Western philosophy – that he developed the virtue theory for modern readers.

MacIntyre felt that we live in ethical confusion and a moral vacuum. He argued that a 'hidden catastrophe' has undermined moral reasoning, with words like 'good' and 'moral' and 'useful' being ripped from their original contexts, and in this sense surviving only as relics. MacIntyre suggested that we live like cavemen in a chaotic science-fiction future, using tools fashioned for complex moral discourse as crude weapons to carry on our Stone Age moral battles.

A moral catastrophe!

In his influential book *After Virtue* (1981), MacIntyre offers us a metaphor (imagining a series of environmental disasters turning the public violently against the natural sciences) to explain why it is that moral debate today rarely leads to consensus – why, in other words, human beings seem utterly incapable of coming to enough basic agreement in matters of ethics to enable us to deal with the moral chaos that surrounds us. MacIntyre argues forcibly that society needs to reassert Aristotle's moral and intellectual virtues in society – in medicine, education, politics and commerce. He identifies some archetypal characters that have evolved in a society lacking virtue.

'The Bureaucratic Managers': the political bureaucrats, the spin merchants, media moghuls, directors of mutinationals, the faceless few who pull the strings on commerce, trade and investment: the 'managers' who match ends to means in the most efficient manner. Their area of expertise is efficient management with no moral strings attached – profit not principle! MacIntyre says the manager is the dominant character in the modern world;

such people are those who think of themselves as 'morally neutral characters whose skills enable them to devise the most efficient means of achieving whatever end is proposed'.

'The Rich Aesthetes': these pursue greater and 'more exciting' pleasures (the image of the ageing rock star fits this bill) in the public glare of a celebrity-obsessed media mesmerized by these people living out their fantasies on our behalf – a celebrity-obsessed culture lacking virtue and meaning.

'The Therapists': these keep the whole show on the road, charging the rich huge amounts of money to listen to their neurotic values (diminished and self-justifying existences), meaningless echoes of their meaningless lives. The society we have created teaches us to value others less and ourselves more.

Nobody understands me!

Key idea

Rather than simply looking to rules for guidance, virtue ethics explores the fundamental issue of what it means to be human.

Word watch

archetypes

Think it through

1 Explain the meaning of MacIntyre's caveman metaphor.

2 Consider whether MacIntyre's use of archetypes weakens his theory in any way.

3 Do you think these archetypes are in fact stereotypes? Are they fair (for example, what about celebrities who work for charity)?

Criticism of virtue theory

- Critics argue that an ethical system built on virtue underemphasizes the substance of an person's action, such as the consequences of that action, and overemphasizes the mere *style* of an agent's conduct.

- Others argue that an ethical system built on virtue is not designed to offer precise guidelines of obligation and fails to address modern dilemmas that arise in applied ethics.
- Other critics feel that virtue ethics could be a harking back to an apparent 'Golden Age' of ethics a sort of romantic nostalgia – not all old ideas are necessarily good ideas and modern ethical theories have their own worth.
- Robert Louden, in *On Some Vices of Virtue Ethics* (1984), argues that some acts are so intolerable, such as murder, that we must devise a special list of offences that *are* prohibited. Virtue theory does not provide such a list.

Think it through

1 Some virtue theorists mention as many as 100 virtuous character traits. How many can you think of? Write down your list and then compare and discuss them with the rest of the class. Which ones do you think contribute to the making of a good person?

2 Virtue theory places special emphasis on education, since virtuous character traits are developed in one's youth – adults, therefore, are responsible for instilling virtues in young people. Do you agree that virtues can be taught? What examples of any particular adults' virtuous qualities have you encountered in your life? Do you agree that the failure to develop and practise virtuous character traits and habits properly will result in people acquiring vices or bad character traits instead? Give reasons for your answers and comments.

3 Do character traits change as people develop? Unless we keep practising virtuous behaviour, do we risk losing our proficiency in these areas? If so, does virtue ethics succeed or do we need a more character-free way of assessing our conduct?

4 Do you agree that practise can make you a better person? Is it ever possible to be perfectly virtuous?

5 Virtue ethics is about 'being', not 'doing'. Discuss with reference to famous people considered to be virtuous.

Key questions

1 Can a person be virtuous and *never* do the right thing?

2 Who is better, the person disposed to do the right thing because he is virtuous, or the person disinclined to do the right thing but does it?

Part 1: Review

The Greeks: a virtue is a characteristic habit of excellence of the soul. A characteristic habit aligns a person in accordance to right reason and to a proper human end (*teleos*) of happiness.

Aristotle: 'We are what we repeatedly do.' Moral virtues are at a mean between more extreme character traits (or vices). Moral virtues are to be understood as falling at the mean between two accompanying vices.

The cardinal virtues: (Latin: *cardo*, 'hinge') virtues because they are 'hinges' on which all moral virtues depend: prudence, justice, courage and temperance.

Alasdair MacIntyre: in *After Virtue* (1981), MacIntyre argued that our current ethical confusion results from a neglect of virtue theory.

Part 2: Social contract theory

> 'No one should ever endorse a social order that he could not accept if he were in the shoes of its most disadvantaged member.'
>
> John Rawls (1921–2002), American philosopher

Objectives

In part 2 of this chapter you will study an ethical theory about social justice by exploring:

- the implications and obligations of a social contract
- the theory of contractualism and the contribution of John Rawls
- the common-good approach to ethics.

Word watch

obligations
social contract

? Key questions

1 What obligations are imposed on parties involved in an agreement or contract?

2 What obligations does the state have towards its individuals and what duties do individuals have?

3 What are the implications of a common-good approach within a global community?

Thomas Hobbes

For more on Hobbes see chapter 7.

In *Leviathan* (1651), Thomas Hobbes (1588–1679) argued that the fundamental legal obligations that a state imposes upon its citizens stem from a tacit (unspoken/unwritten) agreement. This agreement is that the citizens will obey the laws of the state in exchange for the security, comfort and prosperity that the state affords its citizens. In Hobbes's view, we should obey the laws of our government for the same reason that parties to a contract should follow the terms of their contract.

According to Hobbes, a voluntary agreement binds individuals to uphold, in both cases, certain obligations. The one crucial difference is that in the case of the citizens' contract with the state, the agreement is tacit. We do not as citizens actually sign a contract with the state or pledge an oath to follow the laws of the state. Rather, our voluntary choice to live within the boundaries of the state and reap the benefits of the civilized life that it provides constitutes a tacit acceptance of the terms of the social contract.

Key idea

Imagine you have been wrongly treated by a friend. You might suggest to him or her that friendship involves certain reasonable expectations concerning how friends will treat each other and that no reasonable person would enter into a friendship with another person if they believed that these expectations would not be met.

If your friend understands these expectations, these expectations have the force of an agreement. Similar expectations relate to other social relationships. For example, we expect that parents will care for their children and that doctors will use every means available and appropriate to cure their patients.

Think it through

Imagine that you have to put pen to paper and draw up two 'contracts': (a) between you and your best friend, and (b) between you and your parent(s)/guardian. What sorts of obligations would you highlight? What would you regard as unreasonable expectations?

Contractarianism

Tacit social contracts define social relationships. They account for the ways in which our social connections help us to live more satisfying lives. If these expectations are not met, we feel that the offending person has broken a trust with us and thus has acted in violation of his or her moral duty to us. This is a moral judgement. We are making the basic judgement that it is not only explicitly stated agreements between individuals, such as legal contracts, that bind by mutual obligation, but also *tacit* agreements constituted by mutual, reasonable expectations when entering into social relationships with one another. This is the heart of the ethical theory known as **contractarianism**.

John Rawls

The American philosopher John Rawls (1921–2002) was the most famous and also the most controversial political theorist of the twentieth century. His book *A Theory of Justice* (1971) redefined the status of political philosophy in the West,

Key fact

A bill aimed at blasphemous literature passed the Commons in January 1667, and *Leviathan* was one of two books mentioned in it. The bill never passed both houses, but Hobbes was seriously frightened. He is said to have become more regular at church and communion (from *The Internet Encyclopedia of Philosophy*).

Word watch

violation
contractarianism

Key idea

Contractarianism is the idea that we should abide by tacit rules that rational moral agents observe when entering into a social relationship.

giving central focus to the concept of 'liberalism' whereby the liberal democratic state should be the guarantor of social justice. Rawls sketches how such a state could make a positive impact in terms of being 'redistributively just' — that is, how a liberal democratic state could insure that its members were provided with basic rights and more or less equal opportunities.

Justice

In *A Theory of Justice,* John Rawls offered the very plausible suggestion that justice be defined as fairness, which is to be accepted as an intrinsic good. It is the imperative we would follow if we had no starting information about our own future status in life — starting out in a 'veil of ignorance'. By seeing ourselves as potential constructors of a just society in the future, but being ignorant of our racial, social and economic position within that society, Rawls strips away all those pieces of information he considers to be irrelevant to questions of justice. From this 'original position' Rawls considers that the response of a rational person would be to secure two basic principles of justice:

1 A schedule of basic rights: including liberty of conscience and movement, freedom of religion, and so on.

2 Equality of opportunity: the only way to prevent the rich and powerful from overpowering the weak is by enforcing the maxim 'No redistribution of resources within such a state can occur unless it benefits the least well off.'

❛ — Quotable quote

'True **compassion** is more than flinging a coin at a beggar; it comes to see that an edifice which produces beggars needs restructuring.'

Martin Luther King (1928–68)

❜

Think it through

1 An alien – from a harmonious planet where every alien is equal and justice reigns supreme – visits Earth. What might the alien observe about (a) wealth, (b) its redistribution, and (c) about inequality of redistribution? What conclusions might he draw about justice on planet Earth?

2 In your considered opinion, how well does Western capitalism live up to Rawls's theory of justice? Give examples to support your view.

The common-good approach

The **common-good approach** to ethics assumes a society made up of individuals whose own good is linked to the good of the community — all bound together by the pursuit of common values and goals. Given that in the twenty-first century we live in a global community, these common values and goals can be applied internationally – including affordable healthcare, peace among nations, a just legal system, and an unpolluted environment.

The common-good approach appeals to the 'common good', urging us to view ourselves as members of the same community, reflecting on broad questions concerning the kind of society we want and how to achieve it. While respecting and valuing the freedom of individuals to pursue their own goals, the common-good approach also challenges us to recognize and further those goals we all share.

6 — Quotable quote

'The great evils of human history – unjust war, oppression, religious persecution, slavery, and the rest – result from political injustice, with its cruelties and callousness. Once political injustice has been eliminated, these great evils will eventually disappear ... a "realistic utopia". I believe that the very possibility of such a social order can itself reconcile us to the social world. The possibility is not a mere logical possibility, but one that connects with the deep tendencies and inclinations of the social world. For so long as we believe for good reasons that a self-sustaining and reasonably just political and social order both at home and abroad is possible, we can reasonably hope that we or others will someday, somewhere, achieve it.'

John Rawls, *The Law of Peoples* (1993)

Think it through

1. In pairs, list and discuss some of the violations of minimal standards of behaviour that exist in the twenty-first century and give examples of political injustice.

2. Consider (a) why Rawls's ideas have been so influential, and (b) why some people disagree with Rawls.

3. Do you think Rawls's 'realistic utopia' is achievable or is it an idealistic vision that will never come about? Give reasons for your answers.

 **Web quest**

Access Global Issues That Affect Everyone at www.heinemann.co.uk/hotlinks by clicking on this section. See 'Trade related issues' and 'Causes of poverty' and pick out one from any of the following: Structural adjustment; Poverty around the world; Economic democracy; World hunger; Food dumping; IMF and World Bank; or Poverty – facts and statistics. Examine why, how and where Rawls's principles of (a) *a schedule of basic rights*, and (b) *equality of opportunity* are being violated in the world today.

Part 2: Review

Thomas Hobbes: the fundamental legal obligations that a state imposes upon its citizens stems from a tacit (unspoken/unwritten) agreement that the citizens will obey the laws of the state in exchange for the security, comfort and prosperity that the state affords its citizens.

The social contract: a voluntary agreement binds individuals to uphold certain obligations. Our voluntary choice to live within the boundaries of the state and reap the benefits of the civilized life that it provides, constitutes a tacit acceptance of the terms of the agreement, the social contract.

Contractarianism: it is not only explicitly stated agreements between individuals that bind by mutual obligation, but also *tacit* agreements constituted by mutual, reasonable expectations that we all understand when entering into social relationships with one another.

John Rawls: defines justice as fairness. From the 'original position' we can secure two basic principles of justice: a schedule of basic rights and equality of opportunity.

The common-good approach: society is made up of individuals whose own good is linked to the good of the community – all bound together by the pursuit of common values and goals.

Exam questions

1 (a) Explain the theory of virtue ethics. (33 marks)
  (b) How useful, if at all, is the theory of virtue ethics in relation to environmental issues? (17 marks) (OCR, January 2002)
2 (a) What is virtue ethics? (33 marks)
  (b) Discuss the view that it is never virtuous to obtain an abortion. (17 marks) (OCR, June 2002)

REVIEW: applying ethical theories

The dilemma

Colin steals a copy of your final ETHICS exam. He gives your group a copy. You are torn about whether you should look at it or not ... after all, you need to pass this exam!

Relativism:

Rhiannon: Come on, loads of people cheat in exams – there's no particular reason why we shouldn't look at the test.

Roxanne: Yeah, look at all the teachers prowling about during exams – it wouldn't be necessary if they didn't think we were going to cheat! It's like they almost expect it.

Renée: Our year's got a reputation for bucking the system, why change the habit of a lifetime? When in Rome do as the Romans do.

Divine command theory:

Dai: This information has been stolen. Didn't we learn in primary school not to steal?

Damien: Yeah, and if I use this information to get a better mark, aren't I pretending I know more than I do? This sounds a lot like lying, which I've always learnt is wrong.

Declan: But also remember, God helps those who help themselves.

Deontology:

Deiniol: I think I ought to look at some moral rules for a situation like this.

Dyfrig: Yeah, what about justice, equal treatment and refraining from evil?

Dervil: Maybe the best thing to do would be to see which rule you feel most strongly about.

Dafydd: I think this balancing ought to take into account how we are using ourselves and other people ... can the decision we make be applied to others (beyond just us lot) in a situation exactly like this somewhere else?

Utilitarianism:

Uriah: I think the real issue here is do the ends justify the means?

Ursula: OK, maybe stealing is bad, but in this particular case, the greater good might come because I can get a better grade.

Ulrica: When you look at all the alternatives – maybe failing, getting grief from your mates if you turn them in, just using the information – and then you weigh up pros and cons and it seems like just using Colin's information comes out on top for me.

Ulysees: Yeah, keeping quiet offers the greatest benefit for the least cost.

Urban: Maybe for you, but I think the costs of a guilty conscience, for instance, or fear of being discovered, outweigh the risks of telling.

Situation ethics:

Sid: This situation has happened – make the best of it.

Susie: Yeah, I can't love anyone else until I love myself, so I think we should use the paper.

Sandra: I disagree. It's not very loving to take advantage of Colin's theft while students in other schools won't see the paper before sitting the exam.

Virtue ethics:

Vincent: I reckon the best way is to take a long sincere look into ourselves to uncover our real motives.

Valentin: Like if you ratted on your mates just to call attention to yourself, you wouldn't really have made any progress at all ... you would just have done something else wrong.

Vaughan: I'd feel better about myself if I overcame the temptation to use the answers because I knew it was wrong instead of just because I was afraid of being caught.

THEORY	STRENGTH/WEAKNESS	EXAMPLE
ETHICAL RELATIVISM – No principles are universally true. All moral principles are valid relative to cultural tastes.	S – Brings about tolerance of other cultures. W – Confuses what *ought* to be done with what *is* being done.	Some South Seas Islanders have been known to practise cannibalism. Cannibalism is strictly prohibited in Britain.
DIVINE COMMAND THEORY – Moral standards depend on God who is omniscient. Any act that conforms to the law of God is right; any act that breaks God's law is wrong.	S – Standards are from a higher authority than humans. Gives reasons why we should behave morally. Gives worth to all equally. W – Can be arbitrary, depending on interpretation. Can we know what true divine authority is?	Christianity and Judaism teach believers to follow rules like the Ten Commandments.
UTILITARIANISM – Actions are judged right or wrong solely by their consequences. Right actions are those that produce the greatest balance of happiness over unhappiness.	S – Promotes human well-being and attempts to lessen human suffering. W – One person's good can be another's evil. Is also difficult to predict consequences.	The USA dropped the atomic bomb on Japan in 1945 convinced it was worth the loss of life to end the war and stop the potential higher loss of life if the war continued.
DEONTOLOGY – Emphasis is on moral rules and duty. If not willing for everyone to follow the rule, then it is not morally permissible. Emphasis on autonomy, justice and kind acts. People treated as ends, never means.	S – It provides a special moral status for humans. Moral rules are universal. W – It says nothing about other living things. Rules can be abstract.	The Universal Declaration of Human Rights stems from a willingness to reason that justice and equal treatment ought to be applied universally.
VIRTUE ETHICS – We are what we repeatedly do. Excellence is not an act but a habit.	S – Internalizes moral behaviour. W – Offers no specific guidance for resolving contemporary ethical dilemmas.	A journalist with a genuine interest to write the truth deserves more recognition than one who just wants to get promoted to earn more money.

APPLIED ETHICS

> 'The philosophers have only interpreted the world; the thing, however, is to change it.'
>
> Karl Marx (1818–83)

Since the 1960s, academic work in ethics dealing with practical or 'applied' questions has become a major part of both teaching and research in ethics. This development is a revival of an ancient tradition.

Indian and Greek philosophers discussed how we are to live in quite concrete terms (see Chapter 5). Medieval Christian writers were concerned with whether it is always wrong to kill or whether there are times when going to war is justifiable (see Chapter 15). Immanuel Kant in the eighteenth century was interested in, among other issues, the nature of justice (see Chapter 8); and in the nineteenth century, utilitarian philosophers like Jeremy Bentham (see Chapter 9) wrote about legal reform.

However, all this changed in the first part of the twentieth century when philosophers became concerned with the implications of logical positivism and their role became restricted to the meta-ethical task of analysing the meaning of moral terms (see Chapter 2).

This view was finally rejected only when the students of the 1960s demanded courses more relevant to the great issues of the day, which in the USA included civil rights and the war in Vietnam. Issues like the justifiability of war, civil disobedience, and racial and sexual equality, were among the first issues in applied ethics to be discussed by philosophers.

As the environmental movement gained strength too, environmental ethics – which are explored in this book – developed as a new discipline within philosophy in the 1970s. Environmental ethics (see Chapter 14) examines the moral basis of environmental responsibility and how far this responsibility extends, seeking to evaluate past and present attitudes and practices by considering whether feathers, fur, species membership, and even inorganic composition, are not barriers to the range of ethical considerations.

Likewise, the so-called 'sexual revolution' of the 1960s invited people to question the more traditional views of sexuality and sexual ethics has become an increasingly important and fascinating area of study (see Chapter 12).

Again technology and medical science have advanced far more rapidly than our ability to construct a sturdy ethical framework within which such advances can be housed. Each miraculous medical advance brings with it a host of unanswered questions that cut to the heart of what it means to be human. These huge advances throw a challenge to philosophers to find guidelines for issues that are only just emerging – especially in the fields of genetic engineering, cloning and embryo research. We look at these issues in Chapter 13. Whereas in the early 1980s very few medical or nursing undergraduates took courses in ethics, today such courses are widespread. The same is true in schools and this is a major reason why you are reading this book now!

12 Sexual ethics

'If all men and women respected each other, if sex were considered joyful and life-enhancing instead of a wallow in germ-filled glop, if everyone were in love all the time, if, in other words, many people's lives were more satisfactory for them than they appear to be now, pornography might just go away on its own.'

Margaret Atwood, 'Pornography',
Chatelaine, Toronto, 1983

Objectives

In this Chapter you will explore:

- issues relating to sexual ethics
- conservative, libertarian, religious and feminist perspectives on these issues
- the application of natural law, Kantian ethics, utilitarianism and contractualism to sexual ethics and an evaluation of their implications for sexual attitudes and behaviour.

Key questions

1 Given the potentially destructive power of sex, should sexual activity be governed by restrictive rules?

2 Is any sexual activity between consenting adults acceptable?

3 On what basis might a sexual act be regarded as wrong?

4 Is sexual activity permissible only in marriage?

5 How can sexual desire be expressed and satisfied without merely using the other or treating the other as an object? How can sexual desire be expressed and satisfied without treating the self as an object?

6 Are there reasons to suggest that human sexual interaction is essentially manipulative – physically, psychologically, emotionally, and even intellectually?

7 Should the effects of sexual activity on third parties feature in moral evaluations of sexual behaviour, and what effects on third parties count as harm?

Why do we need sexual ethics?

- Sexuality plays a unique role in human life. Sex is, by far, the primary way to reproduce. However, why is the significance of sexuality any different from the significance of eating, breathing, sleeping and defecating? All are instigated by the needs of the natural body. If the desire for sexual pleasure is similar to the desire for food, should sexual behaviour be constrained by moral principles that apply to behaviour in general? Is the ethics of sex no more (or less) important than the ethics of anything else?

- When we acknowledge the destructive potential of sex – rejection and loss, the pain of the sexually exploited, the transmission of sexual diseases – we have reason to believe that sexual ethics is important. Likewise, when we consider the creative potential of making love, the intimacy and trust, the giving and receiving of another, and, ultimately the possible creation of a new life, we have reason to believe that sexual ethics is important.

- Sexual attraction marks the beginnings of potential union, physically, emotionally, spiritually. The ongoing sexual relationship of a couple has the capability of nourishing love, expressing tender concern, eliciting honesty and trust, and renewing commitment. It can bind a couple more closely together. In its full realization it involves entire lives – the emotions, goals and values, the economic resources and social contribution of two people. In this way, it can be seen to defy egoism and point the way to mutual responsibility and service.

- The psychologist Sigmund Freud (see pp. 28–29) suggested that sexual personality resides at the core of moral personality: how we perceive and behave towards sexual partners both influences and is a mirror image of how we perceive and interact with people in general. Our sexuality provides a foundation, or pattern, for acting – morally or immorally – in the world. For many, the failure to learn to control the pursuit of sexual pleasure undermines the achievement of a virtuous character. Some people argue that fostering bad sexual habits or bad patterns of sexual behaviour can destroy the capacity for love.

We can be magnetized and mesmerized by another person's physical strength, charisma and beauty as much as by our own desires. In seeking the pleasure of the body and the comfort of intimacy, do we become vulnerable to betrayal, jealousy, and sorrow?

Key fact

Applied sexual ethics explores a wide range of issues, including bestiality, casual sex, cohabitation, contraceptive intercourse, cyber sex, masturbation, acquaintance rape, making and viewing pornography, sadomasochism, sexual harassment, sexual objectification, sexual exploitation, marriage, divorce, abortion, adultery, prostitution, homosexuality, intergenerational sex, sexual violence, bisexuality and trans-sexuality.

Word watch

eliciting
egoism

'The conflict between ethics and sex today is not just a collision between instinctuality and morality, but a struggle to give an instinct its rightful place in our lives, and to recognize in this instinct a power which seeks expression and evidently may not be trifled with, and therefore cannot be made to fit in with our well-meaning moral laws. Sexuality is not mere instinctuality, it is an indisputably creative power that is not only the basic cause of our individual lives, but a very serious factor in our psychic life as well … our civilization enormously understates the importance of sexuality.'

Carl Jung, *Psychological Reflections* (1953)

Discussion

'The starting point to sex is the sheer desire of a person for the body of another. One wants to feel the skin, to smell the hair, to see the eyes – one wants to bring one's own genitals into contact with those of the other … This gets dangerously close to treating the other as a means to the fulfilment of one's own sexual desire – as an object, rather than as an end.'

Michael Ruse, *Homosexuality: A Philosophical Inquiry* (1988)

'When sex is as much about pleasing another as it is about pleasing oneself, it certainly doesn't involve using another as a means and actually incorporates the idea of respect and concern for another's need … one's humanity is perhaps never more engaged than in the sexual act. But it is not only present in the experience; more important, it is "at stake" in the sense that each partner puts him/herself in a position where the behavior of the other can either confirm it or threaten it, celebrate it or abuse it.'

Jean Hampton, 'Defining Wrong and Defining Rape', in *A Most Detestable Crime: New Philosophical Essays on Rape* (1999)

The conservative approach

St Augustine

It is one thing to argue that evaluating the rights and wrongs of sex is important and another to argue that certain sexual practices must be restricted. Yet, given the psychological nature and potential consequences of sexuality, it could be claimed that sexual activity is **prima facie** morally wrong and is always in need of justification or must be avoided unless stringent conditions are met like marriage. St Augustine (354–430 CE) in *Confessions* (c. 400) provides a classic example of what has come to be known as the conservative approach:

'A man turns to good use the evil of **concupiscence** (lust) … when he bridles and restrains its rage … and never relaxes his hold upon it except when intent on offspring, and then controls and applies it to the carnal generation of children … not to the subjection of the spirit to the flesh in a sordid servitude.'

Word watch

prima facie
concupiscence

Immanuel Kant

Attitudes by Christian thinkers like St Augustine have had a great influence on sexual attitudes and practices in the Western world. Some philosophers, too, have endorsed the view that human sexuality should be governed by restrictive rules. The most striking examples are to be found in Kant's *Lectures on Ethics* (1770):

'If a man wishes to satisfy his desire, and a woman hers, they stimulate each other's desire; their inclinations meet, but their object is not human nature but sex, and each of them dishonours the human nature of the other. They make of humanity an instrument for the satisfaction of their lusts and inclinations, and dishonour it by placing it on a level with animal nature.'

It may appear from a Kantian viewpoint that sexual acts are wrong in themselves because they invariably involve the manipulation of one's partner for one's own pleasure – an idea that appears to be prohibited on the formulation of Kant's principle, which holds that one ought not to treat another as a means to such private ends.

But is Kant right?

As a powerful urge and one open to manipulation and deception, sexual desire could mean we approach another person as an instrument, without regard for the other's needs or ends. Sex for individualistic ends can be manipulative, **chauvinistic** and a destructive power-play that ignores justice, honesty and love.

According to Kant, the quest for sexual pleasure is permissible only when anchored in, or subordinated to, other more valuable goals such as marriage. However, if we begin from another premise, that sex in itself is a wholesome activity, then it becomes easier to justify sexual activity *outside* marriage. Those who assume the worst about sexuality to begin with are therefore more likely to reject casual sex and defend the view that sexuality must be restricted to matrimony.

'Taken by itself, sexual love is a degradation of human nature; for as soon as a person becomes an object of appetite for another, all motives of moral relationship cease to function, because as an object of appetite for another, a person becomes a thing and can be treated and used as such by everyone.'

(Kant, *Lectures on Ethics*, 1770)

For more on Kant see Chapter 8.

Word watch

chauvinistic

Word watch

degradation

Key idea

Conservative views of sexuality: (a) certain sexual practices must be restricted, and (b) sexual activity is prima facie morally wrong and must be avoided outside marriage.

For more on natural law see Chapter 4.

The natural law approach

St Paul first introduced the idea of celibacy to Christianity, cautioning that sex was once pure and uncontaminated. However, with the fall of Adam and Eve came original sin, interpreted as burning sexual desire tainted with evil, with original sin passesing from one generation to another through sexual intercourse (thus Jesus' birth by a virgin, not through sexual intercourse, ensured in Christian tradition that he was 'free from sin').

Celibacy was therefore confirmed by the Christian Church as the highest ideal and sex within marriage regarded as a necessary evil for the continuation of the species. Such views influenced later thinkers in the Christian tradition, the general view being that sexual activity should only take place within the confines of marriage and that all sexual expression undertaken without human reproduction in mind – masturbation, anal sex, oral sex and the use of contraceptive devices – are 'unnatural' and therefore 'immoral'.

St Thomas Aquinas

For more on St Thomas Aquinas see p. 42.

The sexual ethics of St Thomas Aquinas (1224–74) are central to the natural law tradition. They are also reflected in the Roman Catholic Church's view that sex has a particular function – the procreation of children. In *Summa Theologica* (1265), Aquinas argues that sexual acts can be morally wrong in two different ways:

Word watch

deviance

- First, sex is wrong when 'the act of its nature is incompatible with the purpose of the sex act (procreation). In so far as generation is blocked, we have unnatural vice, which is any complete sex act from which of its nature generation cannot follow.' Aquinas gives four examples: 'the sin of self-abuse' (masturbation), 'intercourse with a thing of another species' (bestiality), acts 'with a person of the same sex' (homosexuality), and acts in which 'the natural style of intercourse is not observed, as regards the proper organ or according to other rather beastly and monstrous techniques' (deviance).
- Second, sexual acts can be morally wrong even if natural; in these cases, 'conflict with right reason may arise from the nature of the act with respect to the other party', as in incest, rape, seduction and adultery.

Is the natural law approach reasonable?

Word watch

consummated

Natural law raises two important questions:

1 Is an 'unnatural act' always morally wrong, even if it is consummated with mutual and informed voluntary consent?

2 Are there some non-procreative sexual acts that might actually be natural to human beings? For example, the great varieties of our desires and pleasure fulfilments might be quite natural inclinations. Different forms of sexual expression might, after all, be how humans were fashioned by God following a principle of variety.

Think it through

1 Is an 'unnatural act' always morally wrong? Are there some non-procreative sexual acts that might actually be natural to human beings?

2 Discuss the view that the only immoral thing in human sexuality is activity that causes someone mental or physical pain.

3 Explain why there are differing moral attitudes to non-marital sexual acts. Can you suggest any way of reconciling these attitudes?

4 'Human relationships are too complicated to be controlled by practical rules.' Discuss.

5 We engage in many morally acceptable activities unaccompanied by love or intimacy. Discuss reasons why sex should be any different.

6 Can pleasure – without love and intimacy – serve as a legitimate goal of sex?

The libertarian approach

A grim and conservative characterization of sexuality and the restrictive sexual ethics it implies are rejected by the libertarian approach. This views sexual desire as not being intrinsically sinful or selfish. Sexuality is a natural bonding mechanism that, through the power to produce pleasure, forges a psychological joint interest out of two (or more, presumably if they are very liberal!) independent desires. At least, the self-interested drive for sexual pleasure can, either by its nature or by proper education, incorporate a drive for the satisfaction of another's desire. Further, sexual pleasure is a good and beautiful thing in itself, an activity that ought to be encouraged with appropriate arrangements to make sexual activity less likely to lead to damaging or harmful consequences. Liberal philosophers argue that there is nothing about a virtuous life lived well that excludes seeking sexual pleasure for its own sake.

Key idea

Natural law tradition: sex has a particular function – the procreation of children. According to Aquinas, masturbation, bestiality, homosexuality and deviant sex are immoral because they are not in accordance with the purpose of the sex act (procreation).

Word watch

intrinsically

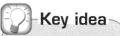

Key idea

The sexual liberal emphasizes autonomous choice, self-determination, freedom, respect for persons, and pleasure, in contrast to a tradition that justifies a more restrictive sexual ethics.

Word watch

reciprocity

Many human relations – including, for example, most economic transactions – involve 'using' other individuals for personal benefit. These relations are immoral only when they are one-sided, when the benefits are not mutual, or when the transactions are not freely and rationally endorsed by all parties. The same could be seen to hold true of sexual acts, with a central principle governing them of the demand for reciprocity in sexual relations. One must recognize one's partner as a subject with demands and desires. By yielding to these desires – by allowing oneself to be a sexual object by giving pleasure – ensures that the pleasures of the act are mutual. It is this kind of reciprocity that forms the basis for liberal morality in sex and that distinguishes right acts from wrong, not whether people are married or not.

The sacred sex approach

Matthew Fox (b. 1940), a contemporary Christian thinker, believes that religion itself has demystified and devalued the true meaning and purpose of sex. Fox argues that the Western Church has followed St Augustine in basically 'regretting the fact that we are sexual, sensual creatures'.

> *Telling us all the sins we are capable of performing with our sexual organs does not enlighten us about our sexuality. Those who reduce a mystery to a problem are guilty of "intellectual perversion".'*
>
> Matthew Fox, *The Coming of the Cosmic Christ* (1988)

Fox reminds us that there is another tradition, one of praise, beautifully expressed in the Song of Songs (1: 2, 4: 1, 7: 2–3) in the Old Testament:

> *'Your lips cover me with kisses; your love is better than wine … How beautiful you are, my love! How your eyes shine with love behind your veil … The curve of your thighs is like the work of an artist. A bowl is there, that never runs out of spiced wine. A sheaf of wheat is there, surrounded by lillies. Your breasts are like twin deer, like two gazelles.'*

The Song of Songs praises human sexuality as a sacred gift encountered by lovers in one another. The sexual act is therefore seen as a giving of oneself in a very deep way, a deliberate giving of the 'I am' that is oneself.

❛ Quotable quote:

'Both religion and sexuality heal the split between ourselves and the universe. We discover that we are indeed "part of everything" and one with the mystery of life. To talk about God in relation to our sexuality means to be aware of love moving in us, for in God we live and move and have our being.'

Dorothee Soelle (b. 1944), modern theologian

In the New Testament, while Jesus condemns adultery, he never stigmatizes erotic impulses as evil. Preaching his message of love and focusing on inner motives and attitudes, Jesus condemns sexuality only when it leads to dishonesty or 'sexual addiction'.

The utilitarian approach

A case can be made that a prima facie right to engage in sexual activity can be derived from utilitarianism. Utilitarian reasons for a right to engage in sex are:

- the value of pleasure
- the contribution shared pleasure makes to the value of personal relationships
- that private and consensual sexual activity creates much good and, if harm to third parties is avoided, provides the greatest happiness for the greatest number.

Popular approaches to sexual morality have often argued for extra-marital abstinence in purely consequentialist terms, arising from the fears of *conception*, *detection* and *infection*. Although contraception has greatly reduced the first fear, and more liberal social attitudes have reduced the second, the proliferation of sexually transmitted diseases including HIV and AIDS has led many people to question the consequentialist approach.

Utilitarian arguments also centre on issues around adultery and marriage. Often, debate focuses not on the actual sexual desire of one person for another, nor their marriage partner, nor on the morality of their sexual relationship as such, but on the potential harm to emotional welfare as a result of infidelity, economic insecurity and deceit.

The contractarian approach

The contractarian approach emphasizes the importance of mutual, voluntary and informed consent, highlighting the appropriateness of tolerating sexual diversity as a recognition of human freedom and autonomy.

Sex is morally permissible if, and only if, it is consummated with *mutual* and *voluntary informed consent*, without force, fraud and explicit duress. Therefore, sex is impermissible where one or both parties lack the capacity for informed consent; for example, the under-age, the significantly mentally impaired, or where there are threats or extortion.

Although the contractual approach seems reasonable, this does not mean that the contract is *always* moral: one of the parties may be vulnerable, destitute or enslaved, while the other may have more bargaining power. A middle-aged man can make a 'contract' with a fifteen-year-old refugee who is desperate for money. He can pass her money if she agrees to have sex with him. Although 'a contract' – the passing of money – has taken place, such a contract is certainly not a moral one, for the girl, like most prostitutes, may have been coerced (forced) into prostitution because of uncertain immigration status, poverty or drug addiction.

Hot tip

Although authoritarian and libertarian views on sex are worlds apart, they may well use the same utilitarian methods in assessing a situation. Utilitarian ethics can impinge on a variety of sexual issues and it will be worth your while to apply them when you can. For example, in recent years this has been highlighted by the advertising campaigns about contraception and the risks of HIV infection. The moral arguments in favour of taking a 'responsible' attitude to sex are not necessarily authoritarian but utilitarian, and the shift in less promiscuous sexual attitudes brought about by the threat of AIDS is largely due to the threat of the harmful consequences of promiscuity.

Word watch

utilitarian ethics
promiscuity

Key fact

In the summer of 1999, Cornell University published research purporting to show that love really is a drug. To be precise, it is a cocktail of dopamine, phenylethylamine and oxytocin in the bloodstream that produces the sensation we call infatuation. Love, the researchers argued, was in fact a chemically induced form of insanity. This condition lasts until the body builds up an immunity to the substances involved, which is usually just long enough to meet, mate and raise a child to early infancy.

Nicholas Fearn, *How to Think Like a Philosopher* (2001)

Think it through: consent

1 Is a man participating in a contract with a prostitute fully informed as to the reasons why she finds it necessary to prostitute herself?

2 How *specific* must consent be in order for a person to engage voluntarily in subsequent sexual behaviour: for example, if Ellie consents to have sex with Alan, does she know specifically what sort of sex Alan has in mind?

3 How *explicit* must consent be: for example, can someone think another has consented just by non-verbal behaviour?

4 How *informed* must consent be: for example, does one partner have an obligation to warn the other that their anticipated sexual activity is medically dangerous?

The feminist approach

- Feminists argue that historically men have been in power and it is *socially constructed sexual roles* (by men) that make it difficult for women to identify and nurture their own sexual desires and needs. Women are socialized to meet male sexual desires in order to prove their own value.

- Contractual arrangements are worthless because the social conditioning that limits women's opportunities in the world will affect sexual 'contracts'.

- Male dominance has influenced Western sexual relations and women, politically victimized by their sexuality, will be free from dominance only when they are allowed the power and capacity to define themselves.

- Moral doctrines have emerged from societies in which women's role has been a subordinate one. If the concerns, activities and interests traditionally associated with women were given a superior status to those traditionally associated with men, then moral priorities might become very different.

- Some feminist thinkers, like Martha Nussbaum (b. 1947), argue that it is men who like to invent elaborate, clinical and complex abstract formal 'systems', which they impose on the world with its moral problems. She asks whether there are specific female 'virtues' and questions the predominant patriarchal view that women 'are more intuitive, irrational, gentle, passive, selfless and sympathetic than men', and argues that these so-called 'virtues' have suppressed and restricted women.

- While some feminists reject the view of female 'nature', others argue that it is irrelevant whether female virtues are innate or conditioned and that some of the traditional 'female virtues' of co-operation and caring that operate in the private spheres of life should also be given a much higher priority in the macho and ruthless culture of the 'public sphere'.

❛ Quotable quote

'Women are not the point of pornography. Pornography is the flight from women, men's denial of sex as a medium of communication, their denial of sex as the basis for a relationship, their rejection of fatherhood, their perpetual incontinent adolescence. The victims of pornography are men not women. Pornography makes men leaky vessels and undoes the principal male virtue of **continence**. *As men's real power dwindles, pornography is their refuge. Fear of commitment is inseparable from indulgence in pornography. Masturbation is easy; relationships are difficult. Relationships interfere with masturbation.'*

Germaine Greer, *The Female Eunuch* (1970) ❜

Word watch

continence

Pornography

Pornography derives from the Greek word *pornographos*, meaning *writing of harlots* – literally writing about prostitutes. Thus the depiction of various forms of sexual intercourse on the walls in Pompeii, intended as aphrodisiacs for the orgiastic parties (bacchanals) held there, were literally *pornographos*. Pornography in this sense is identified by its sexually explicit content, its depiction of varied forms of sexual intercourse and sexual passion.

Cultural trends, influenced by media technology like digital and satellite TV and the Internet, have provided the British public with access to material that would not otherwise be shown in British cinemas. However, one person's 'obscenity' might be another's 'art'. Many cultures, although sharing the fundamental concept of the obscene, do not regard pornography, as defined above, as obscene.

Think it through

If there is no necessary connection between the pornographic and the obscene, how did the connection between them arise? One account of the sexual morality behind this connection is given in Catholic Canon Law, which holds that 'complete sexual activity and pleasure is licit and moral only in a naturally completed act in valid marriage'. This view – derived from St Augustine – holds that pornography is therefore obscene, not only in itself because it displays intercourse outside marriage, but also because it tempts people to engage in intercourse outside marriage and masturbation – independently obscene acts because they are forms of sexual conduct that violate minimum standards of proper bodily function (that is, for procreation only).

Summary

During the late twentieth century, modern popular thinking, influenced by developments in psychology, sociology and anthropology, began to question traditional views, asking questions such as why is sex within marriage for the purpose of procreation more in accordance with 'human nature' than sex outside marriage for the purpose of pleasure? This has not been an invitation to promiscuity but a view that sees sexual relations as being morally acceptable if love, trust, loyalty and intimacy are present.

Review

St Augustine: sexuality is always in need of justification or must be avoided unless stringent conditions like marriage are met.

Immanuel Kant: sexual acts are wrong in themselves because they invariably involve the manipulation of one's partner for one's own pleasure, thus violating the principle which holds that one ought not to treat another as a means to such private ends.

However, it becomes easier both to justify sexual activity and to justify sex *outside* marriage if we do not assume the worst about sexuality to begin with.

Natural law approach: sex has a particular natural function – the procreation of children.

St Thomas Aquinas: sexual acts are morally wrong when *'the act of its nature is incompatible with the purpose of the sex act (procreation)'*.

Key question: is an 'unnatural act' always morally wrong? Are there some non-procreative sexual acts that might actually be natural to human beings?

Libertarian view: there is nothing about a virtuous life lived well that excludes seeking sexual pleasure for its own sake. Relations are immoral only when they are one-sided or when they are not freely and rationally endorsed by all parties.

Matthew Fox: the Christian Church has reduced the sacred *mystery of* sex to a *problem about* sex.

Utilitarian approach: sexual ethics for utilitarians can be both restrictive (for example, the consequences of promiscuity or unprotected sex can lead to bad consequences) and also permissive (consensual sexual activity creates much good and, if harm to third parties is avoided, provides the greatest happiness for the greatest number).

Contractarian approach: sex is morally permissible if, and only if, it is consummated with *mutual* and *voluntary informed consent*, without force, fraud and explicit duress.

Feminist approach: *socially constructed sexual roles* and moral doctrines have emerged from societies in which women's role has been a subordinate one. If the concerns of women were given a superior status to those traditionally associated with men, then moral priorities might change.

Pornography: many contemporary views have derived from the natural law theory – not only that pornography is obscene in itself because it displays intercourse outside marriage, but also because it tempts people to engage in intercourse outside marriage, or to masturbation, which are independently obscene acts because they are forms of sexual conduct that violate 'natural' functioning.

Germaine Greer: male pornography use is 'perpetual incontinent adolescence'.

Word watch

consensual

Exam questions

1 (a) Examine the defining characteristics of utilitarianism. (14 marks)
   (b) Consider how utilitarianism can be applied to a moral dilemma related to sexual ethics. (6 marks) (EDEXCEL, June 2001)

2 (a) Explain the religious and ethical principles involved in deciding whether or not to participate in homosexual practice. (15 marks)
   (b) Evaluate the the view that sex before marriage is natural and therefore morally right. (5 marks) (WJEC, June 2001)

3 (a) Describe the essential features of two theories of conscience. (33 marks)
   (b) Assess the role of conscience in relation to pre-marital sex. (17 marks) (OCR, June 2002)

13 Cloning

> 'Human cloning endangers the right of each human life to find its own way and be a surprise to itself.'
>
> Hans Jonas, philosopher, *The Phenomenon of Life* (2001)

Objectives

Each miraculous medical advance brings with it a host of unanswered questions that cut to the heart of what it means to be human. In this Chapter you will learn about:

- three different types of **cloning**
- arguments for and against these types of cloning
- arguments for and against stem cell and **embryo research**.

?= Key questions

1 Do the ends of increased medical knowledge justify any means?

2 Should science be concerned about the greatest good for the greatest number?

3 Could cloning interfere with diversity and destroy the natural order? If human cloning becomes a reality, will failures, such as deformed offspring, be acceptable?

4 Is **genetic engineering** 'playing at being God', or is it an exercise in scientific freedom?

5 Although pre-embryos have no brain, central nervous system, or internal organs, no organs to see, hear, touch, taste, lack a body, head, arms, legs and have no thought processes or consciousness, do they still have rights?

6 Just because some people might misuse the results of scientific advances (for example, by making atomic bombs), should we stop those advances happening? Is this true when we think about cloning and its effects?

7 Will cloning lead to designer babies – 'vanity products'?

Word watch

embryo research

Word watch

genetic engineering
pre-embryos

Introduction

Since the 1950s – when scientists first understood human **DNA**, the molecule of inheritance – advances in genetics and genetic engineering have been breathtaking:

- inherited diseases can be understood, predicted and even cured
- the criminal justice system has improved with DNA fingerprinting
- our understanding of human origins has developed
- biomedical research and the creation of genetically modified animals is developing all the time
- food production with genetically modified crops is becoming a reality.

An ethical minefield

These advances raise a host of ethical questions. Here are just a few:

- Should young people be told they have inherited the gene for Huntington's disease, which will strike them in middle age with a lethal and debilitating mental disorder with no cure?
- Do insurance companies have the right to access such information?
- If some criminals are genetically predisposed to violence, are they morally responsible for their actions?
- Should parents be able to choose the sex of their babies based on a DNA test?
- Should parents be able to alter the genes of eggs or sperm to rid their children of genetic disorders?
- If this is acceptable, why can parents not genetically engineer their children to improve 'cosmetic' traits such as intelligence, height or even sexual attractiveness?

❛ = Quotable quote =

'The ultimate value of human life is the central insight of our culture. If it is lost – as it was under the Nazis – then any evil may ensue. And it will be lost if we abandon ourselves – as we are now doing – to love of the future or to the endless hypnosis of technology. The question for the next 50 years is not how fast our computers run or how high our rockets go, but how good we are going to be as a species. All else is trivial, for it is on that question alone that our survival depends.'

Brian Appleyard, *Brave New Worlds: Genetics and the Human Experience* (1999) ❜

👆 = Web quest =

To visit Welcome to the Future, an informative site on all things new and their ethical implications by Dr Patrick Dixon, visit www.heinemann.co.uk/hotlinks and click on this section.

Word watch

DNA

The Clone Age!
A sheep in sheep's cloning

Cloning was first brought to media attention in 1996 when scientists in Scotland announced that a sheep called 'Dolly' had been cloned using DNA from another sheep. Dolly (1996–2003) was 'made' from the cells from two different sheep. No ram had anything to do with it. Some newspapers commented that if the technique were perfected in humans, the time would come when there would be no need for men to keep the human race going! Is this a wonderful breakthrough in scientific knowledge – or is it science gone mad?

WORLD NEWS
July 5 1996

SCIENTIFIC SENSATION

Dolly and Mum © Roslin Institute

Dolly - the world's first mammal cloned from adult cells - was born at the Roslin Institute in Scotland. Dolly, unlike any other mammal that has ever lived, is an identical copy of another adult and has no father. It took the scientists 277 tries before they got a healthy, viable lamb.

The announcement of Dolly's birth shocked the scientific community, who at the time thought that cloning from adult cells could not be done. The discovery has triggered a massive public debate about the ethics of future cloning practices.

Cloning a sheep was a significant step, but soon things became more controversial. In 1998 scientists in South Korea announced that they had created an embryo from the cells of an adult woman, although they halted the embryo's growth when it consisted of only four cells.

Human cloning

Rumours have since abounded about an Italian doctor successfully initiating a pregnancy through **reproductive cloning**. Controversy erupted, too, in the USA in December 2002, when the birth of the first human clone, a baby girl nicknamed Eve, was announced by 'Clonaid' – a human cloning company founded by a cult called the Raelians. This claim has been met with widespread scepticism by scientists around the world, as there is no scientific proof that Eve is in fact a clone.

Most scientists believe that human cloning will only succeed at a huge cost, with thousands of women going through difficult pregnancies ending in miscarriage or abortion. Some scientists believe that monkey cloning will eventually lead to the first human clone. Critics view the cloning of a new human being as unethical – an offence to human dignity and potentially harmful to human genetic diversity.

These events – and several other successful attempts at cloning mammals – suggest that cloning humans may one day be possible. This possibility has sparked off a debate about the ethics of creating human clones, the circumstances under which human cloning might be used, and the possibility of using the technique to manipulate the traits of children. The issue remains unresolved and will continue to challenge medical ethicists well into the twenty-first century.

Three types of cloning

1 Embryo cloning

Embryo cloning duplicates the process that nature uses to produce twins or triplets. One or more cells are removed from a fertilized embryo and encouraged to develop into one or more duplicate embryos. Twins or triplets are thus formed with identical DNA. This has been done for many years on different species of animals like cattle, but only very limited experimentation has been done on humans.

2 Reproductive cloning

Reproductive cloning is a technique intended to produce a duplicate of an existing animal. It has been used to clone Dolly the sheep and other mammals. The DNA from an ovum is removed and replaced with the DNA from a cell removed from an adult animal. Then the fertilized ovum, now called a pre-embryo, is implanted in a womb and allowed to develop into a new animal. Reproductive cloning is banned in Britain and it is illegal to put any cloned human embryo into a womb. Many other European countries, to say nothing of those further afield, have yet to legislate in this area.

3 Therapeutic cloning

Therapeutic cloning is a procedure whose initial stages are identical to reproductive cloning. However, the stem cells are removed from the pre-embryo with the intent of producing tissue or a whole organ for transplant back into the person who supplied the DNA. The pre-embryo dies in the process. The goal of therapeutic cloning is to produce a healthy copy of a sick person's tissue or organ for transplant. This technique would be vastly superior to relying on organ transplants, reduce animal testing, and the supply would be unlimited, so there would be no waiting lists. The tissue or organ would have the sick person's original DNA; the patient would not have to take immunosuppressant drugs for the rest of his or her life, as is now required after transplants. There would not be any danger of organ rejection. Since 1998 it has been acceptable to clone human material for medical purposes.

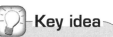

Key fact

Cloning is the production of one or more individual plants or animals that are genetically identical to another plant or animal. Scientists usually do this by taking the DNA from one animal or plant and transferring it to another of the same kind. The greatest advantage of cloning is that cloned material will not be rejected by the body from which the original cell was taken.

Key idea

Critics view human cloning as unethical – an offence to human dignity and potentially harmful to human genetic diversity.

Hot tip

When discussing cloning, always be sure to distinguish between embryo cloning, reproductive cloning and therapeutic cloning before assessing religious and ethical considerations.

Key ideas

Human cloning is intrinsically wrong – a deontological approach.

Human cloning is wrong because it could lead to harmful consequences in the future – a teleological approach.

Cloning is wrong because, from conception onwards, the embryo has full human status – traditional Christian view. Even if the end may be good, the means are not.

 Think it through

Discuss the following viewpoints.

1 'Cloning humans could create psychological problems for the cloned child.'

2 'Disposing of an "early embryo" is an act of killing.'

3 'Human cloning could lead to a twenty-first-century "circus of human curiosities".'

4 'Cloning smacks of scientists "playing God"; interfering with nature and leading to unpredictable and potentially devastating consequences.'

Some objections to human cloning

There are diverse and strongly held opinions regarding the morality of cloning humans. This debate is usually couched in religious and ethical terms. Theologians and ethicists may use different routes to arrive at the same conclusions.

❛ **Quotable quote**

'Every possible act of cloning humans is intrinsically evil and could never be justified.'

National **Bioethics** Advisory Committee (2002) ❜

- Playing God: religions teach that all individuals are valued for their unique worth. Cloning is 'playing at being God' and will ultimately destroy the natural order. Roman Catholics, for example, believe that the soul enters the body at the instant of conception and that the fertilized ovum is in fact a human being: dividing that 'baby' in half would interfere with nature. They also argue that the cloned 'materials' destroyed in the process would be lost human beings. Islam, Judaism and Protestant Christianity also believe that human cloning is morally wrong and would like to see an international treaty to ban it worldwide.

- Health risks: cloning techniques are still very risky. Many attempts at animal cloning produced disfigured monsters with severe abnormalities. There is no guarantee that the first cloned humans will be normal.

- Emotional and psychological risks: cloning may lead to devastating psychological problems and emotional difficulties; for example, a child born from adult DNA cloned from her father or mother would, in effect, be a delayed twin of one of her parents. Emotional problems might arise, too, if a child were to find out that he or she was cloned.

- Sex: human cloning turns reproduction into manufacturing. It turns 'begetting' into 'making'. A human clone becomes a product and a design. Reproduction that does not involve sex is unnatural. The deep inner meaning and mystery of the parent/child relationship – perhaps the most important relationship biologically, psychologically, emotionally and spiritually – is threatened.

- Abuse: a dictator could finance a programme to breed humans with certain characteristics. Once the 'perfect human' or 'perfect warrior' was developed, cloning could produce unlimited numbers of clones. The same approach could be used to create a 'genetic underclass' for exploitation; for example, individuals with subnormal intelligence and above-normal strength. What would Hitler have done if cloning had been available in the 1930s?

- Depletion of genetic diversity: humankind evolves because of diversity in breeding. Small communities with interbreeding soon suffer major problems such as interbreeding within the aristocracy. Large-scale cloning could deplete the human gene pool. If everyone has the same genetic material, what could happen if we lose the ability to clone? We would have to resort to natural reproduction, causing us to inbreed, which will cause huge problems. Also, if we all had the same genetic make-up, it would be easier for a killer disease to wipe out the entire population.

Web quest

Find out the latest research and the Church of Scotland's extensively studied reports on cloning by visiting www.heinemann.co.uk/hotlinks and clicking on this section.

The reports (a) *commend* the principle of the production of proteins of therapeutic value in the milk of genetically modified sheep and other farm animals, (b) *oppose* the application of animal cloning as a routine procedure in meat and milk production, and (c) express the strongest possible opposition to human cloning and therefore urge a comprehensive international treaty to ban it worldwide.

Key question

Is genetic engineering 'playing God', or is it an exercise in morally valid scientific freedom?

Reasons for cloning?

Improve scientific understanding

Research into cloning could greatly advance medical science in showing how organisms develop over time, offering ways of curing diseases, and providing children who need organ transplants to have a clone born to donate organs and so reduce the chances of organ rejection.

Help lesbian or gay couples who want children

DNA from a woman's ovum could be removed and replaced with the DNA from a male. The ovum could then be fertilized with the sperm of the first male's partner. The fertilized 'male egg' could then be implanted into the womb of a surrogate mother. This could produce a child whose DNA came from both of its fathers.

Infertility

Could cloning help infertile couples? Critics have pointed out that anyone who was a clone of one parent would be under unknown psychological pressures throughout childhood. Would such a person feel he or she was living up to the achievements of the 'original'? And how would a woman feel about bringing up a much younger version of the person she fell in love with?

Resurrect the dead

In recent years, some bereaved families have asked scientists to clone a dead child. However, even if human cloning were possible, families might be upset to discover their new baby was not exactly like their dead older brother or sister and the 'replacement' child might suffer feelings of inferiority about being born purely to take the place of a dead sibling.

To replicate the talents of extraordinary human beings

Who is to say, however, that if, for instance, Albert Einstein could be genetically reproduced, his clones might not take up soccer instead of science – subsequently disappointing the people who had put time and energy into 'recreating him'. Manchester United Football Club might appreciate his genius in midfield, however!

❛ Quotable quote

'The most beautiful thing we can experience is the mysterious. It is the source of all true art and science.

Albert Einstein (1879–1955) ❜

Pets

Remember that beautiful dog that used to almost knock you over when you were small? How sad you were when he made that final trip to the vet – and never came home! Well dry your eyes. In future you might never have to say goodbye! Pet cloning might sound trivial but cloning could reduce the number of unwanted animals. Owners might feel happier having a pet neutered if they knew he or she could be cloned. Only one clone would be produced instead of a whole litter and it might also be easier to predict the temperament of a puppy when it grows up.

Farming

Cloning could help to create a mass of elite farm animals with more resistance to common diseases and who produce more meat or milk. Critics worry about the health risks involved in eating food from cloned animals and other health implications like low resistance to disease because of lack of genetic diversity.

Noah's Ark?

Cloning could be a way of recreating animals threatened with extinction. The first clone of an endangered species was a baby gaur, a rare wild ox. Scientists impregnated a cow with a cell cloned from a non-breeding male gaur at San Diego Zoo. Had Noah lived to breed, he would have increased the genetic diversity of the group of gaurs at the zoo. Sadly, Noah died of an infection after two days. Zoo officials saved his skin cells for future experiments.

At the current rate of decline, the wild orangutan will be extinct in ten to twenty years time – could cloning be the answer?

Critics of cloning argue that widespread cloning could considerably reduce genetic diversity, leaving the whole species vulnerable to disease. Also, any resurrected species would probably be condemned to life in a zoo unless a suitable habitat could be found. Animal cloning, too, has a high failure rate: out of 692 fused eggs, 81 grew and divided into 100 eggs. Out of those 100 eggs, 44 were transferred into 32 surrogate mothers. Eight of the cows became pregnant of which five had abortions. Two foetuses were removed to examine the developing baby gaur. That left only one surviving gaur, Noah, who died after two days!

Word watch

surrogate mothers

Web quest

Explore the views of The Ontario Consultants on Religious Tolerance in regards to cloning by visiting www.heinemann.co.uk/hotlinks and clicking on this section.

1 Browse the sections on (a) human cloning, and (b) comments by political groups and religious authorities on cloning.

2 Using information from the website, write an essay highlighting what different individuals and groups say about the ethical dimensions of cloning.

Word watch

embryonic stem cells

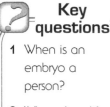

Key questions

1 When is an embryo a person?

2 When does life begin?

Word watch

stem cell research

To obtain stem cells

Scientists have discovered that there are cells of amazing power that could be used to cure a range of diseases, produce new organs and rejuvenate almost any part of the human body.

Potentially, stem cells can develop into virtually every other cell type in the body, such as blood, brain, heart tissue, nerve cells, bones. So, for example, you could take a stem cell from a cardiac muscle cell and inject it into a heart damaged by a heart attack – the stem cells could repair the damaged muscle.

Embryonic stem cells first appear about a week after fertilization and they are the 'parents' of all the cells of the adult body. In animal experiments stem cells placed inside damaged areas of the body seemed to 'know' where they were and turned into new cells of the appropriate type.

Embryonic stem cells have to be harvested from early embryos. However, if you were ill, it would probably be safer to treat you with embryonic stem cells that were genetically identical to you so that your immune system would not reject them. In theory, these could be harvested from an early embryo that was a cloned version of you. This embryo would then be discarded.

Methods may even be found whereby stem cells could be formed into replacement tissue and human spare parts for transplants. They may eventually be used to repair injured or poorly functioning brains and nervous systems. This, scientists believe, would provide the key to an unlimited supply of spare human cells for grafts and transplants. At present, research is hampered by the poor quality of available embryos.

In practise, stem cells are usually extracted from 'unwanted' human embryos. The deliberate 'wastage' of embryos is one reason why therapeutic cloning is controversial.

Supporters of stem cell research argue that these embryos are extras – they will never be implanted and they are destined for destruction anyway, so they might as well be used for the benefit of others. Supporters regard a young embryo not as a full human being; at most, they can become an organ, not a complete living organism, so cannot be considered a form of human life. They argue that stem cells have an enormous potential to benefit humankind and these possibilities should be explored.

Objections to stem cell research

- Conservative Christians believe that an embryo is a human being, so the act of extracting stem cells from an embryo is murder.
- It is possible to 'adopt' those embryos – called 'rescue surrogacy' – and so embryos are not necessarily destined for destruction. They could be implanted and a healthy baby might be born.
- Other methods of obtaining stem cells without 'killing' an embryo should be employed. Practitioners of advanced cell technology claim they have been able

to extract human stem cells by fusing human foetal tissue with parts of a cow's egg. Stem cells can be extracted from brains of cadavers – dead human bodies – and from bone marrow, although with greater difficulty and in smaller quantities. However, research to date indicates that these stem cells are very limited in their potential, compared to cells taken from embryos.

Word watch

cadavers

- Stem cells can also be found in adult bodies where they provide ongoing maintenance and repair. Many people who are worried about wasting embryos would prefer to see the development of treatments that use adult stem cells. They can also be found in the blood collected from a baby's umbilical cord just after birth. Some parents are now choosing to freeze and store this blood so their child will be able to call on a supply of its very own stem cells later in life. These techniques, however, do not have the potential power of embryonic stem cells.

Actor Christopher Reeve who played 'Superman' has a personal interest in embryonic stem cell research. He was paralysed from the neck down when he was thrown from a horse in 1995. In Britain in 2002, the House of Lords Select Committee allowed scientists to conduct research using stem cells derived from cloned human embryos in the earliest stage of development. Reeve said: 'While politically complicated, the medical, moral and scientific case for this decision is overwhelming. Therapeutic cloning and embryonic stem cell research may represent the best hope for the hundreds of millions worldwide who suffer from Alzheimer's, Parkinson's, diabetes, multiple sclerosis, stroke, spinal cord injury, and many other diseases and disorders.'

Think it through

Write a short report to deliver to your class on *two* of the following, assessing the positive and negative implications of (a) cloning animals, (b) cloning humans, (c) therapeutic cloning and stem cell research.

Embryo research

The debate about the rights and wrongs of research using human embryos underlies much of the controversy about stem cell research. In popular usage, the term 'embryo' is often used to refer to any stage of pre-natal mammalian development from 0 to 8 weeks after fertilization. From nine weeks after fertilization until birth, it is called a foetus. Embryology is the study of the changes that occur to an organism from its earliest stages. Embryo research helps detect and treat many diseases and disorders. However, there is much controversy about when life actually begins and whether research on embryos should be carried out.

Word watch

foetus
embryology

Against

- Some critics argue that creating human embryos for the purpose of experimentation and destruction is biotech cannibalism, consuming our young for the sake of our own prosperity. They argue that it does not matter whether it is five or fifteen days old, a human embryo is a human being; that is just what human beings look like at that age.
- Some critics argue that experiments that subject an ovum to any significant risk are the ethical equivalent of Nazi medical experiments in the death camps, in that they too were inflicted on unwilling and uninformed victims. They argue that the scientific ends do not justify the means.
- Individual human beings must not be used or abused for some grand scheme promising 'the greatest good for the greatest number'. If embryologists destroy 'imperfect' embryos with genetic flaws, this has implications for the equal dignity of human beings after birth as well.

For

- A fertilized ovum is only a potential human life. Human life begins either when the foetus can live independently or when the foetal brain develops to the point where it experiences self-awareness, or at some other stage of pregnancy, or at birth.
- Creating embryos and/or performing experiments on existing embryos is justified if the research has a reasonable potential of advancing medical knowledge and enhancing human life, and if the embryos are destroyed before they make the transition to a human person.

A humanist view

Humanists argue that humans have been 'playing God' for a long time, intervening beneficially in reproductive and medical processes. For humanists, the most important consideration in ethical questions on life and death is the quality of life for each individual person. In the case of embryo research, humanists do not regard an embryo as a person and support embryo research. If an embryo's cells can be used to alleviate human suffering, the good consequences seem to outweigh the harmful ones, as long as the legal cut-off point for research is sufficiently early.

Most humanists support therapeutic cloning – new cures for disease are needed and the consequences of producing new treatments seem, on balance, to be good. They feel that human cloning, however, could result in much suffering, with side effects such as premature ageing or infertility and other abnormalities. They also argue that it is unethical to grow human beings experimentally. It is possible that cloned children could suffer psychologically and in many ways cloning seems like a *vanity project* – parents would have to be very confident of their own qualities to want to produce a near identical child and the expectations the parent could have of the child might hinder its healthy emotional development.

Word watch

generic flaws

Key idea

Humanism encompasses atheism and agnosticism with an approach to life based on reason. Humanists believe that moral values are founded on human nature and experience alone. Humanists reject the idea of any supernatural agency intervening to help or hinder human activities and so do not worry about 'playing God'.

Web quest

Examination questions sometimes ask for a non-religious response to ethical issues. To find out more about humanist perspectives visit www.heinemann.co.uk/hotlinks and click on this section.

A Christian view

- Evangelical Christians and Roman Catholics believe that a soul enters the body at the instant of conception and that the fertilized ovum is in fact a human person with full human rights.

- Dividing that 'baby' in half during the embryo cloning procedure, therefore, interferes with God's intent. It is also considered to be human experimentation on live persons. Cloned zygotes that die after a few cell divisions should be considered 'lost human beings'. Their loss should be considered as serious as the death of a newborn baby.

- Conservative Christians also believe that it is wrong to weed out genetically defective fertilized ova in therapeutic cloning procedures. The procedure would result in the killing of one of the clones during the genetic testing. Since they regard each of the clones as separate human beings, this, in their view, would be tantamount to murder.

Word watch

zygotes

Think it through

Write a short report to deliver to your community of enquiry on one of the following: (a) the positive implications of embryo research; (b) the negative implications of embryo research; (c) one religious perspective on embryo research; (d) a humanist perspective on embryo research.

Review

Three types of cloning:

- Embryo cloning
- Reproductive cloning
- Therapeutic cloning.

Objections to cloning: include humans 'playing God' – unleashing powerful forces we do not fully understand; potential health risks and emotional and psychological damage; human cloning turns reproduction into manufacturing – 'begetting' into 'making'; open to possible abuse; could deplete genetic diversity.

Supporters of stem cell research: stem cells have an enormous potential to benefit humankind and these possibilities should be explored.

Objections to stem cell research: an embryo is a human being, so the act of extracting stem cells from an embryo is murder. Other methods of obtaining stem cells should be employed.

Embryo research: controversy about when life actually begins and whether research on embryos should be carried out.

Against embryo research: creating human embryos for the purpose of experimentation is biotech cannibalism; 'human beings' must not be used or abused for some grand scheme promising 'the greatest good for the greatest number'.

For embryo research: a fertilized ovum is not human life; it is, rather, a potential human life. Creating embryos and/or performing experiments on existing embryos is justified if the research advances scientific knowledge and the embryos are destroyed before they make the transition to a human person.

Exam questions

1 **(a)** Examine the views within *one* religion on the ethical issues raised by the increasing possibilities of genetic engineering. (20 marks)

   'Scientists should be given complete freedom to explore cloning regardless of any religious objections.'

   (b) Explain the issues raised by this statement and assess how far you agree with it. (30 marks) (AQA, June 2002)

2 **(a)** Explain any two views of the nature of conscience. (33 marks)

   (b) How far ought conscience to be taken into account when considering the issues of embryo research? (17 marks) (OCR, January 2002)

For more on conscience see Chapter 6

14 Environmental ethics and animal rights

> 'The earth mourns and withers, the world languishes and withers; the earth lies polluted under its inhabitants; for they have transgressed the laws, violated the statutes, broken the everlasting covenant. Therefore a curse devours the earth.'
>
> The Revised Standard Version of the Bible (Isaiah 24: 4–6)

Objectives

In this chapter you will study:

- the environmental consequences of a human-centred approach to the environment and to non-human life
- the meaning and environmental consequences of '**instrumental value**' as against '**intrinsic value**'
- attitudes to the environment, including anthropocentric, non-human rights, eco-holism, religious approaches and **stewardship**
- key facts and opinions about current environmental degradation.

Word watch

instrumental value
intrinsic value
rights
stewardship

Key questions

1 Is the environment simply an exploitable resource for human interests; that is, does the Earth exist just for the benefit of humanity? Or has the Earth a significance all of its own outside any use that might be made of it – a value that ought to constrain certain practices?

2 Is it reasonable to expand the moral framework to nature and counter human chauvinism by showing that non-humans and even inorganic composition are not barriers to the range of ethical consideration?

3 Do other organisms and/or species other than humans have an intrinsic right to exist?

4 Do all life forms that exist deserve moral status simply on the basis that they exist?

5 Do our environmental duties derive from (a) the immediate benefit that living people receive from the environment, (b) the benefit that future generations of people will receive, or (c) both a and b?

Word watch

chauvinism

Hot tip

You will be rewarded in your examination if you remember to apply ethical theories to environmental issues – compare and contrast the ways that the application of Kantian, utilitarian and religious ideas will affect the outcome of these issues. You will also be rewarded if you show some understanding of the issues that affect our planet today; the key facts in this chapter are designed to help you in your exploration.

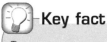

Key fact

Tree sparrow numbers in Britain have declined by more than 80 per cent over the last 25 years.

Word watch

prima facie duty

Discussion

'Human happiness is not as important as a wild and healthy planet. The ecosystem has intrinsic value, more value to me than another human body or a billion of them. Until such time as Homo sapiens should decide to rejoin nature, some of us can only hope for the right virus to come along.'

David Graber, biologist, *Los Angeles Times* (29 October 1989)

Introduction

Environmental ethics examines the moral basis of environmental responsibility and how far this responsibility extends. It seeks to evaluate past and present attitudes and practices to the environment by considering whether feathers, fur, species membership, and even inorganic composition, are not barriers to the range of ethical consideration.

The goal of environmental ethics is not to convince us that we should be concerned about the environment (most of us already are when we think about it): toxic waste, contaminated water, oil spills, nuclear and chemical disasters, fossil fuels producing carbon dioxide, the greenhouse effect, nuclear waste disposal, a depleted ozone layer, extinction of insects, animals and birds, and so on.

In environmental ethics it is important to make a distinction between *intrinsic* value and *instrumental* value.

- Instrumental value: the value of things as a means to further some other ends; for example, certain fruits have instrumental value for bats who feed on them.
- Intrinsic value: the value of things as ends in themselves regardless of whether they are also useful as means to other ends.

Equal intrinsic value: implies species egalitarianism, in other words, all beings, of whatever species, have equal value in themselves for what they are. This is distinguished from any instrumental or use-value they may have to other beings. Thus humans may only interfere with other beings 'at vital need', not just to satisfy their desires. Even non-living beings, like rivers and mountains, have intrinsic value. There is no gradation of intrinsic value – it is absolute.

A certain wild plant may have *instrumental* value because it provides the ingredients for some medicine. But if the plant also has some value in itself independently of its prospects for furthering some other ends such as human health, then the plant also has *intrinsic* value. Because the intrinsically valuable is that which is good as an end in itself, it is commonly agreed that something's possession of intrinsic value generates a **prima facie duty** on the part of moral agents to protect it or at least refrain from damaging it.

Discussion

Read the following and then organize a class discussion on the question 'Is animal experimentation morally wrong?'

Animal experimentation is morally right: instrumental value

Human life has greater intrinsic value than animal life; medical advances using animals have included anaesthetics, open-heart surgery, kidney transplants, high blood pressure drugs, psychiatric drugs, life-support systems for premature babies and gene therapy. Animal testing has helped to develop vaccines against diseases like whooping cough, rabies, polio, measles, mumps, rubella and TB. Antibiotics, HIV drugs, insulin and cancer treatments rely on animal tests. Other testing methods are not advanced enough. Scientists claim there are no differences in laboratory animals and humans that cannot be discovered in tests. Legislation protects all laboratory animals from cruelty or mistreatment. Animals are treated carefully and suffering is minimized. Millions of animals are killed for food every year – if anything, medical research is a more worthy death.

Animal experimentation is morally wrong: intrinsic value

Animals have as much right to life as human beings. Simply because chimpanzees, laboratory rats and farm animals are not members of our species does not give us the right to abuse them and kill them for our own ends. Strict controls have not prevented researchers from abusing animals. There are alternatives to using animals; for example, computer modelling, testing human cell/tissue cultures, test-tube techniques, using synthetic membranes. The stress endured in laboratories can affect experiments, making results meaningless. Animal experiments can be misleading and an animal's response to a drug can be different to a human's. Deaths through research, therefore, are absolutely unnecessary and are morally no different from murder. Animals in these conditions suffer tremendous distress. How can we be sure they do not feel pain?

Key fact

The debate between instrumental value and intrinsic value is nowhere more controversial than in the testing of animals. Britain authorized over 2.5 million live animal experiments in 2000 (including 1.6 million mice, 124,000 birds and 3,700 primates). Millions of animals are being used to test products ranging from shampoo to new cancer drugs. British law requires that any new drug must be tested on at least two different species of live mammal. One must be a large non-rodent. Almost every medical treatment you use has been tested on animals.

Key ideas

Instrumental value: the value of things as *means* to further some other ends; for example, certain fruits have instrumental value for bats who feed on them.

Intrinsic value: the value of things as *ends in themselves* regardless of whether they are also useful as means to other ends.

Key fact

An area of forest equal to twenty football pitches is lost every minute! People destroy forests because, for them, the benefits seem to outweigh the costs. But long-term costs include an increase in atmospheric carbon dioxide concentration (carbon dioxide is the major contributor to the greenhouse effect), depletion of water supplies, soil erosion, silting of water courses and lakes, extinction of species (forests contain more than half of all species on our planet) and desertification.

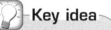

Key idea

Genesis has been interpreted to support the view that humans have a God-given right to control nature.

'Knowledge is power'

The idea that the earth is ours to be exploited has been an enormously influential idea in the contemporary world. Its roots are often located in what is known as the 'scientific approach' that proved so successful in the seventeenth century. First applied to astronomy and physics, it was then extended to everything – including human behaviour, human society and human consciousness.

The British philosopher Francis Bacon (1561–1626), sometimes called 'the father of modern science', was the main instigator of this scientific approach. He argued that the only knowledge of importance to man was empirically rooted in the natural world and that a clear system of scientific inquiry would assure human 'progress' and mastery over the world. Bacon was the originator of the expression 'Knowledge is power'.

Web quest

1 Assess different approaches to the environment in the light of the following discussion stimuli by visiting www.heinemann.co.uk/hotlinks and clicking on this section.

   a What Chief Seattle really said
   b His Holiness the Dalai Lama
   c *Walden* by William Thoreau
   d Arctic ozone layer appears!
   e Kofi Annan's astonishing facts!

2 Write a report on different approaches to environmental ethics in the light of these findings.

Human-centred (anthropocentric) environmentalism

In this pursuit of power – especially since the Industrial Revolution in the eighteenth century – 'progress' has meant that the Earth's natural resources and its non-human inhabitants are being exploited for human advancement. This is an anthropocentric or human-centred approach to the environment.

The anthropocentric approach gained impetus with the emergence of capitalism in the eighteenth century with great emphasis placed on the individual. Human behaviour is seen as flowing from individuals pursuing their interests. The problem of ethical concern is working out how it could ever be sensible for an individual to act in what might appear to be an interest other than his or her own.

Many environmental ethicists argue that the historical roots of the environmental crisis we face today are to be found in the way that successive generations have interpreted the creation story in the book of Genesis, as God giving humankind absolute dominion and supremacy over the natural world.

This view holds that God has made all things specifically for the sake of humans and that the value of non-human things in nature is merely instrumental. The book of Genesis (1: 26, 28) says that 'man' can 'subdue' other life forms:

'Then God said, "And now we will make human beings; they will be like us and resemble us. They will have power over the fish, the birds, and all the animals, domestic and wild, large and small" ... [He] blessed them, and said, "Have many children, so that your descendants will live over the earth and bring it under their control. I am putting you in charge of the fish, the birds, and all the wild animals."'

According to this interpretation, only human beings have intrinsic value, or, a significantly greater amount of intrinsic value than non-human things. The protection or promotion of human interests at the expense of non-human entities is, therefore, deemed ethical. Only human beings are morally significant persons and have a direct moral standing; we need only be careful in our dealings with the environment because our actions may have an impact, sooner or later, upon ourselves. In this interpretation of Genesis, all environmental responsibility is derived from human interests alone.

St Thomas Aquinas

In the thirteenth century, St Thomas Aquinas in *Summa Contra Gentiles* (c. 1260) argued that 'through being cruel to animals one becomes cruel to human beings ... injury to an animal leads to the temporal hurt of man.' Generally, anthropocentric positions like this find it problematic to articulate what is wrong with the cruel treatment of non-human animals, except to the extent that such treatment may lead to bad consequences for human beings.

Immanuel Kant

In the eighteenth century Immanuel Kant, in 'Duties to Animals and Spirits' (*Lectures on Ethics*, 1770), suggested that cruelty towards a dog might encourage a person to develop a character that would be desensitized to cruelty towards humans. From this standpoint, cruelty towards non-human animals would be instrumentally, rather than intrinsically, wrong.

Chernobyl

In our obsession with 'progress' and in our pursuit of power and energy, we are destroying life on Earth, including human life. We have only to look at one very recent environmental catastrophe to see the tragic consequences of this approach.

In Chernobyl in 1986, a nuclear reactor exploded, putting 160 tons of radioactive ash into the air that swept across the land, poisoning 25 per cent of the population and 25 per cent of the land and water of Belarus. Nearly twenty years after the explosive catastrophe, the awful legacy of the radiation is the thousands of people born with deformities and diseases and a dangerous build-up of radiation in food and water.

Hot tip

Examination questions sometimes ask for an assessment of whether (a) religious ideas have a contribution to make in finding a solution to modern environmental problems, or (b) are an obstacle to ethical treatment of the environment. In terms of assessing the Christian religion, the Genesis account of creation and subsequent interpretations of it are key areas of analysis.

Key fact

Surface temperature measurements recorded daily at hundreds of locations for more than 100 years indicate that the Earth's surface has warmed by about one degree Fahrenheit in the past century. This warming has been particularly strong since the 1980s and has been accompanied by retreating glaciers, thinning arctic ice, rising sea levels, lengthening of growing seasons for some, and earlier arrival of migratory birds.

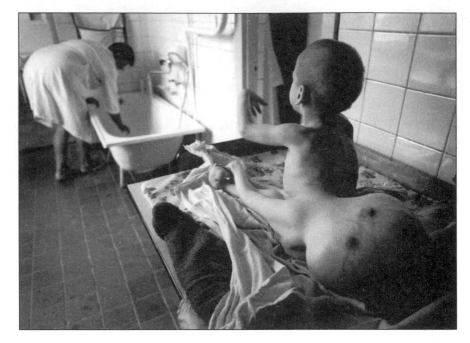

This radiation damages thousands of lives in countless ways. Now the new generation bears the legacy: a bewildering and horrifying array of defects: deformed babies, brain damaged infants, genetic damage, physiological, neurological and psychological damage. They carry the malevolent seeds of Chernobyl that will be passed on to the next generation and again to the next, and the next, and the next.

Web quest

For information about two charities that work to alleviate the suffering of the victims of the world's worst nuclear accident, The Chernobyl Children's Project and Chernobyl Children Lifeline, and about the link between nuclear power and nuclear weapons visit www.heinemann.co.uk/hotlinks and click on this section.

Think it through

After reading about Chernobyl, write a report making reference to the anthropocentric approach to the environment.

Non-human rights

The emergence of environmental ethics in the 1970s posed a challenge to traditional **anthropocentrism** by:

1 questioning the assumed moral superiority of human beings to members of other species on earth

2 investigating the possibility of rational arguments for assigning intrinsic value to the natural environment and non-humans.

Peter Singer: speceism

Australian philosopher Peter Singer (b. 1946) — one of the world's most famous utilitarian philosophers — argues that the 'greatest amount of good for the greatest number' relates not just to human beings' well-being but to the well-being of non-human life forms too:

'If a being suffers, there can be no moral justification for refusing to take that suffering into consideration. No matter what the nature of the being, the principle of equality requires that its suffering be counted equally with the like suffering.'

'Equality for Animals', in *Practical Ethics* (1979)

Singer argues that many members of the scientific community are guilty of **speceism** — a **prejudice** in favour of one's own species and against other species. By posing a key question he asks that we take into account the possible suffering of animals and other **sentient** life forms:

'If possessing a higher intelligence does not entitle one human to use another for his own ends, how can it entitle humans to exploit non-humans for the same purpose?'

'Equality for Animals', in *Practical Ethics* (1979)

Web quest

Read more of Peter Singer's work by visiting www.heinemann.co.uk/hotlinks and clicking on this section.

Tom Regan and the case for animal rights

In *The Case for Animal Rights* (1984), the American philosopher Tom Regan (b. 1938) argues that each *subject of a life* is an individual who cares about his or her life — a life that has *inherent value*. This inherent value is equal among all subjects of a life, since one either *is* a subject of a life or *is not*. Inherent value does not come in degrees and it is not dependent on the individual's experiences or utility to others. Regan does not deny that experience and usefulness to others have value, but he is careful to distinguish this sort of value from the inherent value of the individual.

'What's wrong with the way animals are treated isn't the details that vary from case to case. It's the whole system. The forlornness of the veal calf is pathetic, heart-wrenching; the pulsing pain of the chimp with electrodes planted deep in her brain is repulsive; the slow, torturous death of the raccoon caught in the leg hold trap is agonizing. But what is wrong isn't the pain, isn't the suffering, isn't the deprivation. These compound what's wrong. Sometimes, often, they make it much, much worse. But they are not the fundamental wrong. The fundamental wrong is the system that allows us to view animals as our resources, here for us — to be eaten, or surgically manipulated, or exploited for sport or money. Once we accept this view of animals as our resources, the rest is as predictable as it is regrettable.'

Tom Regan, *The Case for Animal Rights* (1984)

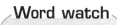

Paul Taylor and respect for nature

In his influential book *Respect for Nature* (1986), Paul Taylor (b. 1943) uses Kantian ethical theory (see Chapter 8) to come to similar conclusions. Taylor argues that an attitude of respect for nature commits us to perceiving animals and plants as having a 'good of their own', which human beings have a duty to respect. By adopting such an attitude, by regarding animals and plants as having a good of their own, we will be disposed not only to give respectful consideration to their existence, but also to see ourselves as bearing a moral relationship to them. This would mean treating all wild living things as ends in themselves rather than as mere means to human ends. It would mean engaging in practices and policies aimed at specific ways of preserving natural ecosystems and of ensuring a physical environent as beneficial as possible to as many species as possible.

By regarding animals as having a good of their own, we will be disposed not only to give respectful consideration to their existence but also to see ourselves as bearing a moral relationship to them

Discussion

Consider this quote with reference to utilitarianism, anthropocentrism and non-human rights:

'But a full-grown horse or dog is beyond comparison a more rational, as well as a more conversable, animal than an infant of a day or a week or even a month old. But suppose they were otherwise, what would it avail? The question is not can they reason? nor can they talk? but can they suffer?'

Jeremy Bentham (1748–1832)

Web quest

Visit the Environmental News Network for up-to-date environmental issues, great links, news stories and much more by going to www.heinemann.co.uk/hotlinks and clicking on this section.

Eco-centrism

Eco-centric approaches include the following.

The land ethic

In his influential essay *The Land Ethic* (1949), American scientist and philosopher Aldo Leopold (1887–1948) argued that we are on the brink of a new advancement in morality, which regulates conduct between humans and the environment – what he calls 'the land ethic': 'The land ethic simply enlarges the boundaries of the community to include soils, waters, plants, and animals, or collectively: the land.' This involves a radical shift in how humans understand themselves in relation to the environment. Originally we saw ourselves as conquerors of the land. Now we need to see ourselves as members of a community that also includes the land. Leopold argues that all species deserve consideration 'as a matter of biotic right', and offers a principle that brings into focus the broader ethical concerns of the environment:

'A thing is right when it tends to preserve the integrity, stability, and beauty of the biotic community. It is wrong when it tends otherwise.'

The Gaia Hypothesis

First put forward by James Lovelock in 1977 (and published in 2000 as *Gaia: A New Look at Life on Earth*), the **Gaia Hypothesis** maintains that our host planet is itself a huge, ruthlessly self-regulating biological organism – a living entity – and one not necessarily committed to the preservation of human life at all! So it may be very much in our interest to convince our planetary host that we are worth keeping on as environmentally conscientious house-guests.

The hypothesis claims that humanity is not indispensable in the great scheme of planetary survival and we need to stop regarding ourselves as superior to other life forms. In an effort to create a powerful image for the damage we are currently doing to our planet, James Lovelock put into currency the idea that the earth is in a sense 'alive' and that we are in the process of killing it.

Deep ecology

The Norwegian philosopher and mountaineer Arne Naess (b. 1912) coined the phrase **deep ecology** to describe deep ecological awareness. Deep ecology can be contrasted with **shallow ecology**. Shallow ecology is anthropocentric or human-centred, seeing humans as above or outside nature, as the source of all value, and ascribes only instrumental, or 'use', value to nature. Deep ecology does not separate humans – or anything else – from the natural environment. It sees the world not as a collection of isolated objects but as a network of phenomena that are fundamentally interconnected and interdependent.

When the concept of the human spirit is understood in this sense – as the mode of consciousness in which the individual feels connected to the cosmos as a whole – it becomes clear that ecological awareness is spiritual. Indeed, the idea of the

Key fact

Oil exploration has permanently harmed the ecosystems of the Arctic. The National Academy of Sciences reported that 30 years of road building, noise, and oil exploration have affected the behaviour of animals, harmed vegetation and caused erosion.

Key fact

World population (currently around 6 billion) is expected to grow to over 9 billion by 2050.

Key idea

Gaia: the earth is a goal-directed system, capable of maintaining its integrity by the operation of a complex of buffering mechanisms. We are currently pushing these mechanisms to the limit. Gaia was a Greek goddess – wife of Uranus – goddess of earth, 'the sure foundation of all that is'. Lovelock uses Gaia to suggest that our current attitudes to the environment will lead to matricide and **deicide**.

individual being linked to the cosmos is expressed in the Latin root of the word religion, *religare* (to bind strongly), as well as the Sanskrit *yoga*, which means 'union'.

Deep ecology recognizes the intrinsic value of all living beings and views human beings as just one particular strand in the web of life. The flourishing of human and non-human life on Earth has intrinsic value. The value of non-human life forms is independent of the usefulness these may have for narrow human purposes.

Discussion

Suppose that putting out natural fires, culling certain animals or destroying some individual members of overpopulated indigenous species is necessary for the protection of the integrity of a certain ecosystem. Will these actions be morally permissible?

Think it through

Eco-centric attitudes have been criticized as being biased, as the theory itself is constructed by human beings, so cannot be absolutely free from prejudice. This is not a strong criticism, but eco-centrism has also been criticized as failing to explain how conflicts are to be resolved between human-centred duties and environment-centred duties. For example, what ought to be done when human-centred duties conflict with environment-centred duties? Think of examples. Can these conflicts between environmental and human duties only be resolved on a case-by-case basis? What implications does this have on the different types of ethical theory you have studied?

Stewardship

Occasionally, apocalyptic visions of humanity acting as its own executioner — by creating a world inhospitable to life — have given impetus and urgency to the idea of stewardship. Stewardship is the idea that human beings are the custodians and trustees of creation. Our role is to act as 'stewards' to the natural world — to look after and maintain Earth for future generations. As such, we cannot escape the duty to act responsibly towards the created world. Such an attitude is popular within Judaism, Christianity and Islam today, and there are many references in the Old Testament in accordance with this view. For example:

'Your land must not be sold on a permanent basis, because you do not own it; it belongs to God, and you are like foreigners who are allowed to make use of it.'

Leviticus 25: 23

Key idea

Shallow ecology: concerned with more efficient control and management of the natural environment for the benefit of 'man', whereas the deep ecology movement recognizes that ecological balance will require profound changes in our perception of the role of human beings in the planetary ecosystem.

Key idea

Deep ecology: rooted in an intuitive awareness of the oneness of all life, the interdependence of its multiple manifestations and its cycles of change and transformation.

Key fact

It takes 1000 tonnes of water to produce one tonne of wheat. But the world's water supplies are dwindling. It is estimated that by 2025, the world could see annual losses of up to 350 million tonnes of food (slightly more than the entire USA annual grain crop) from lack of fresh water.

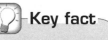

'Even birds and animals have much they could teach you; ask the creatures of earth and sea for their wisdom. All of them know that the Lord's hand made them. It is God who directs the lives of his creatures; everyone's life is in his power.'

Job 12: 7—10

Followers of the world religions all bear witness to the mystery and beauty of the natural world as evidence that the Earth has been created. In the mysterious cycles and patterns of the seasons, in the enormous variety of life, and in the intricate balance of the ecosystem, they see meaning, purpose and interconnectedness. In ordinary life we are not usually aware of this unity and we divide the world into separate objects and events. It is of course useful that our minds do this, but it is an illusion. In reality the universe is one. The principle of unity is apparent to the physicist who explores reality at the atomic level and it becomes even more apparent as she/he goes down into the realm of subatomic particles.

Treat the Earth well – it was not given to us by our fathers but lent to us by our children (Kenyan proverb)

Think it through

Compare and contrast anthropocentric environmentalism, non-human rights, eco-centric and religious attitudes to the environment. Consider which of these approaches focuses on *instrumental* value and which focuses on *intrinsic* value.

Principles versus profits

In 1997, in Japan, the Kyoto Conference on Climate Change took place to cut pollution and fight global warming. The developed countries agreed to specific targets for cutting their emissions of greenhouse gases. The USA proposed just to stabilize emissions and not cut them at all, while the European Union called for a fifteen per cent cut.

In March 2001, USA president George W. Bush (a former Texan oilman) shocked the world when he said that he opposed the Kyoto Protocol. The USA is the most powerful and influential country in the world and, incidentally, the worst polluter. The USA has four per cent of the world's population, yet emits twenty-one per cent of the world's carbon dioxide, just one of many greenhouse gases.

Key fact

When running for election, Bush raised more money than any other candidate in history – 80 per cent from corporations or individuals representing the oil and gas industry (for example, Esso gave $1.376 million!), the car industry, agribusiness, the energy and property industry, and the oil industry, which stands to lose most if the Kyoto protocol goes ahead.

Think it through

1 Discuss this statement: 'President George W. Bush is pursuing a utilitarian approach (the greatest good for the greatest number) in his attitude to the environment.' But whose greatest good?

2 Consider whether Jeremy Bentham's hedonic calculus (see p. 89) could be used to calculate the right levels of use of natural resources by richer nations.

In response to Bush's decision to abandon Kyoto, Peter Singer, in *One World* (2002), wrote:

'We should be developing the ethical foundations of the coming era of a single world community. One great obstacle hinders further progress in this direction. It has to be said, in cool but plain language, that in recent years the effort to build a global community has been hampered by the repeated failure of the USA to play its part. Despite being the single largest polluter of the world's atmosphere, and on a per capita basis the most profligate of the major nations, the USA (along with Australia) has refused to join the 178 states that have accepted the Kyoto Protocol. When the world's most powerful state wraps itself in what – until September 11 – it took to be the security of its military might and refuses to give up any of its own rights and privileges for the sake of the common good, even when others are giving up their rights and privileges, the prospect of finding solutions to global problems are dimmed.'

❛ Quotable quote

'No one expected the Kyoto climate summit to achieve miracles, but the outcome confirmed our worst fears, namely that governments – especially the USA – continue to pander to industry at the expense of the environment.'

Friends of the Earth (2003)
❜

Web quest

Read about the Kyoto protocol, global warming, George Bush and the environment by visiting www.heinemann.co.uk/hotlinks and clicking on this section.

Think it through

1 Consider whether human beings have ethical obligations towards non-humans.

   a If we do, then what do you think is the precise nature of, and basis for, these obligations?

   b Do these obligations vary between different kinds of non-human entities (for example, living and non-living things; individual organisms and species)?

   c Do these obligations vary according to context (for example, between urban and wilderness areas)?

2 If animals have rights, what difficulties arise in claiming that we are entitled to eat non-human animals (but not, presumably, human beings, even if through some accident they are at a similar mental level to the animals we do eat)?

3 Explain how ethical arguments for vegetarianism can (a) be based on the view that we violate the rights of animals when we kill them for our food, and (b) on the more utilitarian grounds that, in raising them for our food, we cause them more suffering than we gain by eating their flesh.

4 Ought governments to be environmentally responsible for the sake of future generations? Do future generations of people have rights any more than a dead person can have rights?

5 Can we justify using up fossil fuels or clearing tropical rainforests for farming so that we gain now when the quality of life of people living in these areas or of unborn generations in the future is impoverished? Is it right to build a dam that will supply water to thousands of people but will destroy the habitat of many plants and animals?

6 Some philosophers have argued that animals have no rights because rights can only exist between *people* who can make moral claims on each other. We have moral capabilities that animals do not have; that is, understanding of free will and moral law. Therefore, animals cannot have rights. In his book *Animal Rights and Wrongs* (2000) the philosopher Roger Scruton argues that animals are non-moral beings because they do not possess rationality and self-consciousness. They are incapable of fulfilling moral responsibility or duty – prerequisites for members of a moral community. What do you think?

Summary

At present, environmental ethics is in the process of evolution, with various strands emerging. Some theorists remain human-centred, some animal-centred, others promote a life-centred ecological holism. They range from utilitarian claims that humans need a healthy environment and so should take care of it, to discussions about the rights of rocks. Whatever approach is accepted, the situation is deemed critical and environmental ethicists ask that governments take environmental issues seriously (particularly the most powerful nations like the USA and China), act responsibly, and adopt far-reaching measures now – before it is too late.

Review

Environmental ethics: examines the moral basis of environmental responsibility and how far this responsibility extends.

Instrumental value: the value of things as *means* to further some other ends.

Intrinsic value: the value of things as *ends in themselves* regardless of whether they are also useful as means to other ends.

Anthropocentric or human-centred approach: all environmental responsibility is derived from human interests alone. Only human beings are morally significant persons and have a direct moral standing.

Non-human rights: environmental responsibility derives from the interests of all morally significant persons, including both humans *and* non-humans.

Eco-centrism: the environment has its own inherent worth and so deserves direct moral consideration. Views include the land ethic, the Gaia Hypothesis and deep ecology.

Stewardship: human beings are the custodians and trustees of creation and as such, cannot escape the duty to act responsibly towards the created world.

Exam questions

1 (a) Describe the nature of the ethical system of *one* religion you have studied. (33 marks)

   (b) Examine the claim that religious ethics are an obstacle to ethical treatment of the environment. (17 marks) (OCR, June 2002)

2 (a) Explain a religious perspective on environmental issues with particular reference to the issue of pollution. (20 marks)

   (b) 'Religion is better than utilitarianism as a guide to making decisions on environmental issues.' Explain and assess this claim. (20 marks) (AQA, June 2001)

15 War and peace

Objectives

In this chapter you will explore whether it is ever right to go to war by looking at:

- the consequences of **militarism** and war
- theories of ethical and religious pacifism and its strengths and weaknesses
- principles of **just war theory** – its application particularly to weapons of mass destruction
- the meaning and implications of '**conscientious objection**'
- the strengths and weaknesses of just war theory
- the meanings of holy war – **jihad** – in the Islamic tradition.

❝ ═ Quotable quote ═

'In starting and waging a war, it is not right that matters but victory.'

Adolf Hitler, quoted in William Shirer's *The Rise and Fall of the Third Reich* (1991)

❞

Introduction

War can be defined as armed hostilities between peoples. War occurs between different nations, between different parties within a nation, as in a civil war, and between one small group and a state, as in a guerrilla war. The supposed aim of war is for one group to win by inflicting maximum damage on the other with minimum damage to itself, an aim only modified when there is a need to preserve some of the enemy as slaves or peasant workers. However, war might also be viewed simply as a baffling process of **reciprocal** destruction.

At one time, individuals like the Greek leader Alexander and the Egyptian King Rameses II were given the title 'the Great' for slaughtering human beings on the battlefield. Today, few would view the killing of vast numbers of non-combatants during wartime as anything other than a crime against humanity. While war can inspire acts of courage and self-sacrifice, it can also destroy conscience and any sense of moral responsibility. Rape is commonplace in warfare: an estimated 20,000 Muslim girls and women were raped during the religiously motivated atrocities in Bosnia in the former Yugoslavia. This was mainly during an organized Serbian programme of cultural **genocide**. One goal was to make the women pregnant and raise their children as Serbs.

A dirty business!

Although war is often glamourized on TV and in films, in reality it is a dirty business. When the Americans waged war in Vietnam in the 1960s their orders were to 'incapacitate' as many civilians as possible and by so doing put intolerable pressure on hospital and health facilities. It takes time, resources and energy to attend to a Vietnamese child with napalm burns.

The Americans dropped napalm bombs on Vietnamese civilians to incapacitate as well as incinerate

Quotable quote

'Perhaps the most gruesome legacy of Agent Orange is to be found in a locked room in Tu Du Obstetrical and Gynaecological Hospital in Saigon. Here the walls are lined with jars containing aborted and full-term foetuses.'

Hugh Warwick, 'The Poisoning of Vietnam', *The Ecologist* (1998)

Many have questioned, too, the ethics of the great bombing raids of World War II, when British and American bombers rained down fire and destruction on millions of German women and children, and the use by the Americans of atomic bombs in Japan in 1945 (see p. 91).

'Enemies'

Enemies are defined by governments and can constantly change. At the beginning of World War II, the Soviet Union was the enemy of Britain, as they had signed a pact with Hitler to carve up Poland between them. In 1941, however, Germany invaded Russia, and the Soviet Union became Britain's ally. After the war, relations between East and West deteriorated and the Soviet Union once again became an enemy. Then, after the collapse of communism and the break-up of the Soviet Union in the early 1990s, the Russians once more became our friends. Britain and the USA found a new enemy in the Iraqi President Saddam Hussein, although before the invasion of Kuwait by Iraq in 1991, he was regarded as a friend by the British and USA governments, who even supplied him with the means to make weapons of mass destruction. Ironically, in 2003 we went to war with Iraq to supposedly destroy Saddam's weapons.

The first casualty of war is the truth!

It is often said that 'The first casualty of war is the truth' and at the opening of the 1991 Gulf War, a Kuwaiti princess appeared on TV to tell the world how, when Iraqi troops had taken over a hospital in Kuwait, they had disconnected the life-support machines for premature babies. This was a lie.

Quotable quote

'Television is a window on war and also a weapon of war.'

Jon Snow, Channel 4 presenter (2003)

At the beginning of World War I, it was reported that when the Germans invaded Belgium they had raped Belgian nuns and forced them to ring church bells to celebrate the German victory. Millions of young men volunteered to kill Germans on the strength of such reports. It was only after the war that they found out that these reports were untrue, a case of 'Chinese whispers' starting with a newspaper report that the Germans had forced a priest to ring church bells.

Key fact

American policy in Vietnam turned a once-pristine habitat to an almost apocalyptic state following the war. Military technologies included 'chemical deforestation techniques which destroyed millions of acres of forest, but it was only later that the carcinogenic effects on humans began to emerge.

Web quest

For some excellent articles on modern warfare and articles on the media, propaganda and war visit www.heinemann.co.uk/hotlinks and click on this section.

Militarism

The glorification of war and heroic self-sacrifice in battle are the hallmarks of militarism – defined as 'the undue prevalence of the military spirit in society'. What are the *values* of militarism?

Special forces in Russia

- Authoritarianism: blind obedience to leaders. Under authoritarian regimes, farmers and fishermen are conscripted or press-ganged into service and forced to kill complete strangers, with whom they have no quarrel, and risk death or mutilation in the process: 'theirs not to reason why, theirs but to do and die' (Tennyson, *The Charge of the Light Brigade*, 1880). In the modern world, authoritarian regimes are more sophisticated, relying on propaganda and fear to programme and control their populations.

- Elitism: militarism depends on a hierarchy of authority, a chain of command that creates sharp divisions in the class system: officers and men, the gentry and the working classes, are separated in order to keep the divide between the leaders and the led. The power of the elite is reinforced by its ownership of land and industry, and by its control of the army and the police.

- Dehumanization: or the brutalizing of feeling. In order to be efficient killing machines, soldiers are trained to suppress their feelings about what they are doing and so they become dehumanized. In turn, the soldiers of the enemy are also dehumanized, making it easier to kill them without compunction. Soldiers in so-called 'special forces' units are subject to shockingly brutal training regimes.

Word watch

authoritarianism
elitism
dehumanization

'He who joyfully marches to music in rank and file has already earned my contempt. He has been given a large brain by mistake, since for him the spinal cord would fully suffice. This disgrace to civilization should be done away with at once. It is my conviction that killing under the cloak of war is nothing but an act of murder.'

Albert Einstein (1879–1955)

Pacifism

- A **pacifist** is a person who is opposed to war and violence. Pacifists believe that it is wrong to harm or kill others and that if killing is wrong, then war must be wrong, as war is basically a matter of killing.

- Many people argue that war is sometimes necessary to protect our family and fellow-citizens, or to defend our ideas of freedom, justice and peace. But pacifists ask how war can establish truth; how war can protect peace; how killing can preserve freedom; how justice is preserved by the evil that is war. Pacifists are often asked, 'What would you have done about Hitler?' They reply that it is necessary to resist evil by non-violent means, always retaining a reverence for life. For if we abhor Hitler because he was a mass-murderer, how can it be right for us to murder women and children in bombing raids in order to defeat him?

- Pacifists believe that war is inhumane, impractical, immoral, unjust and wasteful. Instead of violence they offer non-violence, understood not just as the avoidance of violence, but as the search for positive ways of solving conflicts and achieving lasting peace. A pacifist alternative to the politics of power is to create conditions for social justice, enabling the poor to free themselves from the oppression of moneylenders and landlords; to devote resources to meeting human needs instead of the stockpiling of weapons of mass destruction; to build bridges between communities creating trust and respect, and to develop non-violent strategies for resolving conflicts.

- Pacifists sometimes engage in educational work to spread their ideas; they take part in anti-war demonstrations; they may refuse to pay taxes to buy armaments; or they may practise other forms of civil disobedience to improve society and remove the causes of war – repression, exploitation, injustice. Pacifists try to break the vicious cycle of selfishness, greed and violence that breeds war and revenge. To do this they say we must start by examining our own responsibility for the violence that exists in the world.

But how can pacifism be justified during times of mass deportations, mass exterminations or ruthless foreign domination? If my family is threatened by invading troops and I say to those troops, 'I forgive you for what you are about to do,' and then just walk away, leaving my family to rape, butchery or slavery, is this a display not of pacifism but of cowardice? Reinhold Niebuhr (1892–1971), a

Key fact

During times of conflict, pacifists may become conscientious objectors, join the ambulance service or fire service, or work as hospital porters. Many Quakers (members of the Society of Friends) – in both world wars – joined the ambulance service and cared for the wounded and dying on the battlefield, a job that required as much courage as any soldier's. Conscientious objectors were often treated very badly during war and were imprisoned or forced to do hard manual labour.

Key idea

Conscientious objectors believe that true and lasting security cannot be based on militarism. Killing other people – or preparing for it – does not create protection against real threats like environmental problems or poverty. More likely, war and the arms trade make these problems far worse, wasting billions and billions of pounds and redirecting human resources away from the real issues.

Hot tip

Think of conflict in the world today and apply pacifist and just war principles to evaluate the moral acceptability of going to war to resolve these disputes. See the websites given in this chapter to improve your knowledge of contemporary areas of conflict.

German-American pastor, argued that the usual individual moral rules that prevent us from killing each other do not apply to states – which have a moral responsibility to protect collective national interests. Pacifists expect that 'love will conquer all', but some people argue that, ultimately, people have a moral responsibility to act – even to go to war – to ensure that good overcomes evil.

Think it through

What are the problems if people (a) stand up to, and (b) do not stand up to an aggressor with military force? Try to refer to different ethical approaches in your answer, for example, you can try to apply Kant's ideas as expressed in *Groundwork to the Metaphysic of Morals* (1785):

'Humanity is itself a dignity; for a man cannot be used merely as a means by any man ... but must always be used at the same time as an end.'

Conscientious objectors

- Conscientious objectors: people who, by reason of religious or ethical belief, are 'conscientiously opposed to participation in war in any form'. These people may be discharged from military service. They are exempt from military service in the event of a draft. If called up, they may perform alternative services as civilians.

- Non-combatant conscientious objectors: people who, by reason of religious or ethical belief, are conscientiously opposed to killing in war in any form, but who do not object to performing non-combatant duties – such as being a medic – in the armed forces. These people are reassigned to non-combatant duties in the armed forces or, in the event of a draft, are trained without weapons and assigned to non-combatant service.

- Conscientious objectors to paying for war: people whose consciences forbid them to pay the military portion of their taxes because of ethical and religious beliefs. Many impoverish themselves by living below taxable levels; others face court appearances, property loss, and in some cases, imprisonment as a result of war tax resistance.

- Selective objectors: people whose consciences do not permit them to participate in what they believe to be an 'unjust' war, but that do permit them to participate in what they believe to be a 'just' war.

Web quest

Use the *Internet Encyclopedia of Philosophy* to find out about deontological pacifism, consequentialist pacifism and the just war theory, and visit Third World Traveller to improve your understanding of the militarization of space, state-funded terrorism and genocide by going to www.heinemann.co.uk/hotlinks and clicking on this section.

Think it through

1 What reasons might a pacifist give for saying that war is (a) inhumane, (b) impractical, (c) immoral, (d) unjust, and (e) wasteful?

2 Consider whether pacifism is an irresponsible pipe dream – there will always be occasions when wars have to be fought.

3 On what basis could one assert that it is morally obligatory to use violence in order to defend the weak?

Jesus

Christian pacifism has its roots in the life and teaching of Jesus. Though the Old Testament often saw God as the 'Lord of armies', directing the wars of Israel, Jesus identified himself with another strand of Old Testament thinking, found in the vision of the prophet Zechariah, of a Messiah who would banish chariots and war-horses and 'speak peaceably to every nation'. Jesus took the part of the suffering servant of Isaiah, who would redeem humanity by his own undeserved suffering. At a time when Israel was seething with revolt against Rome, Jesus took care not to identify himself with the revolutionary Zealots and foresaw that the end of armed rebellion would be destruction rather than liberation: that when it came, in 66 CE, the rebellion would 'not leave you one stone standing on another'. Jerusalem was destroyed, and after another rebellion, Israel ceased to exist. Jesus' love was an active benevolence cutting across barriers of class, race and nation. In the Sermon on the Mount (Matthew 5–7), he taught his followers to love their enemies, to forgive those who had wronged them, and to respond to violence with non-violence, returning good for evil.

Quotable quotes

'Happy are those who work for peace; God will call them his children!'

Jesus, St Matthew's Gospel 5: 9

'Violence is a lie … Violence destroys what it claims to defend: the dignity, the life, the freedom of human beings. Violence is a crime against humanity, for it destroys the very fabric of society.'

Pope John Paul II (b. 1920)

'Peace is not the absence of war; it is a virtue; a state of mind; a disposition for benevolence; confidence; and justice.'

Baruch Spinoza (1632–1677)

Holy war

Is the idea of 'a **holy war**' a contradiction? Killing other human beings and causing wholesale destruction seems to be a long way from holiness. But religion and war have gone hand in hand for a long time. Armies go into battle believing that 'God is on our side'. For a war to be a 'holy war', religion has to be the driving force. A 'holy war' has:

1 the achievement of a religious goal

2 authorization by a religious leader

3 a spiritual reward for those who take part.

The philosopher Francis Bacon (1561–1626) argued that there were five causes for holy war (although he wrote in a Christian context, the categories could apply to other faiths): (a) to spread the faith, (b) to retrieve countries that were once Christian, (c) to rescue Christians in countries that were once Christian from 'the servitude of infidels', (d) to recover consecrated places that are presently 'profaned', and (e) to avenge blasphemous acts, or cruelties and killings of Christians.

The Crusades

The great series of Western holy wars were the Crusades (1095–1291 CE). The aim was to capture the sacred places in the Holy Land from the Muslims who lived there, so they were intended as wars to right wrongs done against Christianity. The first Crusade captured Jerusalem after bitter fighting; the residents were subjected to brutal atrocities and slaughter by the Christian invaders. The Crusades were started by Pope Urban II in 1095 with the words:

'Let this be your war-cry in combat, because this word is given to you by God. When an armed attack is made upon the enemy, let this one cry be raised by all the soldiers of God: "It is the will of God! It is the will of God!"'

Key questions

1 Is it ever right to go to war?

2 When is it right to wage war?

3 What is the moral way to conduct a war?

Islam and jihad

One of the responsibilities of a practising Muslim is jihad, 'striving' (to serve Allah), usually translated in the West as 'holy war', which Muslims agree is a fair translation. All Muslims practise jihad to the best of their ability, especially coming to the aid of any fellow-Muslim attacked for practising Islam. Jihad, the defence of Islam, is regarded as just as much a primary duty of all sincere Muslims as prayer and fasting.

In the early years of the Islamic era, jihad was interpreted as the armed struggle against pagans and non-believers, and the followers of Muhammad swept out of Arabia to create an empire that eventually stretched from Spain to Indonesia. The fear created in Europe by the early successes of the armies of Islam still remains, and, consequently, many view Islam as a religion of war and oppression, holding the Muslims responsible for the brutalities of the much later Crusades. However, Western propaganda against Islam – **Islamophobia** – is partly an attempt to divert attention away from the crimes of the Western powers in their treatment of Muslims during the Crusades, when many atrocities were committed by 'Christian' armies.

The teaching of jihad in Islam is based on the teachings of the Qur'an – God's revelation. The study of the Qur'an proceeds from the outer literal meaning to the inner spiritual meaning of the revelation. The Qur'an teaches that the reason for our appearance in this world is to gain total knowledge of things, to become perfected as the 'universal man'. The purpose of the creation is for God to come to know himself through the perfect instrument of knowledge, which is the 'universal man'. God wished to know himself, to see his qualities – power, mercy, intelligence, beauty – reflected in the creation, so he created human beings as the instrument of his self-knowledge. Thus through struggle (jihad) we become a mirror reflecting the divine names and qualities, enabling God to fulfil the purpose of his creation. The inner meaning of the holy war is thus the struggle with immorality.

> ## Think it through
>
> Consider how extremist Muslims have hijacked the teaching of jihad to justify global terrorism as part of a 'crusade' against corrupt capitalist societies.

The just war theory

Why, then, throughout history, have so-called Christians – up to the present day with President George Bush and Prime Minister Tony Blair – gone to war to kill, maim and destroy other human beings? The Early Church took the teachings of Jesus literally and opposed violence and killing for any purpose, but as the Church gradually became more involved in the affairs of state, its teachings began to change. When, in 324 CE, the emperor Constantine made Christianity the state religion of the Roman Empire, the Church turned from pacifism and accepted the use of armed force by the state as justifiable. In time the doctrine of the just war developed.

Is it ever permissible for a Christian to kill?

Word watch

proportionality

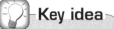

Key idea

The just war theory is not intended to justify wars but to prevent them by showing that going to war except in certain limited circumstances is wrong, thus motivating states to find other ways of resolving conflicts.

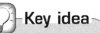

Key idea

The just war theory attempts to reconcile three things:

1 taking human life is wrong

2 states have a duty to defend their citizens and defend justice

3 protecting innocent human life and defending important ethical values sometimes requires willingness to use force and violence.

The Christian just war theory attempts to answer the questions 'When is it permissible to wage war?' (**jus in bello**) and 'What are the limitations on the ways war is waged?' (**jus ad bellum**). For a war to be 'just', three conditions were laid down by St Thomas Aquinas (1224–74): right authority, just cause, and just intention; and later Francisco de Vitoria (1548–1617) and Francisco Suarez (1548–1617) laid down three more conditions – **proportionality** in the conduct of the war, only entering the war as a last resort, and only fighting if there is a reasonable chance of success.

1 The war must be declared by a legal, recognized authority: for example, a government. During most of the time the just war theory has operated, 'declaration by a legitimate authority' has meant declaration by a king or sovereign head of state, or a government.

2 The cause of the war must be just: the war must be fought with the intention to establish good or correct evil. Its purpose must be to promote peace. The war must be carried out with the intention that good shall result rather than evil. A war cannot be just if it is waged with a wrong intention, such as the desire to secure vengeance or to satisfy lust for domination.

3 The war must be the last resort: a state should only go to war *after* all diplomatic negotiations have been tried and have failed. War must only be declared as a last resort. No war is justified if there is *any* chance of resolving the conflict by non-violent means such as discussion, negotiation, the employment of economic sanctions, or other means short of military action.

4 The war must be waged on the basis of the principle of proportionality: the relationship between ends and means must be proportionate; that is, you must use only enough force to achieve your goals, not more. There cannot be excessive destruction for the sake of even small desirable ends. The good to be accomplished must outweigh the otherwise evil acts that will be exercised in bringing about the good end.

5 The war must have a reasonable chance of success: unless there is a reasonable chance that the objective for waging war can be achieved, it is immoral to incur the damage and destruction that will result.

6 Only sufficient force must be used: civilians must not be involved. Warfare must be waged with as much moderation as possible, and so indiscriminate bombing, torture, rape, looting and massacres are prohibited. Care must be taken to see that prisoners of war and people not involved in military activities are not killed. This condition refers not only to the actual war itself but also to the terms of settlement at the end of the war – terms that must include justice rather than vengeance.

Think it through

1 Consider at what point the proportion between military and non-combatant status tips. Is a hospital of 300 patients a legitimate target of war? What if there are two soldiers (uninjured) in the hospital? A platoon? A battalion in full battle gear? A company command post based in the hospital?

2 Consider the idea that some of the causes of war are inside ourselves and some are outside ourselves. Write down what these different causes may be.

3 Consider, which of the following are innocent under the just war theory: (a) politicians who direct wars, (b) civilians who approve of the war but do not take part, (c) arms manufacturers who have no direct involvement in the war but have sold the weapons, (d) medics who heal the combatants, (e) journalists who write propaganda, and (f) munitions workers who are forced to make bombs but who disagree with the war.

4 Ali Ismael Abbas, aged 12 (see photo on p. 5), suffered 60% burns, the loss of both arms and 16 members of his family, including his pregnant mother.

5 Consider whether it is morally just to launch a pre-emptive strike on suspicion that the enemy are about to attack you.

6 Consider whether it is just for a country to go to war with another sovereign state without the backing of international support like the United Nations.

Word watch

pre-emptive strike

Just war and weapons of mass destruction

If we apply the 'just war' theory to the question of whether it is morally justifiable to use nuclear, biological or chemical weapons, we find that while some conditions may be met, other conditions are certainly not. Critics maintain that the just war theory may have applied in the pre-nuclear world, but modern weapons of mass destruction make a nonsense of the theory. There would be no justice afterwards – children (if there were any survivors!) would be born with genetic defects for generations to come and innocent civilians would be killed.

For an analysis of utilitarianism and the atomic bombing of Hiroshima in 1945 see p 91.

Quotable quote

'Nuclear weapons have changed everything, except our modes of thought.'

Albert Einstein (1879–1955)

Against this thesis may be set the numerous arguments supporting the tactical use of nuclear weapons in limited stages of war. In the face of complete lack of experience of such wars, it is impossible to predict consequences with certainty. Even here there are important grades of activity. It is clearly better to destroy military bases than centres of civilian population. It is clearly better to build nuclear shelters, if we may assume that they may give some degree of protection, than to pursue a policy that deliberately solves the problem of emergency food supply by ensuring that 50 per cent of the population will not survive an initial

Word watch

tactical nuclear weapons

Key question

In what way does the just war theory differ from pacifism?

attack. Whatever we may think necessary in an extreme situation, there can be no doubt that any policy that results in the destruction of people is abhorrent.

Problems with the just war theory

- Some philosophers argue that to say war is sometimes *necessary* denies choice, because ethics demands free choice and yet necessity denies choice. There may be reasons for waging war but they can never be *just* reasons, as justice is defined by applying fairness and ensuring equality on both sides, which war cannot do.
- The conduct of soldiers in the heat of war is difficult to control – to expect men who have been ordered to kill, to keep their heads and hearts free of hatred towards the 'enemy' is an almost impossible task.
- It is not always clear who is an innocent bystander in modern warfare. At the beginning of the World War II. German submarines torpedoed unarmed British merchant ships bringing food to Britain – fair targets? Are people forced to work in a munitions factory a fair target?
- An argument against the just war theory is that it sets such high moral standards that no state can follow them; *any* breach of the conditions lays the state open to the sort of challenge it purports to be fighting against. In modern warfare it is civilians who tend to suffer most (see pp. 5, 164), and despite military claims of 'collateral damage' or 'clinical' strikes, civilians undoubtedly get killed, violating the principles of proportionality and **discrimination**.
- Wars are caused by complex reasons and it is unrealistic to see the act of waging war in terms of a single 'just' cause.
- The outcomes (consequences) of war are very difficult to calculate. In the 1991 Gulf War, the USA and its allies blasted Iraqi vehicles with armour-piercing shells made of depleted uranium – the first time such weapons had been used in warfare. Today, parts of Iraq remain a radioactive toxic wasteland and many doctors believe that depleted uranium is responsible for a significant increase in cancer and birth defects in the region. Many researchers also suspect depleted uranium of playing a role in Gulf War Syndrome, the still-unexplained malady that has plagued tens of thousands of Gulf War veterans. Depleted uranium remains radioactive for about 4.5 billion years.

Word watch

Gulf War Syndrome

Think it through

1 'You are just as dead if killed by a bullet as you are from being vaporized by a 5 megaton nuclear blast.' Does this fact prove that the moral issues concerning nuclear warfare are no different from those concerning conventional warfare?

2 Consider whether the term *just war* is outdated.

3 Consider whether it could ever be morally justifiable to use nuclear, biological or chemical weapons.

Key fact: The United Nations

Since the end of World War II in 1945, it has generally been considered that the appropriate authority for going to war should be the United Nations, rather than individual states. United Nations member states are bound by Article 2.4 of the UN Charter, which says that 'all members shall refrain in their international relations from the threat or use of force'. While the UN does not declare war, there have been several recent cases of UN actions that can be regarded as 'lawful authorization'; for example, there were UN resolutions to use force in Bosnia in 1998. Some people have argued that because the UN is now the highest international authority in the world, only a war authorized by the UN is a potentially just war. For example, they say that the USA and the UK could not claim that their pre-emptive attack on Iraq in 2003 was ethically acceptable as a just war because they had not obtained a *specific* UN resolution to authorize it.

Think it through

A war is only a just war if it is waged from the right motives or 'good intentions'. Look at the following and decide which are 'bad intentions' and which are 'good intentions': (a) creating, restoring or keeping a just peace, (b) revenge, (c) preserving or creating colonial power, (d) assisting the innocent, (e) personal or national glory, (f) grabbing land, oil or goods, or enslaving people, and (g) demonstrating the power of a state by using 'shock and awe' tactics.

Web quest

Many aid agencies argue that, given the terrible poverty that exists in the modern world, wars are seldom 'just wars' – war causes poverty and diverts essential resources away from the war on poverty. To find out more look at the War on Want website and look at the consequences of the Gulf War in 1991 by visiting www.heinemann.co.uk/hotlinks and clicking on this section.

Discussion

'*Every gun that is made, every warship launched, every rocket fired, signifies, in the final sense, a theft from those who hunger and are not fed, those who are cold and are not clothed. This world in arms is not spending money alone. It is spending the sweat of its labourers, the genius of its scientists, the hopes of its children. This is not a way of life at all in any true sense. Under the clouds of war, it is humanity hanging on a cross of iron.*'

Dwight Eisenhower (1953)

'*Men love war because it allows them to look serious; because it is the one thing that stops women from laughing at them.*'

John Fowles, *The Magus* (1966)

Review

Militarism: values include authoritarianism, elitism, dehumanization.

Pacifists: it is wrong to harm or kill others, and if killing is wrong, then war must be wrong, as war is basically a matter of killing.

Christian pacifism: rooted in the life and teaching of Jesus – to love your enemies, to forgive those who wrong you, to respond to violence with non-violence – an active benevolence cutting across barriers of class, race and nation.

The just war theory: three conditions laid down by St Thomas Aquinas – right authority, just cause and just intention – and later by Francisco de Vitoria and Francisco Suarez – proportionality in the conduct of the war, only entering the war as a last resort, and only fighting if there is a reasonable chance of success.

Jihad: striving (to serve Allah), usually translated in the West as 'holy war'. All Muslims must wage jihad, especially coming to the aid of any fellow-Muslim attacked for practising Islam. The inner and deeper meaning of jihad is the struggle with our own propensity for wrongdoing.

Exam questions

1 **(a)** Give an account of the view that conscience is 'the voice of God'. (33 marks)

   (b) On what grounds might conscientious objectors defend their attitude to war? (17 marks) (OCR, June 2001)

2 **(a)** Examine the key features of the 'just war theory'. (10 marks)

   (b) Outline what is meant by pacifism. To what extent does this conflict with the just war theory? (10 marks) (EDEXCEL, June 2001)

3 **(a)** Describe the main features of the ethics of any one religion. (33 marks)

   (b) How justified, if at all, is religious pacifism? (17 marks) (OCR, January 2002)

Film archive

Films are a great resource. Here are just some films that are worth watching, either at home or in class. Films marked with an asterix (*) are 18 certificates (you must be eighteen or over to watch these films).

2001: A Space Odyssey (1968): the ultimate trip. (139 minutes)

All Quiet on the Western Front (1930): adapted from a novel by Erich Maria Remarque. A young soldier faces profound disillusionment in the soul-destroying horror of World War I. (131 minutes)

*Apocalypse Now** (1979): based on Joseph Conrad's novel *Heart Of Darkness*. Captain Willard is sent into the jungle with orders to find and kill Colonel Kurtz, who has set up his own army within the jungle. As Willard descends into the jungle, he slowly succumbs to the insanity surrounding him. (150 minutes)

Bowling for Columbine (2002): filmmaker Michael Moore explores of the roots of America's predilection for gun violence. (120 minutes)

Catch-22 (1970): based on the original book by Joseph Heller about an American soldier who discovers that the only way out of the army is to go mad; but if you want to get out, you are not mad! (121 minutes)

The China Syndrome (1979): the story of the cover-up of an accident at a California nuclear power plant entwines with the story of how television bends the news. (123 minutes)

Dead Man Walking (1995): the true story of a nun – Sister Helen Prejean – who tried to end the death penalty in the USA. (122 minutes)

Dr Strangelove or How I Learned to Stop Worrying and Love the Bomb (1963): USA Air Force Colonel Jack Ripper goes mad and sends his bomber wing on a mission. (93 minutes)

Duck Soup (1933): Rufus T. Firefly is named president/dictator of bankrupt Freedonia. (70 minutes)

*Full Metal Jacket** (1987): a group of soldiers develop dehumanized personalities in their training, which surfaces during their tour of duty in Vietnam. (116 minutes)

Gattaca (1997): futuristic story about genetic engineering and 'geneticism'. (101 minutes)

In the Name of the Father (1993): based on the true story of the Guildford Four – a group of Irish men wrongly jailed for the bombing of a British pub in 1974. (133 minutes)

Kandahar (2001): shot on the border of Iran and Afghanistan; a young female journalist who escaped Taliban-controlled Afghanistan must return to rescue her sister who was maimed by a landmine. (84 minutes)

Kundun (1997): the true story of the fourteenth Dalai Lama forced to flee Tibet in the face of Chinese brutality. (128 minutes)

Malcolm X (1992): true story of a man's heroic struggle for justice in racist America. (194 minutes)

Nineteen Eighty-Four (1984): from the original book by George Orwell. Given the huge advances in satellite technology, CCTV and surveillance, Orwell's vision of the future might not be so far-fetched! (110 minutes)

*One Flew Over The Cuckoo's Nest** (1975): a man sent to a mental hospital finds the head nurse more dangerous than the patients. (133 minutes)

Paths of Glory (1957): when soldiers in World War I refuse to continue with an impossible attack, their superiors decide to punish them. (87 minutes)

Platoon (1986): a young recruit in Vietnam faces a moral crisis when a sergeant orders a massacre of villagers. (120 minutes)

Rabbit-Proof Fence (2002): the true story of 'the stolen generation'. A young aboriginal girl leads her younger sister and cousin in an escape from an official government camp, in search of the rabbit-proof fence that bisects the continent and will lead them home. (94 minutes)

Romero (1989): the true story of Archbishop Romero of El Salvador who spoke out against, and was killed by, government death squads in central America in the 1980s. (105 minutes)

*Salvador** (1985): an American journalist in El Salvador chronicles the events of the 1980 military dictatorship, forming an uneasy alliance with both guerillas in the countryside, who want him to get pictures out to the USA press, and the right-wing military, who want him to bring them photographs of the rebels. (123 minutes)

Schindler's List (1993): Thomas Kenneally's true story of Oskar Schindler, a German businessman who saves Jews from the Holocaust. (197 minutes)

Silkwood (1983): the true story of a young woman, an employee in a nuclear processing plant, who dies in an 'accident' just before she is going to talk to a reporter about a safety problem. (131 minutes)

Sophie's Choice (1982): based on the novel by William Styron: a Jewish mother of two is faced with a terrible dilemma in a Nazi concentration camp. (150 minutes)

The great Dictator (1940): Chaplin's satire on Nazi Germany. (124 minutes)

*The Last Temptation of Christ** (1988): based on Nikos Kazantzakis' controversial depiction of Jesus. (164 minutes)

Mash (1970): US staff at a Korean conflict hospital use humour to keep their sanity amidst the horror of war. (112 minutes)

The Matrix (1999): Sci-fi about artificial intelligence. (136 minutes)

The Mission (1986): a Jesuit mission to convert the Indians in the jungles of Brazil in the eighteenth century is threatened by colonists. The non-violent resistance of one priest comes up against the cry for armed resistance. (125 minutes)

To Kill a Mockingbird (1962): a lawyer defends a black man against an undeserved rape charge, coming up against prejudice towards himself, his client and his children. (129 minutes)

Twelve Angry Men (1957): a dissenting juror in a murder trial slowly manages to convince the others that the case is not as clear cut as it seemed in court. (96 minutes)

Welcome to Sarajevo (1997): adrenaline-loving American and British journalists meet the beginning of the Bosnian war in Sarajevo. (103 minutes)

Glossary and index

Use this glossary particularly for revision. Words appearing in bold within an entry have their own entry elsewhere in the glossary. The glossary also functions as an index. The page numbers are given in italics after each definition.

Absolute Perfect in quality, complete, not limited by restrictions or exceptions. This term is often applied to God but can also be applied to 'Truth'. *pp. 35, 37, 101*

Absolutism The theory that morality is **absolute** rather than relative (see **relativism**); that is, there are **moral** truths we must adhere to that particular situations, people or places do not affect. *pp. 30, 36–7, 39, 41, 44*

Act utilitarianism Ethical theory according to which the rightness or wrongness of individual acts are calculated by the amount of happiness resulting from these acts. *pp. 87, 90, 93, 98*

Agape Understanding, creative and redemptive goodwill to all people. An overflowing of love that seeks nothing in return. Theologians call it the love of God operating in the human heart. *pp. 97, 108*

Agapeistic calculus 'There is only one duty and that is to love your neighbour as yourself' (see **situation ethics**). *pp. 99, 109*

Altruism A selfless concern for other people purely for their own sake – considering other people's happiness before one's own. *pp. 11, 65, 67, 74*

Amoral No sense of what is right or wrong, or being indifferent to right and wrong. Babies and people who have been given pre-frontal lobotomies might be in this category. *p. 10*

Analytical ethics Twentieth-century methods of philosophizing, generally characterized by the careful effort to uncover suppositions concealed beneath the superficial structure of statements in ethical language. *p. 13*

Analytical statement A statement true by definition; for example, 'all bachelors are men'. *p. 17*

Anthropocentrism Belief that the non-human world only has value in so far as it is instrumental in satisfying human desires. *pp. 82, 152–4, 156, 161–2*

Antinomian The term 'antinomian' means 'against law'. This approach to ethics argues that the situation itself will show us what we ought to do. Each decision and each occasion is unique. Making a moral decision is a matter of spontaneity. The right thing to do is dependent on things like intuition or waiting for that 'inner voice' to guide us. *pp. 99–101, 109*

Arbitrary A power that is uncontrolled and used without the wishes of others, based on personal opinion or chance rather than reason. *p. 54*

Arete Greek word for *excellence* or **virtue**. *p. 111*

Autonomy The ability to determine one's own course in life freely. Autonomy in **ethics** focuses on the individual's capacity for self-determination. Etymologically: it goes back to the Greek words for *self* and *law*. *pp. 13, 25, 29, 74, 103*

Benevolence An attitude of goodwill. An attribute sometimes given to God. *pp. 46, 52, 60, 70, 103, 169, 176*

Bioethics The application of **ethics** to the biological sciences, medicine, healthcare and related areas. *pp. 140, 145–6*

Calculus A calculus is simply a means of computing something and a moral calculus is a method of calculating what the right moral decision is in a particular case. *pp. 87, 89, 94, 98, 109*

Cardinal virtues In medieval discussions, the particular virtues described by Aristotle and the ancient Greeks became known as the cardinal virtues. They are called *cardinal* (Latin: *cardo*, hinge) virtues because they are 'hinges' on which all moral virtues depend. *pp. 112, 115*

Categorical imperative 'I ought to do such and such regardless of my own wishes.' The key principle of **Kantian ethics** – essentially that an act is **immoral** if the rule that would authorize it cannot be made into a rule for everyone. *pp. 77–9, 82, 86*

Celibacy A state of not engaging in sexual relations. *pp. 7, 128*

Chauvinistic Unreasonable and unfounded view that one is 'superior' to another. *pp. 127, 149*

Civil rights Legally enforced and protected **rights** belonging to people by virtue of their membership of a state. *pp. 63, 85, 118*

Cloning A form of **genetic engineering** that can produce one or more individual plants or animals that are genetically identical to another plant or animal. The three distinct types of cloning are: (a) **embryo cloning**, (b) adult **DNA** cloning (**reproductive cloning**), and (c) **therapeutic cloning**. *pp. 123, 136–48*

Common-good approach Assumes a society comprising of individuals whose own good is inextricably linked to the good of all (the community). Community members are bound by the pursuit of common goals and values. The common-good approach focuses on ensuring that the social policies, social systems, institutions and environments on which we depend are beneficial to all. Examples of goods common to all include free health care, effective public safety, peace among nations, a just legal system, and an unpolluted environment. *pp. 69–71, 118–9*

Compassion An emotional attitude towards another person, characteristically involving an active regard for the other person's good. *p. 118*

Concupiscence Lust. *p. 126*

Conscience St Thomas Aquinas named conscience as 'the mind of man making moral judgements other definitions include 'the voice of God within' (Joseph Butler). *pp. 55, 57–63, 66, 163*

Conscientious objection A form of dissent against an institution's rules, policies or practices; often refers to refusal to participate in military service on ethical and/or religious grounds. *pp. 163, 167–8*

Consistency The absence of contradictions. *pp. 7–9*

Continence The ability to control oneself, especially one's bodily desires and feelings. *pp. 126, 133*

Contractarianism An activity is morally permissible if there is mutual agreement or consent between the participating parties. *pp. 116, 117, 120, 124, 131, 135*

Courage One of the **cardinal virtues** – also known as fortitude – a characteristic that enables the individual to regulate pain and strive towards the mean between cowardice and recklessness. *pp. 11, 111, 112*

Cultural absolutism The belief that there is a **universal moral** order at work and that some ethical beliefs are identical irrespective of differing cultural beliefs and practices. *pp. 35, 38*

Cultural relativism The belief that ethical values depend upon, and vary with, cultural conditioning and **moral** training, and so no moral belief system can be universally true. *pp. 32–4, 36*

Deep ecology View that the world is not a collection of isolated objects but a network of phenomena that are fundamentally interconnected and interdependent. *pp. 157–59*

Deicide The death of God. *p. 158*

Deontological theories Ethical theories that maintain that an action is good or bad, right or wrong, by something within the action itself. *Deon* comes from the Greek meaning **duty**. (Contrast with **teleological theories**.) *pp. 76–7, 85, 88, 97, 121–2*

Descriptive ethical relativism Claims that different people have different moral beliefs, but takes no stand on whether those beliefs are valid or not. *p. 31*

Descriptive ethics A term to express ethics as it identifies and compares different ethical systems that exist in different cultures. Compare with **normative ethics**, which seek to determine the rightness or wrongness of actions. *pp. 4, 10, 12, 15, 19, 20, 31*

Determinism The belief that acts of will, natural events, or social changes are settled and decided by earlier causes. *pp. 22–3, 27, 29*

Dharma Indian principle of **universal moral** order. *pp. 46–7, 55*

Discrimination (a) The ability to choose the best by seeing small differences, (b) treating things or people in different ways. *p. 174*

Divine command theory An act is morally right if God has commanded it and morally wrong if God has forbidden it. *pp. 45, 50, 54, 55, 119, 121–2*

DNA Complex two-stranded molecule that contains, in chemically coded form, all the information needed to build, control and maintain a living organism. *pp. 137–41*

Duty A motive for acting in a certain way that indicates moral quality. *p. 84*

Egoism Theory concerned with self-interest. The word *egoism* is often used in a pejorative sense to mean 'excessive self-regard'. *pp. 67–75, 125*

Egoistic hedonism To act only in your own interest to get maximum satisfaction. *pp. 88, 98*

Embryo cloning One or more cells are removed from a fertilized embryo and encouraged to develop into one or more duplicate embryos.

Twins or triplets are thus formed with identical **DNA**. This has been done for many years on species of animals, but only very limited experimentation has been done on humans. *p. 139*

Embryo research In popular usage the term 'embryo' is often used to refer to any stage of pre-natal mammalian development from 0 to 8 weeks after fertilization. Embryo research is the study of the changes that occur to an organism from its earliest stages and research into the detection of diseases and disorders. *pp. 82, 123, 136, 145–6, 148*

Embryonic stem cells First appear about a week after fertilization – 'parents' of all the cells of the adult body. *pp. 136, 139, 143–5, 147*

Emotivism Ethical theory based on people's emotive response to other people, situations, principles and viewpoints. *pp. 10, 18, 19, 21*

Enlightenment (a) An intellectual movement in modern Europe from the sixteenth until the eighteenth centuries that believed in the power of human reason to understand the world and to guide human conduct; (b) for Buddhists, the state of Enlightenment or *nirvana* is the goal of human existence. *p. 47*

Environmental ethics Concerned with issues arising out of human interaction with the environment. *pp. 123, 149–62*

Epistemology Branch of philosophy that studies knowledge. It attempts to answer the basic question 'What distinguishes true (adequate) knowledge from false (inadequate) knowledge?' *pp. 17, 21, 31*

Equal intrinsic value Implies species egalitarianism, in other words, all beings, of whatever species, have equal value in themselves for what they are. This is distinguished from any **instrumental value** or use-value they may have to other beings. Thus humans may only interfere with other beings 'at vital need' not just to satisfy their desires. *p. 150*

Equality Although we are all different in terms of physique, skills, and so on, in some ultimate ontological sense, we are all equal and this equality is more important than any empirical differences. *pp. 8, 118, 123*

Eros Sexual affection, passion or desire. *p. 108*

Ethical egoism Theory that, in its most common version (*universal ethical egoism*), states that each person ought to act in his or her own self-interest. (See also **psychological egoism**.) *pp. 67–8, 75*

Ethical naturalism Belief that all objects, events, and values can be wholly explained in terms of factual and/or casual claims about the world, without reference to supernatural powers or authority. *pp. 10, 16–17, 21*

Ethicists Thinkers who attempt to bring clarity of thought to ethical issues: to define clearly the language that is used to discuss **ethics**, to reveal the forms of **inference** that underlie our reasoning about them, and to determine and justify principles that can provide guidance in resolving these issues by bringing into consistency our best thoughts and intuitions on these matters. *p. 13*

Ethics A branch of philosophy that aims to understand the meaning of right and wrong. The word *ethics* comes from the Greek *ethos* meaning 'character'. But how do we *know what is right or wrong*; how do we *define good and bad*? These sorts of questions make up the greater part of the study of *ethics*. There are two approaches to ethics: the scientific (or **descriptive**), as used by social science, and the philosophical, which includes **normative ethics** and **meta-ethics**. When used in its ordinary sense, however, ethics, like morality, means the values by which human beings live in relation to other human beings, nature, God, and/or themselves. *pp. 2, 46, 75*

Euthyphro's dilemma 'Is conduct right because the gods command it or do the gods command it, because it is right?' The Euthyphro dilemma is found in Plato's *The Last Days of Socrates*

(c. 360 BCE) and concerns Socrates' discussion with a young man, Euthyphro. *pp. 45, 51–2, 55*

Fallacy The point of an argument is to give reasons in support of some conclusion. An argument commits a fallacy when the reasons offered do not support the conclusion. *p. 70*

Formula of universal law One of Kant's formulations of the **categorical imperative**: act as if the maxim of your action was to become through your will a universal law of nature; that is, we should act in such a way that we can will that the **maxim** under which we act should be a general law for everyone. *pp. 78, 85*

Free will Actions are the result of free rational choice on the part of agents, who are not compelled to act by forces outside their **moral** consciousness. *pp. 22–4, 27, 29*

Freudianism Human beings are determined by inner drives and unconscious motivations to behave the way they do. *pp. 28–9*

Gaia Hypothesis Theory that the earth's living and non-living systems form an inseparable whole that is regulated and kept adapted for life by living organisms themselves. The planet functions, therefore, as a single organism. *p. 158*

Genetic engineering A term that describes genetic manipulation, including **cloning**. *pp. 95, 123, 136, 140–1*

Genetics The study of human variability in terms of its causes and effects. *pp. 27, 140–1, 145–6*

Genocide The deliberate and systematic destruction of a racial, political or cultural group. *p. 164*

Golden mean Moral virtue that is always the mean – a middle way – between excess and deficiency. *pp. 110, 111, 115*

Golden rule The principle common to all world faiths that we should treat others as we would wish to be treated. *pp. 38, 96*

Good An action is judged 'right' or 'wrong' depending upon whether or not it is a 'good' or 'bad' thing to do. 'Good' can be defined in **absolute** terms (it is good in its particular context). It can also be defined in what it can achieve, so an action is 'good' if the result of that action is 'good'. Aristotle describes good as something that fulfils its purpose. This formed the basis of the **natural law** approach to ethics. *pp. 4, 11, 15, 42, 47, 49, 53, 84, 118–19, 167*

Grace The state of the soul when freed; the mercy and help of God. *pp. 59, 74*

Hard determinism People do not have free will. All moral actions have uncontrollable prior causes. *pp. 26, 29*

Hedonic calculus Jeremy Bentham's utilitarian calculation, whereby the good or bad effects of an action can be measured. *pp. 87, 89, 94*

Hedonism A term used to describe an attitude that makes happiness the goal of life. *Hēdonē* is the Greek word for pleasure. *pp. 88, 98*

Hedonistic Of – or pertaining to – pleasure. *pp. 88–9*

Holy war A war fought out of the belief that it is approved or commanded by God. *pp. 169–71, 176*

Hypothetical imperatives 'If you want to play professional football, practise your skills.' Hypothetical imperatives are based on an 'if'. We can reject the command to practise if we resist the 'if' on which the command rests. **Moral** imperatives, by contrast, do not depend upon our having particular desires – they are categorical. *pp. 78, 86*

Immoral That which is bad or wrong, such as a bad person or a wrong action; used interchangeably in this book with 'unethical'. *pp. 1, 10*

Inference The act or action of inferring – to draw the meaning from something. *p. 69*

Instrumental value The value of things as *means* to further some other ends; for example, certain fruits have instrumental value for bats which feed on them. *pp. 149–51, 162*

Integrity Wholeness, soundness, uprightness, honesty. *pp. 9, 62*

Intention In ethics, questions of intention can be very important; if someone does a good act but their intention – their inner motive – is suspect, then it could be argued that this is a bad action. *p. 24*

Intrinsic goodness Good in itself without reference to consequences. *pp. 89, 103, 118*

Intrinsic value The value of things as *ends in themselves* regardless of whether they are also useful as means to other ends. *pp. 82, 129, 149–51, 161–2*

Intuitionism The claim that we grasp basic moral principles by *intuition*. W.D. Ross claimed that there *are* 'facts' about what is morally right and wrong and that our understanding of these facts is sufficient enough to deserve the title 'knowledge'. *pp. 10, 19–21, 60, 66*

Islamophobia A climate of distrust of and **prejudice** against the Muslim community. *p. 170*

Jihad 'Holy war'. A jihad may be undertaken to defend Islam against external threats or spread the religion among non-believers. The term is also used to mean effort in the cause of Allah and can encompass struggle against resistance to the rule of divine law within oneself. *pp. 163, 170–71, 176*

Jus ad bellum Justice in the decision to wage war. *p. 172*

Jus in bello Justice in the way war is conducted. *p. 172*

Just war theory War is justified and morally acceptable if it meets certain conditions. *pp. 163, 171–5*

Justice As rational beings, we should treat others as we would like to be treated unless there is some reasonable ground for difference in treatment. Justice is a social as well as an individual virtue. It is the excellence of the soul that distributes each according to his dessert and a characteristic that enables the individual to direct his will appropriately to relate properly to others. *pp. 46, 48, 80, 96–7, 103, 111, 112, 118, 172*

Kantian ethics The ethical theory devised by Kant consisting of the primacy of **duty**, goodwill and the **categorical imperative**. *pp. 62, 77–86, 124, 127, 134, 153, 156*

Kingdom of ends One of Kant's formulations of the **categorical imperative** on which all moral commands are based: 'So act as if you were, through your **maxims**, a law-making member of a kingdom of ends.' Kant envisages rational agents acting as if they were making laws for themselves based on reason. By doing this they will become 'law-making members of a kingdom of ends'. The laws adopted by all members will be the same because they are all based on reason. If there are disagreements, rational discussions should be able to resolve these. *pp. 78, 84*

Legalism A type of ethic that seeks to prescribe rules for every conceivable occasion of **moral** choice. *pp. 100, 101, 105, 109*

Libertarianism The view that humans are free to make moral choices and are therefore fully responsible for their actions (in contrast to **determinism**). *pp. 22, 26–7, 29, 124, 129, 134*

Logical positivism Logical positivism emerged during the early part of the twentieth century when philosophers attempted to establish criteria so that they could *talk meaningfully* about the world. They argued that the only meaningful propositions are those that can be verified empirically, and those that cannot are neither true nor false, but simply meaningless. (See **verification principle**.) *pp. 10, 17, 21, 123*

Marxism Karl Marx – founder of Marxism – argued that morality is simply ideology in disguise and that it exists to serve the interests of the ruling class. Underlying society's beliefs about everything is one thing: economics. Basically, capitalism has survived so successfully because the dominant class has monopolized education, religion, the law, the press and even morality itself. *pp. 30, 40–1*

Maxim A general principle. According to Immanuel Kant, a maxim is the **subjective** rule that an individual uses in making a decision. *pp. 7, 78, 79, 86*

Meaningless statement A statement that cannot be verified. *p. 17*

Means Philosophers often contrast *means* and *ends*. The *ends* we seek are the goals we try to achieve, while the *means* are the actions or things we use in order to accomplish those ends. Immanuel Kant argued that we should never treat human beings merely as means to an end. *pp. 79–82*

Meta-ethics The analysis of ethical language – the study of the meaning of ethical statements. *pp. 10, 13, 20, 123*

Militarism The undue prevalence of the military spirit in society. *pp. 163, 165–6*

Moral That which is good or right, such as a good person or a right action. Used interchangeably in this book with 'ethical'. *pp. 7, 10, 30, 57, 84, 101, 123*

Moral agent A phrase used to describe one who can make moral decisions and who can be judged on moral grounds. *p. 86*

Morality A set of beliefs accepted by a given culture concerning what we ought or ought not to do in moral situations, whether these beliefs are a product of critical reflection or not. Refers to the first-order beliefs and practices about good and evil by means of which we guide our behaviour. Contrast with **ethics**, which is the second-order reflective consideration of our moral beliefs and practices. *pp. 19, 20, 36, 123, 173*

Natural law In ethics, believers in natural law hold (a) that there is a natural order to the human world, (b) that this natural order is good, and (c) that people therefore ought not to **violate** that order. *pp. 37, 43*

Natural law theory Theory that everything is created for a particular purpose and fulfilling this purpose is the 'good' to which everything aims. *pp. 41–4, 54, 99, 124, 128, 134*

Naturalistic fallacy The naturalistic fallacy is a meta-ethical theory, proposed by G.E. Moore in *Principia Ethica* (1903), that the notion of moral goodness cannot be defined or identified with any property. Moore argues that 'goodness', like 'yellowness', is not capable of being explained in terms of anything more basic. We intuitively recognize goodness when we see it, as similarly we recognize yellowness when we see it. But the notion of 'goodness' itself cannot be defined. *pp. 4, 15–16*

Non-moral Some things are outside the realm of morality altogether (for example, inanimate objects such as a stick are non-moral – the person using the stick, however, may use it immorally by hitting somebody with it!) but the stick itself remains non-moral. Animals, plants and inanimate objects are essentially non-moral. *p. 10*

Normative ethical relativism Claims that each culture's or group's beliefs are right within that culture and that it is impossible to judge another culture's values from the outside. *p. 31*

Normative ethics The setting up of norms or value systems that prescribe how human beings should behave (also known as **prescriptive ethics**). All ethical systems such as ethical **egoism**, **natural law theory**, **utilitarianism** and **Kantanian ethics** are normative. *pp. 13, 20, 31, 111*

Objective Outside or external to us rather than within us. (See **subjective**.) *pp. 33, 38–9, 56–7*

Obligations Responsibilities we have towards one another (by morality, laws or traditions) to see that the just **rights** of others are protected. *pp. 3, 82, 116*

Omnipotent All-powerful – an attribute given to God. *p. 50*

Omnipresent Present in all places at all times – an attribute given to God in Judeo. *p. 50*

Omniscient All-knowing – an attribute given to God. *pp. 50, 53, 105*

Pacifist Someone who believes it is wrong to harm or kill other people, and if killing is wrong, then war must be wrong, as war is basically a matter of killing. *pp. 163, 166–9*

Personalism The ethic that demands that humans are not treated as **means** but are subjects. *pp. 68, 102*

Philios Love between friends. *p. 108*

Philosophy Literally means 'love of wisdom'. If you are being philosophical, you are wondering about thoughtful questions and trying to find answers to them. For example, one philosophical question might be: 'What is wisdom?' It is philosophical because people might have different opinions about it. There is no single answer – it needs to be discussed or 'enquired about'. *pp. 1, 9, 48*

Positivism Belief that natural science, based on observation, compromises the whole of human knowledge. Positivists reject as meaningless the claims of religion. The most influential twentieth century version is **logical positivism**. *p. 102*

Postmodernism A movement that arose in the 1980s, postmodernism is hard to define but is a concept that appears in a wide variety of disciplines. Generally, postmodernists are sceptical about the existence of an **objective** reality like God or the possibility of using reason to understand it. There is no supreme principle that can tell us which ethical system is the best or truest one; we live in a relativistic universe where there are only human truths and human ethics. *pp. 30, 40*

Pragmatism Philosophical theory that explains both meaning and truth in terms of the application of ideas or beliefs to the performance of actions that have observable practical outcomes. *p. 102*

Predestination Belief that God has decided everything that will happen and that no human action can change things. (Compare **free will**.) *pp. 25, 29*

Prejudice An injury, detriment or damage caused to a person by judgements or actions that disregard his or her **rights**; 'a previous judgement' due to a preconceived opinion. *pp. 155, 159*

Prescriptive ethics An ethical theory that maintains that moral statements do not describe an opinion, but have an intrinsic sense that others ought to agree and follow (contrary to **descriptive ethics**). *pp. 4, 10, 13, 15, 20, 21, 104*

Prescriptivist A name commonly given to those with views which hold that **moral** judgements are in some special sense 'action-guiding'. *pp. 3, 13, 19*

Prima facie A duty 'at first glance'; that is, all other things being equal, we ought to do it. In the original Latin, this phrase means 'at first glance'. In ethics, it usually occurs in discussions of duties. *pp. 126, 131*

Prima facie duty A duty that appears binding but that may, upon closer inspection, turn out to be overridden by other stronger duties. *p. 150*

Proportionality/proportionalism St Thomas Aquinas in the **just war theory** argues that any warring activity should be proportionate to the aggression made and not excessive to that aggression. Proportionalism as an ethical theory maintains that basic moral laws which exist may be broken in exceptional circumstances. *pp. 172, 176*

Prudence One of the **cardinal virtues** – also known as practical wisdom: gives an individual the capacity to deliberate well about what is good and advantageous for the self in practical affairs. *p. 112*

Psychological egoism The doctrine that all human motivation is ultimately selfish or egoistic: 'everyone will ultimately do what is in his or her own self-interest.' *pp. 68–9, 72, 75*

Reciprocal To give and receive in turn – a mutual exchange. *pp. 130, 163*

Relativism In ethics there are two main type of relativism. **Descriptive ethical relativism** simply claims as a matter of fact that different people have different moral beliefs, but it takes no stand on whether those beliefs are valid or not. **Normative ethical relativism** claims that each culture's or group's beliefs are right within that culture and that it is impossible to judge another culture's values from the outside. *pp. 30–7, 44, 102, 121–2*

Reproductive cloning Technique intended to produce a duplicate of an existing animal. It has been used to clone a sheep and other mammals. *pp. 138–9, 147*

Responsibility From the Latin *respondere*, 'to answer' – inferring accountability, being answerable for one's actions. *pp. 22–4, 167*

Retributivism The use of deserved punishment in the law. *p. 80*

Rights Powers or privileges to which an individual has a just claim such that she or he can demand that they not be violated or suspended. Rights involve a mutual recognition on the part of each individual of the claims or rights of others. Rights are thus related to duties. Some rights, like human rights, belong to everyone by nature, or simply by virtue of being human; other rights, like legal rights, belong to people by virtue of their membership in a particular state. *pp. 82, 85, 118, 122*

Rule utilitarianism If following a rule will result in more happiness than not following a rule, then we should adopt the rule as a **moral** principle and always act in accordance with it. *pp. 87, 98*

Sanctioned With permission, approval or acceptance; adhering to a law or standard. *p. 56*

Scepticism In ancient Greece the sceptics were thinkers dedicated to the investigation of concrete experience and suspicious of theories that might confuse that experience. In modern times, sceptics have been wary of the trustworthiness of sense experience. *p. 35*

Sentient Having feelings and some kind of consciousness or the power of self-perception. *p. 155*

Shallow ecology A human-centred or anthropocentric way of viewing the world; starting from an assumption that human beings are the central species in the Earth's ecosystem, and that other beings are of less importance or value. In its extreme manifestations shallow ecology sees other beings (and features of the Earth) as resources for human use and fails to see their **intrinsic value**. Shallow ecology concentrates on quick-fix solutions to pollution and resource depletion, in contrast to **deep ecology**. *pp. 157–9*

Sin From the Greek word *hamartia*, which literally means to *miss the mark*; to go against divine law or principles of morality. *pp. 42, 128, 130*

Situation ethics A situationist enters into a moral dilemma with the ethics and principles of his or her particular tradition, but is prepared to set these laws and principles aside in the situation if love seems better served by doing so. *pp. 99–109, 121*

Social contract The view that 'society' originated when individuals agreed to surrender some of their 'natural **rights**' and social **obligation** was born. *pp. 73, 116–20, 132*

Soft determinism The claim that we are sometimes free even though all events are the result of previous causes. The distinction between **libertarianism** and soft determinism is the latter's insistence that sometimes we are free even though *all* events are determined. *pp. 22, 27–8*

Speceism A **prejudice** towards the interests of one's own species as against the interests of other species. *p. 155*

Stewardship The idea – prevalent in contemporary Christian views on the environment – that we are trustees of creation and cannot escape the **obligation** to act responsibly. *pp. 149, 159–60, 162*

Storge Instinctual love. *p. 108*

Subjective Coming from within us rather than from outside. (Compare **objective**.) *p. 19*

Subjectivism An extreme version of relativism, which maintains that each person's beliefs are relative to that person alone and cannot be judged from the outside by any other person. *p. 19*

Synthetic statement A statement that might be true or false, but one that can be demonstrated using sense experience. *p. 17*

Tautological statement An unnecessary repetition of the same idea in different words; for example, 'he sat alone by himself', which does not make the meaning clearer. *p. 17*

Teleological theories Actions are judged good or bad by reference to the end to which they aim. These theories are sometimes called consequentialist (for example, **utilitarianism**). (Compare with **deontological theories** of ethics.) *pp. 48, 67, 72, 76, 85, 87–8, 97*

Teleos A Greek word meaning 'end' – in ethics, used to describe a theory of morality that derives **duty** or **moral obligation** from what is good or desirable as an end to be achieved. *pp. 48, 88, 111, 115*

Temperance One of the **cardinal virtues** – a form of self-control; a characteristic that enables individuals to strive towards the mean between insensitivity and self-indulgence. *pp. 111, 112*

Therapeutic cloning Procedure where the stem cells are removed from the pre-embryo with the intent of producing tissue or a whole organ for transplant back into the person who supplied the **DNA**. The goal of therapeutic cloning is to produce a healthy copy of a sick person's tissue or organ for transplant. This technique would be vastly superior to relying on organ transplants and also reduce animal testing. Since 1998 it has been acceptable to clone human material for medical purposes – but not human clones! *pp. 139, 146*

Universal Applicable to all human beings, situations and places. A **moral** rule that is 'universalizable' is one capable of being applied to all human beings without self-contradiction. *pp. 13, 30, 35, 67, 80, 170–1*

Universalizability Immanuel Kant used this term when discussing the **maxims**, or subjective rules, that guide our actions. A maxim is universalizable if it can consistently be willed as a law that everyone ought to obey. The only maxims that are morally good are those that can be universalized. The test of universalizability ensures that everyone has the same moral obligations in morally similar situations. *pp. 78–9, 82, 94*

Utilitarianism A moral theory which says that what is morally right is whatever produces the greatest overall amount of pleasure (*hedonistic utilitarianism*) or happiness (*eudaimonistic utilitarianism*). Some utilitarians (*act utilitarians*) claim that we should weigh the consequences of each individual action, while others (*rule utilitarians*) maintain that we should look at the consequences of adopting particular rules of conduct. (See **deontological theories** in contrast.) *pp. 55, 76, 88–96, 98, 121–2, 124, 130, 135, 155, 156*

Verification principle A tool used by logical positivists for the elimination of nonsense of every sort. The principle itself is a simple test. A.J. Ayer describes it thus: 'We say that a sentence is factually significant to any given person if, and only if, she knows how to verify the proposition which it purports to express – that is, if she knows what observations would lead her, under certain conditions, to accept the proposition as being true or reject it as being false.' *p. 18*

Vice A wrong habitually carried out. *pp. 111–12*

Violate To disregard or act against something promised or accepted as right. *pp. 37, 117*

Virtue Any kind of excellence (translated from the Greek word *arete*). A virtue is a characteristic habit of excellence of the soul that aligns a person in accordance to right reason and to a proper human end (*teleos*) of happiness. A virtue has both individual and social dimensions. *pp. 22, 47, 48, 111, 132–3*

Virtue ethics Ethical theory that claims that being good demands practising virtuous behaviour, or as Aristotle put it in his *Nicomachean Ethics* (350 BCE), 'We are what we repeatedly do.' *pp. 49, 110–15, 121–2*